hester.

MUNICH:

THE ELEVENTH HOUR

MUNICH:

THE ELEVENTH HOUR

BY
ROBERT KEE

HAMISH HAMILTON
LONDON

HAMISH HAMILTON LTD

Published by the Penguin Group
27 Wrights Lane, London W8 5TZ, England
Viking Penguin Inc, 40 West 23rd Street, New York, New York 10010, U.S.A.
Penguin Books Australia Ltd, Ringwood, Victoria, Australia
Penguin Books Canada Ltd, 2801 John Street, Markham, Ontario, Canada L3R 1B4
Penguin Books (N.Z.) Ltd, 182–190 Wairau Road, Auckland 10, New Zealand

Penguin Books Ltd, Registered Offices: Harmondsworth, Middlesex, England

First published in Great Britain 1988 by
Hamish Hamilton Ltd

British Library Cataloguing in Publication Data

Kee, Robert, *1919–*
  The Munich crisis.
  1. Europe. Peace. Maintenance. Treaties:
  Munich Agreement
  I. Title
  940.53′12

  ISBN 0–241–12537–5

Typeset in Ehrhardt at The Spartan Press Ltd,
Lymington, Hants
Printed and bound in Great Britain by
Richard Clay Ltd, Bungay, Suffolk

CONTENTS

LIST OF ILLUSTRATIONS

Chamberlain's triumph (*Topham Picture Library*)
'Peace with honour' (*BBC Hulton Picture Library*)
Hitler in the Sudetenland, October 1938 (*Robert Hunt Library*)
German troops in Prague, March 1939 (*Popperfoto*)

'In dealing with the grievances of post-war Germany, His Majesty's Government have always advocated coming to terms with her whenever possible. From the earliest years following the war it was our object to modify those parts of the Treaty of Versailles which we knew to be untenable.'

Foreign Office Memorandum, February 3, 1936
circulated to the Cabinet as C.P. 42 (36)

'I said . . . I had been thinking the situation over and wondered whether it might not be possible for Great Britain and France to concert with Germany in seeking to find a satisfactory solution to the [Sudetendeutsche] problem.'

Anthony Eden, Foreign Secretary

Report of a conversation with the French Foreign
Minister, Delbos, November 4, 1937

FOREWORD

THIS BOOK, WHICH HAD ITS ORIGINS IN A TELEVISION DOCUMENT-
ary, has been written for the fiftieth anniversary of the Munich
Agreement of September 29, 1938, to provide a narrative of what
happened and why, for those who may have forgotten or never have
known precisely. I have used only published sources. These include
the monumental series of Documents on British and German
Foreign Policy published by H.M. Stationery Office.

It was an astonishing event, to appreciate which requires an
understanding of the background in many preceding years. It is my
own view that clues to an explanation of 'Munich' are scattered
more liberally and less obviously than is sometimes recognised in
the years 1932 to 1936, a period of which the details can often seem
of small significance when viewed, as they usually are, from the
outbreak of the Second World War. I have therefore here devoted
rather more space to these years than might have been thought
necessary in a book of this length, though the survey they receive is
still cursory. A satisfactory definitive history of the origins of the
Second World War has yet to be written, and this period will, it is to
be hoped, then receive much more careful attention. Who, for
instance, now remembers that the man who expressed as much
consternation as anyone over the mildness of the British response to
Hitler's introduction of conscription in 1935 was Mussolini, the
'honest broker' of Munich?

My thanks for support, cooperation and assistance are due to Gill
Coleridge, Judy Mooney, Christopher Sinclair-Stevenson, Kate
Trevelyan, and the always expert and friendly staff of the London
Library.

Phillip Whitehead and Cate Haste, of Brook Productions, made for Thames Television a documentary for the fiftieth anniversary of 'Munich', to which I supplied linking and other commentary. I am grateful to them and to all who worked on the programme for their collaboration in that enterprise and for providing transcripts of the interviews which they recorded.

Detailed notes on sources may be found at the end of the book.

Robert Kee
London, June 1988

EUROPE, JANUARY 1938

The Rhineland was remilitarised in March 1936, Austria annexed to Germany in March 1938.

Inset: the Sudetenland of Czechoslovakia as finally transferred to Germany under the Munich Agreement

PART I

CHAPTER ONE

'MUNICH'

AT 2.40 P.M. ON SEPTEMBER 28, 1938, ADOLF HITLER WAS STILL eating lunch in his Chancellery in Berlin when the Italian Ambassador to Germany, whom he had already seen twice that morning, was shown into the room. After their first meeting, Hitler had postponed by twenty-four hours plans to cross the frontiers of Czechoslovakia on October 1 which had brought him to the point of war with the democracies of Britain and France. Now the Italian announced in his imperfect German: 'Tomorrow eleven o'clock Munich!'[1]

At Munich the next day Britain and France negotiated an Agreement which permitted the German armies to cross the frontiers of Czechoslovakia on October 1. France had been under a treaty obligation to defend Czechoslovakia against aggression. Czechoslovakia was allowed no part in the negotiations.

After fifty years, it is still quite difficult not to make this appear a grotesque event.

To approach any landmark in history is to risk being told, like the man in the old joke, that one should not have started from here. This is particularly true of 'Munich'. In the democracies, 'Munich' was seen at the time very differently by people viewing it, often passionately, from different angles. For a short time it could be seen as the event which saved the world from a Second World War. It could also be seen as the event which made that war inevitable, a view superficially confirmed when the Second World War broke out within a year. Thereafter, many saw 'Munich' chiefly as having provided Britain with a breathing space in which to rearm and subsequently win that war with the support of powerful allies. It has now come to be seen pejoratively, as the symbol for an ineffectual and even unprincipled attempt to stave off catastrophe by making the sort of concessions which in fact render catastrophe certain. At a distance of fifty years all such views can be seen simply as different aspects of historical truth.

On the surface it is not difficult to sustain the charge that 'Munich' was unprincipled. The Agreement, concluded without consulting Czechoslovakia, led within six months to that state's total dismemberment and occupation by Germany, though as part of the Agreement Britain and France had declared themselves ready to guarantee the truncated state which it produced. But, before that happened, 'Munich' could be justified logically at least as an attempt to save Czechoslovakia from collapsing under her own internal tensions. In any case, a greater principle had been at stake, that of trying to save European civilisation from the horrors of a Second World War. It was such considerations which led the English historian, A. J. P. Taylor, who had severely condemned Munich at the time, to classify it in 1962 as 'a triumph for all that was best and most enlightened in British life', a verdict which dismayed – as it was meant to dismay – many firmly committed to the pejorative view.[2]

Certainly the failure to achieve high-principled objectives cannot fairly be attributed to lack of principle, though an assessment of the likely outcome of any action must play some part in assessing its morality. But morality in any case is not the historian's chief concern. This must be to find out what happened and why, and, perhaps particularly in the case of 'Munich', to speculate about what might have happened if chance or human personality at the time had been different.

CHAPTER TWO

VERSAILLES

To obtain a historical perspective on the event it is necessary to go back to that hour on which the First World War ended in 1918, that hour of which the poet Siegfried Sassoon wrote: 'Everyone suddenly burst out singing,' and concluded: '. . . the singing will never be done.' The Treaty of Versailles with which peace was proclaimed in the following year was intended to make the song endure. There had been a unique sense of horror about the four years of slaughter through which European civilisation had just passed. This civilisation had imagined itself to be based on order, enlightenment and the inevitability of human progress. It had revealed itself capable of something so foul as to call in question the very nature of the civilisation itself. As another poet of that war, Edmund Blunden, was to put it: 'This was not what we were formerly told.'

The trauma of this First World War was to haunt people long after a Second had far exceeded it in terms of casualties. Seventy years after the second battle of Passchendaele a man who had been sent there as a boy of nineteen after training in model trenches in the chalk downs of Hampshire vividly conveyed in a letter to *The Times* something of the universal horror which Europe had experienced.

The July 1917 offensive had failed so the high command decided on a second attempt in September. By then it had rained incessantly and thousands of men went 'missing', choked to death as they lay helpless and sinking unseen in waterlogged craters.

Forward positions were reached only by a long and perilous trek for miles on duck boards. Slippery foothold on the planks and shrapnel overhead took a heavy toll before we could reach (or even

5

find) the men waiting to be relieved after standing soaked and caked in mud without sleep for 48 hours.

We had to get to them somehow and in that merciless hell we were ordered not to stop to attempt the rescue of any who slithered or fell off the duckboards into the mire. Their heart-rending cries for help had to go unheeded until the stretcher bearers came to their rescue in the rear of the long single file column making slow progress up the line.[1]

No fair understanding of 'Munich' can be achieved without taking into account how much more vividly still such horrors haunted many men's minds only two decades after it had been vowed that they were at an end for ever.

In 1919 the experience was both physically and psychologically so devastating that for the victors the need to exorcise what in fact could never now be exorcised dominated their making of the peace. In the first place such a thing was never to happen again, and very elaborate precautions were taken to see that it did not. Secondly, the victors could partly dissociate themselves from what had happened by branding with the mark of Cain those whose armies had started the war and now stood defeated.

The great Austrian and Turkish empires were broken up into a number of smaller states, constructed around various ethnic populations on the principle of 'self-determination'. But it was the Germans upon whom the weight of guilt was made to fall and who were made to pay the price for what had happened – literally in money and other material 'reparations'. At the same time Germany's ability to disturb the peace of Europe again was removed by reducing her armed forces to insignificant proportions and restricting their deployment even within Germany's own frontiers.

The financial reparations were specified in detail. Twenty billion gold marks were to be delivered by Germany to the Allies within two years, though the entire gold reserve of the German State Bank then stood only at 2.4 billion marks. Other economic means of compensation included the monthly delivery to Belgium for three months of farm animals (500 stallions, 30,000 mares, 90,000 milch cows, 100,000 sheep, etc) and, over a period of ten years, the delivery of some 20 million tons of coal to France, Belgium and Italy.[2]

The precision with which retribution was sought was typified by Article 247 of the Treaty. This required the supply to Belgium of 'manuscripts, incunabula, printed books, maps and other objects of collection corresponding in number and value to those destroyed in the burning by the Germans of the library of Louvain'. Similarly, while Germany was to be stripped of all her colonies, the British government also demanded the return of 'the skull of the Sultan of Mkwawa removed from the Protectorate of German East Africa and taken to Germany'. With such meticulous detail was the humiliation in other clauses of the Treaty underlined.

Germany was to be allowed no merchant fleet. Her navy was restricted to 15,000 men and none of her ships could exceed 10,000 tons. The ships themselves were limited to six battleships, six cruisers, twelve destroyers and twelve torpedo boats. She was allowed no submarines. No naval fortifications could be built within fifty kilometres of the German coast.

Her army, which although defeated in the field had not been pursued beyond her frontiers, was to be reduced to 100,000 men – seven divisions of infantry and three of cavalry, with no more than 4,000 officers. To prevent the formation of any effective reserve, these officers, if already in service, had to remain there until they were forty-five, while new officers had to engage for twenty-five years. For the same reason, conscription was forbidden. The German General Staff was dissolved. Germany was to be allowed no air force.

Nor were these the only punitive restrictions intended to ensure that she could never again wage war in Europe. Few even in Germany regarded as unreasonable the return to France of Alsace-Lorraine, taken in the war of 1870. But not only were Allied occupation forces to be placed for up to fifteen years in the Rhineland and in bridgeheads on the Rhine itself, but the whole of the Rhineland was to remain demilitarised, even after the withdrawal of the occupation forces. Neither on the west bank of the river nor in a further strip extending to a breadth of fifty kilometres on the east bank of the Rhine could any German forces be stationed or manoeuvre, nor could any military installations be built there. The resulting weakness of Germany's western frontier was seen both as giving protection to France and at the same time as providing a safeguard against any possible German aggressive adventure in the east since she was thus made vulnerable to instant Western reprisal. The demilitarisation of the Rhineland was in fact a lenient compromise on an earlier French demand for its permanent occupation.

So harsh were these terms that Philip Scheidemann, the Socialist Chancellor of the government of the new German Republic which had replaced the Hohenzollern monarchy, denounced them at once as making 'slaves and helots' of the German people. When the Allies refused to amend the terms and sent a five-day ultimatum demanding signature, he resigned. The Social Democratic President of the new State, Carl Ebert, was also reluctant to accept the terms. Desperately trying to assert the coherence of the new German Republic against anarchic forces of left and right, he went so far as to consult the army, the one relatively stable element in the state, about the possibility of taking up arms again. He was told that the chances of effective success were nil. He advised his new Cabinet to accept the terms.[3] The German delegation which then travelled to Versailles and signed the Treaty declared dutifully that they signed 'without any mental reservation' and that what they were signing they would carry out, but they added that they thought the victors would 'in their own interests, find it necessary to change some of the terms which they will come to see as impossible of execution'.[4]

The victors were themselves under no illusions about the severity of the Treaty. That indeed was its point. The British Prime Minister, Lloyd George, described it as 'stern' and 'terrible'. 'The terms,' he told the House of Commons to whom he successfully recommended the Treaty, 'are in many respects terrible terms to impose upon a country. Terrible were the deeds which it requites.'[5]

But General Smuts, who signed for South Africa, was concerned for the future. He said he signed not because he considered it a satisfactory document but only because it was necessary to bring an end to the war. The Treaty did not yet achieve 'the real peace to which our peoples were looking' and he spoke of the need for 'a new spirit of generous humanity'. 'There are,' he said, 'territorial settlements which will need revision ... There are indemnities stipulated which cannot be enacted without grave injury to the industrial revival of Europe and which it will be in the interests of

8

all to render more tolerable. There are numerous pinpricks which will cease to pain under the healing influences of the new international atmosphere.'[6]

Smuts was expressing at once sentiments which were to stir increasingly in the minds of many on the victorious side and to be expressed with intellectual vigour by J. M. Keynes in his publication in 1919 of his book *The Economic Consequences of the Peace*. But for a while the public were content to see victory consolidated and the Great War's sacrifices confirmed in glory by this triumph in the ancient Roman style. Only as both the sense of triumph and the need to vindicate it faded with the passage of time, did the victors' uneasy sense that Versailles had not in fact represented a wholly satisfactory or just peace develop a certain honourable hold.

Like many significant processes in history, this was gradual enough to be unremarkable until obviously there. It was accompanied by another process which also worked gradually but more discernibly: a change in attitudes towards each other of the nations which had combined to win victory. Many of the events of the 1930s, culminating in 'Munich' itself, seem virtually inexplicable unless the steady working of these two processes is remembered, together with the sense of continuing revulsion from the nature of modern war.

Even during the war the attitudes towards each other of the victorious Powers had not always been harmonious, governed as they were by individual interests as well as by the common interest in victory. Peace, by loosening the common interest, encouraged individuality.

France, already invaded twice by German armies in less than half a century, had on this occasion lost over a million and a quarter dead and missing and had suffered greater material damage than any of her allies. Looking in 1919 chiefly for security and protection against any repetition of the experience, she wished to establish permanent occupation of the Rhineland. But in this she had been opposed at the Peace Conference by Britain, and had had to accept instead the compromise of the Rhineland's complete demilitarisation. By 1923, when Germany was already hopelessly failing to meet the set target of reparations, France sent her troops with those of Belgium into the Ruhr to collect

9

reparations for herself. Britain gave no support and tactfully expressed regret at the action.

After 1918, British foreign policy again concentrated instinctively on the principle which had governed it for centuries and for which indeed Britain had fought the war, namely that no foreign power should become too strong in Europe. Germany was now weak. Since the seventeenth century the foreign power whose strength she had most consistently contested had been that of France. There were people in Britain in 1919 who could remember the building of forts against the French along the Thames in 1859. No one any longer seriously thought of France as a potential enemy, but a supposedly salutary distancing of British foreign policy from France was to determine much of the story that ended in Munich.

Italy, the other important victorious Power after the withdrawal into isolationism of the United States, had her own reasons for dissatisfaction with the Treaty of Versailles. She had been brought into the victorious alliance during the war by suggestions of territorial gain in the Eastern Mediterranean and in Africa at the expense of defeated enemies. But the Dalmatian coast which she coveted was made part of the new state of Yugoslavia, while Albania, which she had hoped to absorb as a protectorate, became another new state under its own name. None of the former enemy African colonies came Italy's way. She received some compensation in the extension of her Austrian frontier to the Brenner Pass, thus acquiring a disaffected population of some 250,000 Germans. But she retained an understandable ambivalence towards the 'justice' of the Treaty of Versailles.

When Hitler came to power in 1933, most of the security provisions of the Treaty of Versailles were still intact. Those which had already been partly subverted by the German army (the Reichswehr) through secret military training could have been re-imposed without difficulty. Even during the first three years of Hitler's dictatorship the former victors, with the requisite will, would have had little physical difficulty in re-imposing the restrictions on Germany's power which he had set about removing. And yet within a few more years the precise situation which the Treaty of Versailles had been designed to prevent had come about.

It is difficult not to ask the simple question: 'How could they not have taken the necessary steps to stop it happening?'

The question is too simple. Pursuing their own interests and absorbed by new internal problems, 'they' were no longer a coherent force. An awareness that it was only a relatively short time since their interests had closely coincided often confused their picture of events; a nominal sense of obligation to act as if they were still allies persisted. Sometimes they deluded themselves that they were acting in accordance with their old community of interest; at other times they deluded themselves that they were playing a diplomatic game alone. Only Hitler had a consistent perception of what the game was.

CHAPTER THREE

WEIMAR

THE HUMILIATION INFLICTED ON THE GERMANS BY THE TREATY
of Versailles was something which all Germans found painful
whatever their political inclinations – and there were many different
political inclinations in the early days of the new Republic which
received its constitution at Weimar in 1919. Further humiliation,
both material and psychological, followed with the economic
consequences of the Treaty. Reparations at the level on which they
had been demanded soon proved a quite unrealistic concept. Not
only was Germany unable to maintain the required payments but
the attempt to do so led in 1923 to a devastating inflation which,
while permitting skilled financial manipulators to make great
fortunes, introduced into the everyday lives of most ordinary
Germans a distressing sense of insecurity and personal need.

The war itself had brought about a German inflation of more
than 100 percent. In January 1919 the value of the mark stood at 89
to the dollar. By January 1922 it stood at 191.2. Just over a year
later, when the French went into the Ruhr to try to seize the reparations they were not receiving under the Treaty, the mark had fallen
to 17,972 to the dollar. Eight months later the figure was 4.5
million, by September nearly 100 million, and by mid-November
4,200 million.[1] People were paid twice a day with an interval for
buying goods the price of which rose wildly in the course of it. Quite
apart from the economic distress there was something deeply dis-
orientating about the collapse of what one modern historian has
aptly called 'the one commodity which more than any other serves
man as a means of rational measurement of his situation'.[2] The
psychological trauma, compounded by the hurt to national pride of
the French occupation of the Ruhr, affected particularly the middle

12

classes brought up on moral principles of thrift and ordered living hitherto regarded as sound. That trauma continued long after the nightmare itself had come to an end.

A new currency, the Rentenmark, based on solid assets, was introduced in 1924 and rigorous government economic measures ensured its success. By the end of 1924 the inflation was cured. But although the Weimar Republic was then to enjoy some years of stability and even prosperity, the memory of the inflation and the way in which it had undermined the average German's belief in the state which had allowed it to happen was less easily erased.

The problem of reparations was eventually resolved over a period of many years in the course of gradual negotiations with victors who became psychologically readier to make concessions with the passage of time. A full moratorium was not granted until 1932, by which time the psychological effect on the Germans of each stage of negotiation had been rather to remind them continually of the burden of Versailles than to impress them with any generosity in the lightening of it. German concurrence with the last but one reduction in 1929 had indeed been rewarded by the removal in 1930 of all occupation troops from the Rhineland. (The French had withdrawn from their independent occupation of the Ruhr as part of an earlier adjustment in 1924.) The final withdrawal in 1930 carried with it, under Article 431 of the Treaty of Versailles, acknowledgement that Germany had correctly fulfilled the Treaty's terms. But the Germans still had to wait another two years for the full moratorium on reparations. The continuation of any reparation payments at all at a moment of world economic crisis which hit Germany particularly severely kept traditional resentment of the Treaty alive to overshadow for many the moratorium itself. In any case official fulfilment of the Treaty was seen by many not as a wiping clean of the slate but as painful confirmation of all the other blows to national pride which it enshrined and which continued: namely, the saddling of Germany with sole responsibility for the war, the humiliating restrictions on her army and navy, and the permanent weakening of her western frontier by the non-militar-isation of the Rhineland. There was, too, another aspect of Versailles which not only Germans saw as hypocritical and unjust.

'Self-determination' for ethnic nationalities had been one of the broad principles on which the peace was based: a question largely of accommodating in new states of their own the various groups of non-Russian Slavs previously incorporated in the German, Austrian and Russian Empires. Thus Poland regained her ancient independence; Yugoslavia was created for Serbs, Croats, Slovenes and others as the country of the Southern Slavs; and Czechoslovakia, a product of the Czech nationalism proclaimed by Thomas Masaryk and his pupil Edward Beneš, placed Czechs, Slovaks, Germans, Hungarians, Poles and Ruthenians together within what seemed the most suitable natural economic and geographical boundaries for a newly constructed state.

The trouble with 'self-determination' was that, like other high-minded principles such as 'disarmament' invoked by the Treaty of Versailles, it was invoked one-sidedly on behalf of the victors. The benefits of self-determination were not extended to Germans. A logical extension of the principle, if applied to the rest of the Austro-Hungarian Empire, would have been to allow the ten million Germans within that former state to join others of the same nationality in the new sanitised Germany which the Treaty had theoretically established. Not only however were the Austrian Germans now excluded in a new republic of their own but considerable numbers of other Germans were kept separated from the main body within other states: 180,000 of them in the city of Danzig alone and the corridor created for the new Poland between east and west Prussia; more than three million in the new Czechoslovakia and a quarter of a million in that part of the Tyrol newly awarded to Italy.

German national consciousness had all the political sensitivity of a newcomer on the European power scene. Any German over the age of sixty could remember the time before Germany was a political nation at all. Prussia's war of 1866 had been not just against Austria but against Germans in Bavaria, Baden, Württemberg, Saxony and other smaller states. The German Reich, which Bismarck had been able to create after that war and after the war of 1870 against France, thought of itself as possessed of a fresh and forward-looking national dynamic by contrast with that of the older states of Europe. It was this dynamic which had been subjected to the abrupt and humiliating halt of 1919.

Even before the 1871 victory over France was complete and Bismarck's new German Reich had been proclaimed one German writer, Gustav Rümelin, ecstatically expressed the mood of the time.

14

History, he said, hardly provided a more impressive event 'than this change of scene in the world theatre as the hitherto dominant people steps behind the curtain and another, long kept standing in the wings, steps to the centre of the stage'. The effect was, he concluded, 'a doubly sublime . . . a divine judgement . . . inscribed in letters of fire upon the tablets of history'.[3] Within less than a life-time such notions, heady enough in the first place, had been consigned by the defeat of 1918 to realms where the dividing line between reality and fantasy was dangerously obscured.

On February 24, 1920 a German army corporal, holder of the Iron Cross First and Second Class, who had been severely gassed in the final British offensive of 1918, addressed the first mass meeting of a new and insignificant political party in the Hofbrau Haus in Munich. This was Adolf Hitler. As Rümelin had done, Hitler viewed that German Reich which had just disintegrated only fifty years after the glory in which it had been founded as a phenomenon of almost mystical superiority, handed over after 'an unparalleled series of victories . . . as the guerdon of immortal heroism to the children and grandchildren of the heroes'. He echoed Rümelin by ascribing to it 'an aureole of historical splendour such as few of the older states could lay claim to'.[4] The meeting he addressed that February evening in 1920 was attended by only about 2,000 people, some there out of curiosity, others from hostility. He explained methodically the new party's task which was to win over to the ideal of a reconstructed German nationalist state those broad masses of the German people temporarily seduced by the illusions of internationalist Marxism. The objective, he insisted, was one not to be achieved by half-measures; there could be no compromises. No sacrifice would be too great.[5]

An essential prerequisite was to purify the German national blood and 'get rid of those foreign germs in the national body which are the cause of its failings and its false ways', i.e. the Jews. The masses were to be made national 'in the extreme and vehement sense'.[6] Expediency was to be the guiding principle of the movement which must be 'anti-parliamentarian . . . and if it takes part in the parliamentary institution it is only for the purpose of destroying this institution from within'.[7] The movement must use primitive propaganda where necessary, and not be afraid of intolerance or 'the cult of the personality'. It should regard struggle 'as something to be desired in itself'.[8]

When Hitler left the hall that evening in 1920 after speaking for some hours he felt that he had won his audience over. 'A fire was kindled,' he wrote, 'from whose glowing heat the sword would be fashioned which would restore freedom to the German Siegfried and bring back life to the German nation.'[9] Within thirteen years he had succeeded in winning over the German nation itself to his ideal or rather to the belief that his ideal was, after the experience of those thirteen years, sufficiently close to their own national aspirations to justify support for him. And, having won that support through the parliamentary system to which he had from the first declared his hostility, he logically proceeded to dismantle it.

So all-pervading in this time was that German national dynamic of which Hitler made himself master that it was to work equally powerfully in the minds of Germans who were opposed to him. The lawyer and diplomat Adam von Trott was eventually to lose his life in trying to rid his country of Hitler's dictatorship. A close friend of von Trott's wrote of his attitude in the late 1930s that, as a Third German Reich was indeed successfully reconstructed, von Trott 'became not less but more German, and more defensive. As German strength expanded, he seemed to feel more strongly the wrongs, sufferings and grievances of his country, and to be more ready than ever to put the blame on others for the leaders his country had chosen.'

Von Trott himself wrote of foreign reaction to Hitler's international successes:

> I resent as utterly hopeless and damaging the high-handed denunciation of a people ... which have been defeated and silenced by economic depression and not least by the leading spirit of Europe [presumably France] wanting to perpetuate Germany's defeat in 1918.[10]

Ironically this letter of von Trott's was addressed to an English-woman. Her country's Government had, at the time it was written, conscientiously done much to help Hitler lead Germany to greatness again.

CHAPTER FOUR

FROM WEIMAR TO THIRD REICH

LONG BEFORE HITLER AND THE NATIONAL SOCIALIST PARTY HAD become a significant part of the German political scene, the restructure of the currency and the end to the demoralising inflation had enabled the Weimar Republic to develop at last some credible political stability. The faith of those relatively few Germans who had believed in the Republic from its earliest precarious years began to seem justified. Most Germans had merely accepted it for want of anything better, or had just acknowledged its existence because it was all there was. Now, in the mid-1920s, for the first time, Weimar began to offer Germans a better life than any they had experienced materially and psychologically since the war. It developed something of a liberal culture of its own in the arts, the cinema and an often attractively heterodox individual lifestyle. Whether the ambivalence towards it which had always underlain the support of the Reichswehr and other powerful forces in the country would now finally resolve itself in the Republic's favour was a question only likely to be determined by the ability of this improved state of affairs to continue and to improve further.

An example of such ambivalence, even on the part of the organs of state themselves, had been the relatively mild sentence given to Hitler when in November 1923, in pursuit of his National Socialist party's goal, he had attempted a political *coup d'état* in Munich. His march on the War Ministry there had been halted by police bullets which had killed a number of his supporters, but he was sentenced, after trial, to only five years' imprisonment; his offence – an attempt to overthrow the Weimar Constitution by force – carried a life sentence under the penal code. He was released after nine months into a more confident climate for the Republic which allowed the

17

National Socialist press to continue though it banned Hitler himself from public speaking for two years.

Just as a realistic conservative-minded banker, Dr Hjalmar Schacht, had paved the way for Weimar's economic stability, so now a realistic conservative-minded politician, Gustav Strese-mann, first as Chancellor and then as Foreign Minister, helped stabilise the Republic politically. By negotiating honourably with the victor Powers at a time when reconciliation was at last in the air he secured a new and respected position for Germany on the international scene. A Pact between Britain, France, Italy and Germany signed at Locarno in 1925, while re-affirming security provisions of the Versailles Treaty such as the demilitarisation of the Rhineland, did so in a framework of mutual respect. It specified *mutual* guarantees against unprovoked aggression for the frontiers of Germany, France and Belgium, and removed some occupation troops and the military Control Commission from German soil. Germany's status was that of an equal partner in the Pact by contrast with the *Diktat* which had been imposed on her at Versailles. 'We were a people of helots,' the Chancellor Hans Luther, who accompanied Stresemann to Locarno, declaimed to nationalist critics, 'and today we are once more a state of world consequence.'[1] The next year, 1926, Germany was admitted to membership of the League of Nations.

Certainly Stresemann met with opposition from traditional nationalist circles for having not more summarily swept away Versailles. He himself was to be disappointed that Locarno was not as quickly followed as he had hoped by the further withdrawal of occupation troops. But Locarno was a sufficient international success to enable him to remain in office as Foreign Minister for the next four years and provide a consistency to Germany's new status after years in which Germans had felt the lack of any real status at all.

In the Reichstag elections of 1928 the Social Democrats emerged as the largest party with more than nine million popular votes. Stresemann, who was himself a member of the conservative German Peoples' Party, remained Foreign Minister in the coalition which took office. In these elections the extreme National Socialist Party, on the organisation of which Hitler had been working since his release from prison in 1924 and the relaxation of his own speaking ban in 1927, won fewer than a million of the popular votes and only 12 of the 491 seats in the Reichstag. The Communist Party won four times that number of votes and 54 seats in the Chamber.

In the autumn of 1929 Stresemann died of a stroke. His death coincided almost exactly with the great Wall Street crash of 1929, and the world's plunge into a major economic depression.

Within three years there were six million unemployed in Germany. The new-found stability of the Weimar Republic had proved untrustworthy after all. The Republic about which many Germans had felt ambivalent even while the good times lasted and of which so many others had earlier painful memories had to take the strain without Stresemann to help it. In the Reichstag elections of autumn 1930 the National Socialists suddenly won six and a half million of the popular votes instead of less than a million two years before and nearly ten times the number of seats – 107 out of 491. The Communists, who were as determined in their own way as the National Socialists to destroy the Republic, also gained votes and seats, though the National Socialists were now ahead of them in both.

What might have been passed off as the natural democratic volatility of the Weimar Republic's multi-party system was revealed as fundamental political instability. The instability was fundamental because, except in the case of certain high-minded Social Democrats who themselves saw the Republic as only the precursor of something nobler still, the Republic was nowhere firmly grounded in popular political faith.

Even Stresemann, whose exertions on behalf of the Republic had cost him his life, had been a monarchist at heart and had worked for the Republic only because the practical alternative to it – dictatorship of left or right – seemed worse. His own party had become increasingly uneasy about his association with the republican idealist Social Democrats. The Reichswehr, upon whom ultimately the safety of the state depended, had always regarded Weimar as an aspect of that humiliation which Versailles had imposed on Germany and in particular on themselves. 'They regarded the Republic as a provisional arrangement, dictated by the enemy, with which they must go along for a while; then they would see.'[2] With more than half the Reichstag members (National Socialists and parties of the right as well as Communists) now actually hostile to the Constitution, the time for the Reichswehr to have another look had plainly come.

No one was more acutely aware than the leader of the National Socialist Party of the need to take the Reichswehr into account if his own ambitions for Germany were to be realised. But they were only the most important of a number of uncommitted political factors to be considered. As the world recession tightened its grip and his storm troopers fought the Communists in the streets for, as they thought, Germany's future, he saw a sizeable proportion of the more moderate electorate turn to his party as a possible outlet for their own frustrated personal and national feelings.

The President of the State itself, elected after the death of the Social Democrat Ebert in 1925, was the most revered soldier in Germany, one-time faithful servant of the Hohenzollerns, the old warrior-victor of the battle of Tannenberg in 1914: Field Marshal von Hindenburg. Hindenburg's conservative military nature ensured an obligatory loyalty to a Constitution over which he had been elected to preside, particularly since he had taken office just as Germany began to hold up her head in the world again. But when the economic environment deteriorated and political instability returned his was the sort of mind to deplore the indiscipline endemic in pluralistic democracy. He had no shortage of advisers to foster doubts about the political structure within which it occurred. Duty remained his personal imperative. But it was a curious twist of historical fate which decreed that he of all people should be the last symbol of the democratic German Republic to which its supporters would be able to turn in their hour of need. This was now fast approaching.

Adolf Hitler had for many years made clear what he meant to do once National Socialism became an effective force in German politics. He had said at one of his very first meetings in 1920 that the movement would be anti-parliamentarian. He had written this down when his first attempt at power by extra-parliamentary means in 1923 had brought him to prison and given him time to begin his book *Mein Kampf*. But to a fellow prisoner at that time he had also articulated the need to be more subtle in his methods in future. 'Instead of working to achieve power by armed coup,' he had said, 'we shall have to hold our noses and enter the Reichstag against the Catholic and Marxist deputies. If outvoting them takes longer than outshooting them, at least the result will be guaranteed by their own constitution. Any lawful process is slow . . . sooner or later we shall have a majority – and after that Germany.'[3] And this was what was to happen within three years of the elections of 1930.

The National Socialists never actually achieved an overall majority of seats in the Reichstag, although by 1932 they were the largest party there. But in 1933, after Hindenburg had finally called Hitler to the Chancellorship, the Reichstag voted Hitler a statute enabling him to take dictatorial powers by the constitutionally required two-thirds majority. It is one of the black ironies of history that the horrors of Auschwitz, Maidanek, Treblinka, Sachsenhausen and the rest were to be perpetrated under the technical legality of the liberal Constitution promulgated at Weimar.

Details of the manner in which Hitler manipulated the minds, instinct and political will of the German national centre and right into granting him full power (even using Communist votes in the Reichstag at one stage in the process before setting about the physical destruction of that party) are no part of this story of Munich. The manner itself, however, is very much part of the story; for over the next six years he was to employ very similar techniques against democratic statesmen on the international scene. Those with whom he dealt in both situations adopted towards him a similarly misjudged attitude, accepting his preparedness to abide by the rules at its face value when it suited their vision of their own purposes to do so. At the same time they ignored his own frequent statements that he would pursue his objectives by more ruthless methods than any which could be contained within rules.

Before his first triumph in the Reichstag elections of 1930 he had said openly in the course of the campaign: 'We know that in this election democracy must be defeated with the weapons of democracy.'[4] And after he had secured a sizeable section of the electorate to vote for such a policy he reassured them: 'If today our action employs among its different weapons that of Parliament, that is not to say that parliamentary parties exist only for parliamentary ends . . . We are not on principle a parliamentary party – that would be a contradiction of our whole outlook – we are a parliamentary party by compulsion . . . The constitution compels us to use this

21

means . . . It is not for seats in Parliament that we fight, but we win seats in Parliament in order that one day we may liberate the German people.'[5] He was to employ an identical tactic within the framework of international diplomacy.

At one crucial stage in 1932 during the intricate machinations for power which took place in the last months of the Weimar Republic, Hitler whose National Socialist votes and Reichstag seats had then more than doubled since 1930 received a temporary setback; he was at first turned down by Hindenburg for the Chancellorship just as it seemed to be within his grasp. Strong pressures from radical elements in the party's vast private army, the Sturm Abteilungen (S.A.), urged him to come to power by a *putsch* against the Republic. Knowing that there were conservative elements in the state and particularly the army who would disapprove of such action and whom he could not afford to antagonise, he insisted on proceeding through 'legality', though there were doubts at moments as to whether the impatient storm troopers could be held. When in November 1932 in new elections for the Reichstag the National Socialists actually dropped two million popular votes, while the Communists made gains, Hitler continued to hold firm for the parliamentary legality he despised. On January 30, 1933 a reluctant Hindenburg accepted that only Hitler was capable of commanding a coalition majority in the Reichstag and called him to the Chancellorship of the German Reich. Six months later the National Socialist Party legally proclaimed itself the only political party in Germany. Anyone who attempted to start another was to be 'punished by penal servitude . . . if the action is not subject to a greater penalty according to other regulations'.[6]

Thanks to his use of legality and his insistence on appearing to play by the rules, Hitler had achieved even greater power than the bare political facts of his dictatorship indicated. For he had managed to gather behind him a great body of German opinion which was not necessarily dedicated to the party's full political philosophy and which even disapproved of some of its radical methods, but was nonetheless able to see in National Socialism and its leader the means at last for redressing those grievances of national and personal pride which had smouldered for the past fifteen years. The humiliations of Versailles had always been as painful in the memories of those who had opposed him as in the memories of those who had supported him, not least because many of the humiliating limitations imposed on Germany by the Treaty persisted. Further humiliating memories of inflation and unemployment also waited to be redeemed in some sort of proportionate future glory. To 'liberate Germany' had been Hitler's one proclaimed objective. Liberation from an inconclusive recent past was what people wanted. Millions could see in him what they wanted to see.

A combination of Hitler's oratorical and political skills enabled him to foster this sensation of credibility while obscuring the truth of what else he stood for. Soon one democratic statesman of Europe in particular was to be in thrall to the same experience.

CHAPTER FIVE

FRENCH SECURITY V. GERMAN 'EQUALITY OF STATUS', 1932–4

ON OCTOBER 14, 1933 GERMANY UNDER HER NEW DICTATOR-Chancellor withdrew from an international conference on disarmament which had been in session at Geneva for over a year and a half. Simultaneously she announced her intention to withdraw from the League of Nations of which she had been a member since 1926.

The British Chancellor of the Exchequer of the day was Neville Chamberlain. In a speech at Nottingham he urged his audience not to be put out by this apparently unwelcome news. With that gift for homely aplomb which was later often to characterise his utterances on international affairs, he cited a dictum of the former British army commander, Field Marshal Earl Haig:

'No news is ever so good or so bad as it seems at first sight.'[1]

Another Conservative, the junior minister Mr Alfred Duff Cooper, speaking the same night struck a different note.

'Never,' he said, 'in the history of the world has a whole nation prepared for war with the same unanimity and the same enthusiasm as that which is inspiring the German nation at the present time.'

He cited the widely-held view that the recent Great War would never have come about if Germany had known for certain that Britain would intervene, and continued:

'Let us not make the same mistake as we made in 1914 . . . Let us make it plain that we will obey all the treaties we have signed, and that we will maintain our old tradition of preventing any Power from seeking to uproot the balance of Europe to their own advantage.'[2]

In the light of later events, Duff Cooper's words seem more prescient and intelligent than those of Neville Chamberlain. But history does not proceed by the light of later events. In the context of the autumn of 1933 it was Chamberlain's unhurried response which seemed the more pertinent and balanced. Duff Cooper's, by contrast, could almost be reckoned alarmist. Germany after all had already withdrawn from the Disarmament Conference once before, in 1932; she had come back to Geneva a few months later in return for an important concession in her favour. She was even now, under Hitler, to continue negotiating about disarmament for several months independently of Geneva and her eventual second return remained the hope of European governments for years.

The Geneva Disarmament Conference had begun on February 2, 1932, almost a year before Hitler was made Chancellor. Opening it, Arthur Henderson, a former British Foreign Secretary, had refused to contemplate even the possibility of failure. 'If we fail,' he said, 'no one can foretell the evil consequences that might ensue.'[3]

At the heart of this Disarmament Conference lay a new acknowledgement by the former Allies that the time had come to adjust the working of the Treaty of Versailles. Article 8 of that Treaty had proclaimed that the maintenance of peace required 'the reduction of national armaments to the lowest point consistent with national safety' and that the Council of the League of Nations should 'formulate plans for such reduction'. Article 164 had specified that '*up to the time at which Germany is admitted a member of the League of Nations** the German army must not possess an armament greater than the [very restricted] amounts laid down'. Germany had by now been a member of the League of Nations for nearly six years. The very part of the Treaty which tabulated the restrictions on German armament contained a preface which gave as their rationale: '. . . to render possible the initiative of a general limitation of the armaments *of all nations* . . .'†

The conclusion to be drawn from all this was clear enough. It had long been drawn by Germans of every political standpoint. If the apparent moral obligation for the victorious Powers to reduce their own armaments had not been fulfilled (and except to a very limited extent, and mainly by Britain, it had not been) then both equity and lip service to the sanctity of treaties demanded that the restrictions on German armaments should in turn be lifted. In this area

*Author's italics.
†Author's italics.

significant differences in attitude to Germany between Britain and France began to assert themselves.

Some early progress in the Disarmament Conference seemed made when a formal German claim to equality of status in armaments within a framework of general disarmament was received with sympathy by both British and American delegates. The French were less favourable, even apprehensive, particularly when proposals were advanced for specific limitation of those very armaments of interest to land powers like herself while those of interest to naval powers like Britain and America were to be unaffected. The French argued that they could not let themselves be deprived of guns and manpower essential to their own security while other nations geographically farther away from the danger of sudden attack retained all that they felt necessary.[4] Two disparate themes then began to dominate the Conference: Germany's claim for that equality of status in armaments which she enjoyed in other respects as a member of the League of Nations; and France's claim to have safeguards for her own security treated as a first priority.

Britain expressed at first a certain non-committal approach to both claims. In French eyes this became easily interpreted as veiled hostility. However courteously members of the British Government might talk in Parliament (and they often did) about their 'sympathy and understanding' for 'our friends in France', such phrases could not disguise the fact that French and British Government thinking about Germany was moving in divergent directions. Independent Conservatives like Winston Churchill might regret 'any approximation in military strength between Germany and France', adding: 'To those who would like to see Germany and France on an equal footing I would say: "Do you wish for war?" For my part I earnestly hope that no such approximation will take place during my life-time or that of my children.'[5] The British Government preserved a far less dogmatic approach.

In this way, months even before Hitler had taken charge of Germany, those fissures in Anglo-French 'sympathy and understanding' of which he was eventually to take good advantage were gently widening on the European scene for all the occasional applications of cosmetic diplomacy. When, in September 1932, the German delegation made their first protest and left the Conference over its failure to progress with their claim to equality of status, the

London *Times*, which was to be seen increasingly, if not always correctly, as an articulator of British Government policy, spoke out plainly. French fears, it said, over clandestine infractions of the Versailles terms allegedly taking place were 'clearly exaggerated'. It went on to give unequivocal support to the view that the diminished role imposed on Germany by Versailles should be adjusted.

'In this country at all events the great body of opinion holds that the time has come to recognise the impossibility of keeping a great country in a perpetual inferiority of status.'

The paper acknowledged that there were 'unfortunately' deep misgivings in France about replacing the Versailles restrictions with a new disarmament convention and that for her no reduction in armaments was possible without increased guarantees of security. (One such guarantee proposed by France was an international military force.) But it continued:

> In this respect it would be folly to mislead the French Government and public into believing that Great Britain is prepared to undertake any further commitments on the Continent of Europe. The obligations of Locarno are the utmost that this country can properly assume. Any more far-reaching promise of help in unknown and unforeseeable circumstances might at the critical moment find Parliament and people unwilling and unable to answer it.[6]

Contemplation of such statements in France began to encourage an impression that the Entente might not, in the last resort, be France's most reliable line of defence. The first seeds were being planted of what, in the sharper context of Hitler's Germany, was to become that introvert response to the need for security later thought of as 'Maginot-mindedness', after the War Minister responsible for those powerful fortifications on the German frontier which were already under construction in 1932.[*]

In 1932 the Disarmament Conference was still the framework within which international security was being sought and in December of that year Britain eventually persuaded France to concede the general principle of the German claim to equal status

---

[*]Maginot, a war veteran from Lorraine, won legislative approval for the line named after him in 1930. It was under construction when he died in January 1932.

in armaments. It was a claim, wrote *The Times*, regarded in Britain as being 'substantially a good one'.[7] The Germans returned to the Conference.

The concession meant that either the former victorious Powers must now proportionately disarm to Germany's level or that Germany had the right to rearm to theirs. The stages by which these things were to happen could be a matter for negotiation, and it was in this area predictably that French wariness was displayed. But clearly there could be little question of maintaining the restrictive military clauses of the Treaty of Versailles if the Conference were to fail to agree on a new international disarmament convention. Indeed there could be little question of trying to maintain these much longer anyway now that the general principle of equality of status had been concluded.

Less than two months later Hitler became German Chancellor. He himself was the first to admit that his success was primarily based on the German people's passionate revolt against earlier political failure to change Versailles.[8] The British-inspired concession at Geneva made it easy for him to begin to implement his programme with apparent diplomatic propriety.

The core of the issue was theoretically the speed at which the agreed levelling up, or levelling down, of armaments was to proceed. But particularly in the new German atmosphere of heightened national agitation and enthusiasm, with the formerly clandestine minor evasions of the Versailles restrictions becoming daily less circumspect, and a semi-military force of a million or more Nazi storm troopers embodying the new German state's ideology in addition to the Reichswehr, France's wariness about her own security became more sensitive than ever.

It can now be seen easily enough that concession of the principle of equal status on armaments had come too late. If made in the wake of the Locarno Pact when Stresemann was Foreign Minister, while the Weimar Republic enjoyed some stability, the future history of Europe might have been different. There was, as *The Times* said on the day after Hitler became Chancellor, 'in fairness to the Nazis' little more in what they had to say about German disability over armaments than had been said by most of the constitutional parties of the Weimar Republic.[9] The trouble was not only that they were saying it more loudly but that the loudness suggested a new

28

expansive direction for German foreign policy in tune with the objectives which the Nazi leader himself had made plain enough in his ideological treatise *Mein Kampf*. Expansion of German living space eastwards and the national unity of all Germans in a new Reich were the proclaimed ideals.

Everyone knew that the recipe for political success was always to proclaim more than you could hope to achieve. But the extent to which the principle of full equality of status awarded to Germany in December 1932 could be safely implemented in the new situation created by Hitler's success was the problem which the former victors now had to face. It was a problem not to be conclusively resolved, and then only by events, until the end of the decade.

Of course the extent to which it was a problem was in 1933 not so clear as historical hindsight now makes it seem. There were misgivings and there were hopes and both fluctuated. But it was in France above all that the misgivings predominated. Within a few months of the Germans' first withdrawal from the Conference the French had seen Germany's national flag altered from the Republic's black, red and gold tricolour to the former Imperial black, white and red with a central Iron Cross. They heard President Hindenburg, who had ordered the change, declare that it 'gave visible expression to the resurgent national forces of the German people' and that 'in spite of all its heavy shackles the German Reichswehr has in the difficult post-war years preserved the martial idea in the German people.'[10] They heard the wily von Papen, whom Hitler had out-manoeuvred on his way to the Chancellorship but who still clung to marginal office, laud 'the old military axiom "There is no better death than to be slain by the foe"' and revile those who could not understand 'the ancient German aversion from death on a mattress'. Fathers, he added, 'must fight on the battlefield in order to secure the future of their sons'.[11] And while, on return to Geneva, Germany pressed for immediate implementation of the equality principle, and the French insisted that it could only be implemented by stages which in any case could involve only disarmament and exclude any rearmament whatever, they heard the German Foreign Minister, von Neurath, state threateningly outside the Conference that, if the other powers did not disarm, Germany would have to have her own air force again despite the Versailles clauses.[12]

There were misgivings about the new German attitude in Britain too but of a much more flexible kind. They were modified partly by traditional detachment from any too close involvement in the European scene and partly by a prejudiced inclination to think the French neurotic about their security. On the other hand the crude style of Nazi political methods particularly in expression of their anti-Semitic philosophy could often antagonise a basic British sympathy towards German claims.

Neville Chamberlain's brother, Austen, who as Foreign Secretary had once said he was not prepared to sacrifice 'the bones of a single British Grenadier' to prevent the Germans in Danzig from re-joining their fellow countrymen, declared of the new German régime in May 1933: 'I still feel, and cannot but feel that the spirit which manifests itself in the proscription of a race within the boundaries of Germany is a spirit which if allowed to prevail in foreign affairs would be a menace to the whole world.'[13]

It was precisely this intermingling of moral and diplomatic judgements that his brother, on becoming Prime Minister, would scrupulously exclude.

Sometimes British misgivings were themselves actually made the basis for understanding the German point of view. *The Times*, condemning von Papen's speech, wrote that its tone could hardly have come as a surprise to those who knew the essential militarism of the German people and who realised that 'a sorely stricken nation – for Germans have certainly suffered very terribly for the consequences of their own military folly in 1914 – is apt to express in moments of desperation the dominant features of its character.'[14]

Such contorted apologia made small appeal to French reasoning. Nor were the French likely to be attracted by the updated logic of the former British war leader, Lloyd George, the man who at the time had justified 'the stern and terrible' conditions of the Treaty of Versailles. Speaking a few days after von Neurath's threat to build an air force he asked: 'If you are going to apply sanctions to people who break a treaty, who is going to enforce sanctions against France, Czechoslovakia, Italy, Poland, the U.S.A. and us who promised to disarm but who all, except ourselves, have increased their armaments?' Lloyd George concluded by asking for 'fair play for the 600,000 Jews in Germany and fair play also for the 60,000,000 of Germans inside Germany'.[15]

On October 14, 1933 the irreconcilability of the French and German positions on German rearmament led, despite British efforts at mediation, to the second German withdrawal from the Geneva Conference (this time reinforced by notice of withdrawal from the League of Nations). *The Times*, noting with regret that Herr Hitler was introducing more and more into foreign policy those methods which had served him so well in internal politics in Germany, advised the governments of the world to show him 'that the ways of the swashbuckler and the hothead will bring him no success in diplomacy'.[16] But within a month it was using the very danger likely to follow if such advice were not heeded as an argument to support Hitler's case. It was clear, said the paper, that the Nazis were determined that, if they could not obtain a diplomatic hearing, then military methods would have to be employed. It found it natural enough that this prospect, and the claim to include within Germany all Germans of the German race, should arouse deep misgivings in neighbouring states. 'What really matters, however,' it concluded, 'is that those other countries should make up their minds in which respects and to what extent the present position of Germany – 15 years after the close of the war – does not in fact befit the dignity of a great nation, *and should put no obstacles in the way of her recovering her proper position.*[*] There can be no tranquillity or equilibrium in Europe so long as a guilty sense of inferiority agitates one of its most important states.'[17]

There could be no clearer synopsis of the attitude in which British Government foreign policy was to be reasoned for the next five years. Misgivings about the way in which Germany under Hitler might conceivably misuse her proper position jostled secondarily with the concern for a new balance of European power.

The attitude of the official British Labour Opposition was straightforward enough. Though in theory appropriately opposed to Government foreign policy, the form which this opposition took equally helped to promote the German Government's diplomatic case. Labour argument was concentrated in ideological theory. Internationalist and anti-militarist by tradition, the Party had called at the time of Versailles for 'an immediate revision . . . of the harsh provisions of the Treaty as the first step towards the reconciliation

[*]Author's italics.

31

of peoples and the inauguration of a new era'.[18] For all its dislike of Nazi suppression of fellow socialists in Germany and persecution of the Jews, it fully supported in principle Germany's claim to equality of status. While opposing any rearmament for Germany it wanted all nations to disarm to Germany's level, the alternative which even the German Government theoretically accepted. On the same day as *The Times* defined the British establishment attitude to the new Germany, the Labour Party tabled a vote of censure on the British Government for not reducing its own armaments further. Its prescription for any abuse by the Nazis of Germany's equality of status was not resort to the force of sovereign nations but to the principle of collective security enshrined in Article XVI of the Covenant of the League of Nations.

In this the Labour Party were in tune with much British public opinion at the time. The Government,* while concerned to give Germany new status, was anxious to keep Britain's defence at a plausible level. Their majority in the House of Commons was enormous as a result of the landslide election of 1931. But at a by-election in East Fulham in October 1933, the Labour candidate, a former Royal Navy man who campaigned on the need to preserve peace through the League of Nations instead of by national expenditure on armaments, succeeded in overturning a Government majority of 14,000 and winning by 5,000. A similar swing against a Government prepared to spend a limited amount on armaments continued into 1934 at seven following by-elections.

More robust opposition to a foreign policy which might too easily be discounting the dangers of the new Germany continued to come only from Winston Churchill and a few other Conservatives who, like him, seemed out of joint with the time.

The French, viewing this scene from across the Channel, could reasonably feel a need to look to themselves. It was true that under the Locarno Pact of 1925 Britain was bound by treaty to come to France's aid either if Germany attacked her or if Germany militarised the Rhineland. But there were other circumstances in which France might find herself at war with Germany which were not covered by Locarno.

*A 'National' Government – of which Ramsay MacDonald was Prime Minister until May 1935, when he was succeeded by Stanley Baldwin. Baldwin was to be succeeded by Neville Chamberlain in May 1937.

In the original concept of the peace of 1919 an additional Treaty had been agreed between France, Britain and the United States by which the last two countries undertook to guarantee the security of the first. But this treaty had fallen through owing to the failure of the United States Congress to ratify it along with the Treaty of Versailles itself. In the 1920s, as part of a precautionary strategy to reinforce Versailles in her own interest, France had concluded treaties of mutual assistance with countries on Germany's eastern frontiers; with Poland in 1921, with Czechoslovakia in 1924, with Rumania in 1926 and with Yugoslavia in 1927. Within the structure of this alliance, any German aggressive move eastwards would involve France in war with Germany but this would not automatically bring Britain to her aid under Locarno. The obvious remedy was some new wider Franco-British mutually defensive guarantee to supplement the theoretical collective security of the League of Nations, but of this, in the prevailing mood of the British Government and people, there was no likelihood whatever.

Lord Beaverbrook, who controlled an important section of the British popular press in the *Daily Express* and the *Evening Standard*, was busy actually calling for Locarno itself to be repudiated. It was, he said, already a dead letter since, far from enabling the armed nations of Europe to scrap their war material as had been intended, it had led to France increasing hers. France had therefore herself rejected the document and if the Germans did the same and militarised the Rhineland the obligation on Britain to intervene no longer applied.[19] When in the middle of 1934 Anthony Eden nevertheless clearly restated at a garden fête the British Government's commitment to the Locarno treaties, he did so adding '. . . but we are not prepared to extend our commitments in respect of those treaties to other parts of Europe with which we are not so intimately concerned.' He was able to conclude confidently: 'No one I think will quarrel with us for this.'[20]

Eden was indeed merely affirming a theme which was to remain a consistent principle of British foreign policy for nearly five more years. One such 'other part of Europe' with which Britain did not feel intimately concerned was the new state of Czechoslovakia created fourteen years before at Versailles.

CHAPTER SIX

CZECHOSLOVAKIA: 1918–33

ONLY BY UNDERSTANDING THAT CZECHOSLOVAKIA WAS TO BE, FOR British foreign policy, never more than a potential if increasingly awkward irritant, is it possible to make the otherwise grotesque story of Munich begin to fall into place. As that story reached its climax four years later, Neville Chamberlain, by then Prime Minister, made a reference to Czechoslovakia which is now notorious in which he spoke of 'a quarrel in a far away country between people of whom we know nothing'. But this was no more than the unvarnished truth. Of the quarrel certainly few British people knew anything, though it had existed in one form or another for over 300 years.

The conflict between the Czechs and the Austrian Germans among whom they had lived so long, which the Munich Agreement claimed to resolve, had at its roots all the strength of an ancient antagonism. To try to resolve it at all could be regarded as a laudable endeavour. Looked at in this narrow context, the Munich attempt was simply a fundamental revision of another fundamental revision made twenty years before at Versailles.[1]

The idea for an independent state to be formed from the three 'historic provinces' of the Austrian Empire, Bohemia, Moravia and Southern Silesia, together with that Empire's predominantly Slovak territory in Hungary, had been agreed in principle by 'the Allies' just before the end of the war in 1918. The two Czechs who in Paris had successfully pressed the case for such a state rather than autonomy within a preserved Austrian Empire were Thomas Masaryk, a Professor of Philosophy at Prague University and his one time pupil Edward Beneš. Both had been Austrian citizens who until 1914 had hoped for some form of satisfactory feudal solution within the Empire for the old nationality problem.

34

Centuries before it might theoretically have been possible for an individual Bohemian personality of mixed German and Czech to evolve. But this had not happened. The subsequent conflict between some ten million Germans and seven million Czechs in a German(Austrian)-run Empire had been over political, linguistic, educational and social status, and the Czechs had inevitably come off second best.* Though Czechs had occupied many of the junior posts in the Imperial civil service they felt themselves with reason to be second-class citizens. Their language, once that of a proud Bohemian nobility and for a long time reduced almost exclusively to peasant and artisan usage, had undergone conscientious revival by German-speaking Czechs of the middle classes in the nineteenth century but continued to be treated by many Germans with contempt as 'a servant's language' which symbolised the inferior cultural status to which Germans felt the Czechs belonged. Czechs had educational and language rights and their own representation at local, regional and Imperial levels, but 'Bohemia' was for many Germans a German concept even for areas in which Czechs were in the majority. In the circumstances Czech culture seemed not only inferior but an incipient political threat.

Tension within the difficult relationship had varied over the years in differing political climates. But the war of 1914, in which the ten million Germans of the Empire allied themselves with sixty million other Germans, inevitably aggravated it and brought it to breaking-point. The Czechs saw the Empire's enemies as their potential liberators from oppression and inferiority; the Germans saw Czechs as traitors to a state into whose structure they had long been integrated. Czech units in the Imperial army deserted to the Allies *en masse*. Oppression of Czechs became a necessary form of German patriotism. In 1916 German was made the only official language and even in Prague the police were known to attack people speaking Czech in public. An extreme nationalist German deputy in the Imperial Parliament said of Czech aspirations to autonomy in Bohemia that there was 'a sweetness in which one can perhaps indulge in highly civilised circles, but which one cannot show towards tigers. In a menagerie one does not work with politeness and caresses, but with the whip.'[2]

*Approximate figures for the end of the nineteenth century.

Suddenly, with the military and political disintegration of the Austrian Empire, Germans accustomed to being in the majority and feeling superior to Czechs found themselves about to become a minority in an independent state run by Czechs and their Slav cousins the Slovaks. So unthinkable to them did the prospect seem that, though a Czech National Committee took control of Prague at the end of October 1918, Germans in areas of the 'historic provinces' where they were in a majority declared themselves part of an autonomous 'German Bohemia', and sent their own representatives to the expiring Imperial Parliament in Vienna. Even after the new Czech troops had, in accordance with the terms of the armistice, occupied all such territories, the German 'provisional governments' continued to function as such for some weeks. The largest of these, that of former Austrian Silesia, North Moravia and Eastern Bohemia, calling itself, after the mountains of the latter, the Sudetenland, continued to meet as a body for three months and to press unsuccessfully for autonomy within the new state.

On the whole the dramatic transition from one political dimension to another (from Austrian Empire to Czechoslovakia) took place calmly, but not without bloodshed. A new solely German state had been formed in Austria, a democratic Republic whose Chancellor proclaimed proudly to the delegates of the Provisional Parliament in the hope of an *Anschluss* or union with Germany: '. . . in this hour the German people in every district shall know that we are one race and share one destiny.'[3] The Sudetenland Germans responding to his word expected to be able to take part in the elections for the first Austrian republican Parliament. But the new Czech authorities forbade this. Protest meetings against the ban were held throughout the Sudetenland for the day on which the new Parliament in Vienna met, March 4, 1919. Czech forces reacting nervously fired on the demonstrators in a number of places and fifty-two Germans were killed, twenty of them in one small town alone.

For all the bitterness which this event lodged in Sudeten memory, there were factors, principally economic, which inclined many of the less politically-minded German population to accept with the grace of inevitability their membership of the new Czechoslovak state. In the course of the summer of 1919 the state's frontiers with Germany and Austria were carefully scrutinised, particularly in relation to awkward salients in the territory of those countries. The Czechs were prepared to give up some of these. But the Sudetens – a term increasingly applied generally to all Germans living within the former provinces – came to realise that the larger their numbers within the new state, the greater could be their strength there. Marxist dangers, too, from across the borders of the new Germany in the early days inclined German industrial interests in Czechoslovakia to opt for bourgeois stability even if a Czech one.

But the principal consideration was that there was no alternative. The Allies' power from the Versailles Peace Treaty was total. The Austrian Empire had gone for ever. The new Austrian Republic and the new Weimar Germany were far too weak for any pan-German emotions to be practically relevant. There was no one to whom the Sudeten Germans could possibly appeal for an alteration of the framework within which they now had to live. What they had to accept became something they accepted.

It would, of course, have been logically tenable for the Allies to solve the old problem the other way round: to incorporate most of the predominantly German areas within the new Germany and the new Austria. But this would itself have been contrary to the overriding logic of Versailles. As one of the French delegates to the frontier study of 1919 put it: 'He could not allow Germany to be fortified by populations taken from what had been Austrian dominions, taken, moreover, from Bohemia which he trusted would remain an ally of France, and handed over to Germany which, as far as he was concerned, still remained a country to be feared.' It was further accepted as a guiding principle at these discussions that to cut away the frontier areas of the new Czechoslovak state would have left it 'so entirely defenceless as to be incapable of independent life'.[4]

The Constitution of the new state within which the three million Germans of the former 'historic provinces' now formed just under a quarter of the population was promulgated in 1920. It was in spirit meticulously democratic and liberal and it laid down appropriate provisions for the treatment of minorities, in regard to proportionate political representation, schools and the use of language with particular reference to the large German minority. Forcible denationalisation of communities was made a crime. Dr Beneš at Versailles had written rashly of the new Czechoslovakia becoming 'a sort of Switzerland', implying apparently some notion of cantonal equality for all areas and a parity of status for all languages. The suggestion which was to be assessed later by critics as a calculated deceit was more probably an insufficiently calculated expression of euphoric good intention at the moment of final success. But, although the proper liberal tolerance of minorities was expressed in the Constitution, there was no question of the new state regarding them as anything but minorities. It was a Czech state, of which Czech was to be the official first language. Its first President, Thomas Masaryk, in his speech after election said: 'We have created our state, and that will determine the political status of our Germans who originally came into the country as emigrants and colonists.'[5] Though there was partial truth in the final words of this sentence, it was galling for Germans who had lived in German-populated Bohemia for six hundred years, or even a hundred, and thought of themselves as Bohemian Germans, to have to hear them. It seemed an ominous indication of attitudes to come.

Further small indications of an underlying need for Czechs to get their own back on Germans who had for so long seemed to despise and humiliate them could be found in the order of the wording on the state's new bank notes. This was in four languages and German was placed third after the Cyrillic script of the Ruthenians, a minority of some five hundred thousand compared with the three million Germans. Though all deputies to the Parliament in Prague were entitled to speak in debates in their own language, the official parliamentary reports of the debates were available only in Czech. The Mayor of Prague forbade shop signs in German though not in any other language, despite or rather because of the fact that 50,000 Germans lived and worked in its one million population. This absurdity becomes at least comprehensible if it is remembered that, only a quarter of a century before, Germans, with a similar proportion of the city's population, had claimed parity for their language there with Czech.

That there were in the early days of the new Czechoslovak state many instances of German-Czech friction at both national and local levels, aggravated by the traditional chauvinism of elements on both sides, is perhaps less remarkable than the fact that there were not more of them. After all, people of German blood, long proud of their ancestry, now had to describe their citizenship as that of a race

38

they had been brought up to think of as inferior. To have to call oneself a Czechoslovak citizen at all was for many Germans the first insult. That this should be regarded as an insult was itself an insult to Czechoslovaks.

But eventually what had been a politically negative attitude to the state on the part of Germans in the early years began to wane and to be replaced by a positive preparedness to make something of their integration within it. Already after the elections of 1925 fewer than half of the seventy German Deputies in the Prague Chamber of Deputies could be reckoned in sharp opposition to the Government; six of these were members of the National Socialist Workers' (Nazi) Party which was twinned with the party of similar name being organised by Adolf Hitler in Germany. It proclaimed the same aims of pan-German unity and displayed the same uniforms and swastika flags. Another ten extreme German oppositionists were the conservative Nationalists, the German National Party, also twinned with the Nationalist Party of the same name in Germany. But, even together in extreme opposition to the Czech Government, the two represented only an insignificant proportion of the German electorate of the Czechoslovak state. Within a year of these 1925 elections there were two Germans in the new Government itself: the Minister of Justice and the Minister of Public Works.

After the 1929 elections the intransigent German opposition among the Deputies shrank from sixteen to fifteen, though the National Socialist Workers' Party increased their representation from six to eight. Two Germans again became members of the Government: one the previous Minister of Public Works from the Agrarian Party and the other the Minister of Social Welfare from the Social Democrats, the largest German party in the state. The two largest German political parties in Czechoslovakia were thus by 1929 themselves part of the Czechoslovak Government. Ten years after the foundation of the Czechoslovak state the old German-Czech rivalry seemed no longer in itself a factor to bring about the state's likely political disruption. It remained, however, a factor potentially susceptible to external events.

At the end of 1929 the Wall Street crash and the world-wide industrial depression which followed had particularly severe effects in the industrial Sudeten areas of Czechoslovakia. Greater distress was on the whole caused among Germans than among Czechs, partly because the character of the Czech population was more agricultural and partly because much of the industry in which Czechs did engage was domestically orientated and thus less vulnerable to the slump.

Within a few years another change in the European scene which interacted with this economic distress had special significance for the old 'historic provinces'. Germany emerged as a power which could increasingly effectively speak for Germans. With Adolf Hitler's assumption of the Chancellorship in January 1933, the Germans of Bohemia, Moravia and Southern Silesia could, if they wanted to, once again realistically look elsewhere than to the Czechoslovak state. How likely were they to want to? How interested would the new Germany be in them?

Many Czechoslovak Germans, particularly the young, had in recent years consciously diverted their pride in German nationality away from immediate practical politics altogether into the more congenial and often headier fields of comradeship in cultural, gymnastic and sporting associations of a sort which had figured since the nineteenth century in the life of the 'historic provinces'. Except insofar as membership of such German associations signified in itself a lack of identification with Czechoslovak politics, political aspirations within them were in general either often absent altogether or, where present, focussed widely and often at variance with each other on different aspects of Germanic idealism. One such, the *Kameradschaftsbund*, founded in secret in 1926 and emerging into the open in 1930, still looked back towards Vienna in hope of some sort of authoritarian revival of the Holy Roman Empire. Another, the *Volksport*, was the most obviously political and, as the sporting organisation of the relatively small Sudeten Nazi Party, looked towards the party of the same name in Germany whose racial and nationalistic aims it shared and whose propaganda chief, Josef Goebbels, it had invited to address its meetings in 1927. Members of the *Volksport*, who wore the same brown uniforms as the Nazi storm troopers, attended the Nazi rally in Nuremberg in 1929, marching under the slogan *Treu zu Hitler*.

In 1931 the Czechoslovak authorities banned the wearing of *Volksport* uniforms and in 1932 put seven of its members on trial for planning the destruction of Czechoslovakia by armed rebellion – a charge which, for lack of concrete evidence, had to be watered down into mere conspiracy against Czech democracy. Relatively mild sentences eventually passed in October 1933 were widely resented among many Sudeten Germans.

Hitler had already been in power nine months in Germany. The potential danger to the Czechs of their own internal Nazi Party was obvious enough. Its legal proscription was clearly imminent. The Party and the *Volksport* took the tactical step of disbanding themselves. The *Kameradschaftsbund* did the same.

It was at this sensitive moment, with the economic crisis biting more deeply than ever into the lives of Sudeten Germans, that a thirty-five-year-old instructor from one of the German gymnastic associations which had had links with the *Kameradschaftsbund* came into the Czechoslovak limelight. His name was Konrad Henlein. Son of a German father and a Czech mother, he had been a front-line officer of the Austrian army during the war, and a clerk in a Sudeten German bank for some years afterwards, before devoting himself professionally with petit-bourgeois zeal to gymnastics. A man apparently of no more than average intelligence and personality, he had for some time been expressing an opinion about the lines along which German consciousness should pursue its destiny, and he now came forward to propose a movement to be known as the Sudeten German Home Front.

'Men,' Henlein had already written in 1931 in an article entitled 'The National Significance of Physical Training', 'Men wish to be led in manly fashion . . . We all know that an un-German parliamentarism, an un-German party system, which divides our people into organic parts, will and must break down some time . . .' At a great gymnastic festival in the Sudetenland he had been hailed by the crowd as 'Führer'. Now in October he appealed to the Sudeten Germans to rally round this new association altogether, the Sudeten German Home Front.

'I appeal above all parties and estates,' he declared, 'and put myself at the head of this movement.'[6]

It was in effect a new political party, only 'above parties' inasmuch as these had hitherto been part of the 'un-German parliamentarism' of the Czechoslovak party system. Members of the now dissolved former Czech Nazi Party quietly joined it. But it was still far too early for this new party to have at its centre any very coherent political identity other than German consciousness. It would not for years be clear to its leader Henlein in which direction he should or could lead it.

CHAPTER SEVEN

BRITAIN AND FRANCE – 'A CLEAVAGE', 1934–5

DURING THE WINTER OF 1933–4 HITLER'S GERMANY, FOR ALL HER official departure from the Disarmament Conference, continued intermittent negotiations with France about how the military clauses of Versailles might be adjusted to suit both France's demand for security and Germany's demand for rapid 'equality of status'. While such negotiations continued, Britain maintained a cooperative stance more or less in the wings. What had happened could be seen at the time – Neville Chamberlain had so seen it – as just one more disturbing phase in the Disarmament Conference's already chequered and languid progress. But it was during this time that the pattern of British foreign policy which was to make possible the Munich Agreement began to set.

It was becoming plainer, *The Times* argued that winter, with every successive phase of the Conference, that no substantial progress was likely to be made until the question of the revision of Versailles was settled in one sense or the other. So long as a mere negative was returned to Germany's desire for revision there was likely to be no relaxation of the tension which was tending to divide Europe into opposite camps.[1]

Relaxation of such tension in the interests of the stability and prosperity of Europe and thus the British Empire now became British policy's main concern.

As Anthony Eden, then Lord Privy Seal, put it in January 1934, using a word which had not then yet acquired a vestige of pejorative sense: 'If the nations could be assured of a period of real appeasement, international confidence would gain thereby just the encouragement it needed.'[2] Quite apart from having themselves conceded and brought the French that winter to concede the

43

principle of equality of status for Germany, the British Government had already formulated concrete proposals which involved a revision of Versailles. Their first-draft disarmament convention of March 1933, presented while the Germans were still at Geneva, had suggested among other ambitious projects such as 'abolition of bombing from the air' that Germany should now be permitted a conscript army (forbidden in any case by Versailles) of 200,000 men for eight months' service, whereas Versailles had stipulated, to prevent the building of reserves, only a long-service army of 100,000. France had eventually come to agree such figures though deadlock continued on other aspects of the proposals. Germany, in the course of these winter negotiations with France, now stipulated a conscript army of 300,000 men with a twelve-month period of service.

On February 1, 1934 the British Government in their mediatory role produced a White Paper which modified the earlier draft proposals, emphasising that it was the principle of parity in armaments that was now important and that it should not for instance be too difficult to find an accommodation between 200,000 and 300,000. 'The Government,' it added, with a further pointer to the direction in which it was leaning, 'would be prepared to acquiesce in the longer period of service if such is the general desire.'[3] It was a neat way of by-passing, without apparent offence, the desire of the French.

The new proposals envisaged further revision of the military clauses of Versailles in Germany's favour by allowing the new German conscript army tanks up to six tons, anti-aircraft guns and artillery of a calibre of 155 mm – all forbidden to her under the Treaty. If by the end of two years there had been no All-Power Convention to abolish all military and naval aircraft then *all countries* would be entitled to have naval and military aircraft. Later that week in the House of Commons the British Foreign Secretary Sir John Simon emphasised the British Government's main point. 'Germany's claim,' he said, 'to equality of rights in the matter of armaments cannot be resisted and must not be resisted.' He made a face-saving gesture in the direction of Versailles by adding the further principle that in pursuit of equality of rights you could not bring everyone down at once to the level permitted by that treaty.[4] What he did not actually say – and a great deal of British policy in these years was to be detectable from what it did not say – was that it was therefore only realistic in the current hyper-nationalistic climate of the new Nazi Germany to accept that Germany would have to come up.

Stanley Baldwin, the Lord President of the Council, had recently analysed the available options with realistic simplicity. Either, he said, all countries had to disarm to the level of existing German armaments, *or* the heavily armed nations must disarm to a point up to which Germany would be allowed to rearm, *or* there would be an armaments race. The last option had to be avoided at all costs, the first was 'unattainable for the moment', which left only the second, with its awkward rider, which he did not specify, that the French would never agree to disarm at the same time as the Germans were allowed to rearm.[5]

The Times had already reported in December 1933 that, in spite of the Versailles prohibition, the German General Staff had been reconstituted under the cover of the Troops Office (*Truppenamt*) and that although Germany was officially allowed no air force men whom the paper called 'Goering's boys in grey-blue' could be seen frequently on short strolls in Berlin or marching in the road in squads of a couple of hundred at a time.[6] Indeed, in *The Times* of January 24, 1934 there appeared an excellent photograph of them on parade in uniform virtually indistinguishable from that of the future Luftwaffe, though the caption described it as 'similar to that of the British Royal Air Force'. They were being organised by Goering under cover of the so-called 'Air Sport Federation' whose leaders bore titles such as Air Vice-Commander, and whose machines were often potential military machines in commercial disguise from the factories of Junkers and Heinkel.

It was noticed that industrial plants such as the Karlsruher Industrie Werke which made small arms and the Bayerishe Motorenwerke which made aircraft engines had recently greatly increased their profits while there had been an enormous expansion in German imports of such commodities as copper, cotton, nickel and aluminium. In March 1934 official budgetary statistics published by the Germans themselves revealed as estimates for that year an increase in expenditure of 40 percent for the Reichswehr, 30 percent for the German navy and 150 percent for the Air Ministry.[7] The last was solemnly accounted for by German officials as being for air transport and air raid protection. The naval expenditure was said to be for purposes of renovation, and it was true that the German navy had in fact never hitherto armed up to its permitted level. The army expenditure was said to be required for adaptation of the Reichswehr to a new short-service army, a change which both France and Britain had certainly proposed but which had never been officially agreed and which therefore in itself already represented a technical unilateral infringement of Versailles.

The publication of these estimates, though received with appropriate disapproval by official circles in Britain, told no one anything they did not know before. Two months earlier *The Times* had appraised straightforwardly enough the dilemma which the figures now made real. 'What,' it wrote, 'will rearmed Germany do? Her leaders claim that with the open acknowledgement and open attainment of her right to practical equality in armaments the sense of grievance will disappear, that there will be better hope of lasting peace in Europe than ever before. Her uneasy neighbours recall that Germany also has territorial claims' – the leader-writer had read *Mein Kampf* – 'and ask whether the sense of grievance would not simply transfer itself to these . . .' And he added cold-bloodedly as if Britain might count herself aloof: '. . . It is for other nations to discover whether the motive for German rearmament is really the sense of grievance, or the desire to create a strong backing for the further aims of German policy.'[8]

Evasively equivocal as the British establishment might be, there was one neighbouring nation in no doubt whatever about how to appraise the dilemma. Invaded twice by Germany in the lifetime of many still living, uncertain of the extent of British support in every eventuality, France was in no mood to take chances, in view of what was happening in Germany, with proposals for further German rearmament.

Earlier in the month in which the German estimates were published, Goering, to celebrate the official absorption of Prussia into the Reich as part now of a single administrative unit, had made just the sort of speech which would have aroused France's worst fears if she had not been alert already. He reminded the world that it had often derided the spirit of Prussian Potsdam, its militarism and its goose-stepping, but it should not forget that it was precisely this steadfast soldierly streak which had been able to defy the world. The world had stopped laughing when the tread of those Prussian Grenadiers had resounded over the battlefields. 'And so again would this very steadfast and soldierly stock bring Germans again to greatness.'[9]

The French reply to the new British draft proposals was delivered on March 19 and published on the 23rd. It summed up, in more positive terms than at any time since theoretical equality of status had been accorded to Germany, France's deep concern for her own security. France, it said, could accept no proposal which required her to disarm while permitting Germany to rearm within limits which were hardly to be relied on since that country was already rearming in violation of other treaties. Doubt was cast on the validity of any possible future arms convention. Since the military clauses of Versailles had not been observed, how could there be any faith that a new convention would be upheld? The British memorandum had spoken of 'consultation' in the event of violation of such a convention. France now said that positive guarantees were essential. 'When an engagement has been contracted towards the international community, its violation ought to be considered as a threat to that community itself.' There was an 'imperative duty to rectify without delay that infraction by all methods of pressure which would be recognised as necessary'.

The exchange of views between French and Germans themselves had already again reached deadlock. This French note of March 19, 1934 to the British Government signalled clearly enough that the whole process by which, since the beginning of the Disarmament Conference, Europe had been trying to reorganise itself in a new stability was coming to an end. The French Government, the note concluded, could 'neither understand nor admit that exaggerated pretensions to rearmament put forward on one side should constitute an argument for asking other powers to agree to reductions of armaments which do harm to the interests of their security'.[10]

The French *Journal des Débats* put the argument more directly. 'Security,' it declared, 'will never be established until Great Britain realises that the only danger of war that can threaten Europe results from the danger of Germany, acts accordingly, accepting and preparing methodically her instant military action for the event of

47

aggression. Until then she has no right to ask ourselves that we should weaken ourselves in the face of the Reich, and she assumes a grave responsibility in doing so.'[11]

In other words Hitler had made 'equality of status' talk out of date. Baldwin's third option could be said, in theory at least, now to be in play.

The French note, wrote *The Times* peevishly, 'shows not the slightest inclination to base a new system upon a new convention'. It reported 'considerable disappointment that the French Government have so far felt unable to make a better response'.[12]

When the German response to the British proposals came in on April 16 it was much more favourably received. The Germans maintained their claim for a conscript army of 300,000 men for a period of twelve months' service. In the air, however, while saying they could not wait two years before being allowed a defensive system, they claimed only the right to a purely defensive air force consisting of short-range machines and no bombers. They were prepared to accept a numerical air strength which would not exceed 30 percent of the combined strength of Germany's neighbours or 50 percent of the French air force, whichever were the lesser, and they were prepared to accept this inferiority for a period of five years. They would agree to accept international inspection which could ensure also that the Nazi S.A., a body of a million men whom the French assessed with disquiet as a paramilitary force, would neither have arms nor be commanded by military officers. Finally they would agree that the disarmament of other powers down to their own level should be postponed for a period of five years.

'It is really impossible to describe the German thesis as unreasonable,' wrote *The Times*, adding a few days later: 'It is time that . . . all countries should squarely face the fact that Germany is morally if not judicially entitled to possess the means of self-defence, and is in fact providing herself with them.'[13]

The French had already faced the latter point squarely enough, coming to a diametrically opposite conclusion. With a final note to the British Government on April 17, they delivered the *coup de grâce* to the whole process which had begun at Geneva more than two years before. Making full use of the figures revealed in the recent German budgetary statistics and of their own detailed intelligence about what was actually happening in Germany the note castigated the German Government for, 'without waiting for the results of the negotiations which were in progress', continuing every form of rearmament in contempt of the Treaty of Versailles. 'The German Government,' continued this final note, 'intends to increase immediately on a formidable scale, not only the strength of its army, but also that of its navy and its aviation. So far as this last is concerned, it is all the less permissible for the neighbours of Germany to disregard the menace that hangs over them, in that numerous aerodromes have recently been organised in the de-militarised zone also in violation of the Treaty . . .'[14]

When what was to be the last significant meeting of the Disarmament Conference took place at Geneva at the end of May the French Foreign Minister Barthou vigorously criticised both the British Foreign Secretary, Simon, and British policy, saying that the British proposals were no longer regarded by France as a basis for agreement even if they were accompanied by guarantees. *The Times*, commenting that 'some of M. Barthou's shafts were more sharply barbed than the representative of one friendly country usually aims at the representative of another', concluded that 'the cleavage' between the French and British positions was 'complete'.[15]

Of the now forgotten Disarmament Conference of 1932–4 it can at least be said that it brought about one positive result: the end of Versailles as an easily defensible position. Regrettable as any future unilateral revision of that Treaty by Germany could properly be said to be, it would from now on always be the unilateral nature of the act of revision rather than the revision itself which would be the cause for reproach. This inevitably weakened the case for, and certainly the will for, strong response to the act.

There was another effect too of the year and a half of negotiations since equality of status for Germany had been accepted in principle. A certain self-deluding sense of realism now entered the minds of both British and French as they looked over their shoulders at each other while facing Hitler. It was self-deluding inasmuch as each felt they could safely concentrate on their own emphasis in policy while in the long run clinging to a preconditioned belief in their old alliance. The full scope of the delusion was not to become apparent until the summer of 1940.

CHAPTER EIGHT

REVISION OF VERSAILLES; APPROVED APPEASEMENT, 1935

IN THAT SUMMER OF 1934 THE FRENCH FOREIGN MINISTER Barthou came to London to discuss the separate way in which he now intended to go, pursuing a pact or series of mutually defensive pacts on Germany's eastern frontiers. It was an aim roughly categorised as a sort of 'Eastern Locarno'. But Britain was exclusively party to the Western Locarno. While concerned to have the British Government's goodwill, Barthou could be under no illusions about reservations it attached to the new venture.

Just before his arrival Eden, then Minister for the League of Nations, had made the garden fête speech in which he spoke of standing by Locarno but being 'not prepared to extend our commitments to other parts of Europe with which we are not so intimately concerned'.[*] And Neville Chamberlain, Chancellor of the Exchequer, in his own style now delivered a similar reassurance to his constituents in Birmingham.

'Efforts,' he said, 'have been made to frighten people into thinking that the forthcoming visit of the French Foreign Minister has some connection with some sinister attempt to commit this country to some new Continental alliances. There is not a word of truth in any story of that kind. We are not going to enter into any new alliance, neither are we going to relax our efforts in the cause of peace.'[1]

The Times was sharper.

'Any talk of an alliance between Britain and France,' it wrote, '. . . is altogether beside the mark. Neither the British Government nor British public opinion is in any mood for alliances . . . The

*See above, page 33.

50

British Government consider their existing commitments under the Treaty of Locarno to be quite sufficient . . .' And the paper spoke further of 'the steady British refusal to assume further responsibilities in Europe'.[2]

What, though, apart from maintenance of a non-committal stance was Britain actually doing in the way of 'efforts', as Chamberlain put it, in the cause of peace? There were those that summer of 1934 who thought that, apart from keeping a benevolent eye on what the French were doing, it was not particularly necessary to be doing anything, because Hitler's own position in Germany had begun for a moment to seem less secure. The alleged attempt by the leader of the Nazi Sturmabteilungen (S.A.), Ernst Röhm and his million or more fanatical supporters, to usurp the role of the army and possibly replace Hitler himself had only just been put down in the bloody 'Night of the Long Knives' of June 30. *The Times* at least still thought Germany might be 'heading for chaos'. It decided that there was 'little one can do but wait with patience and calmness'.[3]

Sir John Simon, the Foreign Secretary, talked in terms of contemplation. What was contemplated, he told the House of Commons, after Barthou's visit, was a five-element mutual assistance pact involving the Soviet Union, the Baltic States, Poland, Czechoslovakia and Germany and at the same time a linking-up of the Soviet Union to the Locarno Pact. This was in fact what Barthou was contemplating and Simon hurried to make one thing about the project clear: 'I do not think any Government in this country could lend any countenance or any encouragement or moral support to a new arrangement between states in Europe which would be of a definitely selective character in the sense that they were taking up one commitment as against another.'

This implied assurance that Britain would not be party to any system designed specifically to protect countries from Germany unless there were also reciprocal guarantees for Germany drew cheers from all parts of the House of Commons. He emphasised that he had made it his business to make this entirely clear to M. Barthou. Something else he made clear was that, even should France be successful in organising an Eastern Locarno along British-approved lines, it would have from Britain no more than approval, well deserved though that might be.

'Whatever may be the interest or encouragement which this

country may be prepared to offer this new Pact we are not undertaking any new obligation at all.'

Here again there were universal cheers, which Simon acknowledged with the words: 'That is quite clearly and definitely understood, and there is no possible question or challenge about it.'

So what then, apart from avoidance of such pitfalls, was Britain herself contemplating in the form of foreign policy?

Simon spelt it out: '. . . a reasonable application of the principle of German equality of rights in a régime of security for all nations.'[4]

In fact Barthou was to fail in his attempt to achieve an 'Eastern Locarno' basically because both Germany and Poland refused to consider any sort of alliance with the Soviet Union. But his initiative was to lead to the sort of 'selective' pact of which Simon did not approve and to lay the groundwork for an all-important new departure on the European scene. In the following year, 1935, Barthou's successor, Pierre Laval, was to agree a straightforward Franco-Soviet Pact clearly angled for defence against Germany. Though this was not to be ratified by the French Parliament until March 1936 it was to erect, in conjunction with a Czech-Soviet Pact also agreed in 1935, France's long-standing alliance with Czechoslovakia and Czechoslovakia's own 'Little Entente' with Yugoslavia and Rumania, a theoretical European security structure independent of one to which Britain might or might not be prepared to contribute.

Before that, however, in 1934 both Britain and France were watching Germany continue, by more or less open 'secret' rearmament in the wake of the collapse of the disarmament negotiations, unilateral revision of the military clauses of the Treaty of Versailles. Either this mattered or it did not matter. British policy proceeded as if it were possible to take up both attitudes at once.

Sir John Simon, who would almost certainly have seen the uniformed German Air Sport Federation on parade in *The Times* photograph of the previous December, conceded calmly in the House of Commons in July 1934 that Germany had 'probably the most highly developed commercial air service in Europe'. He was proposing a modest expansion of the Royal Air Force at the time. His attitude to Germany could be said to be resolute compared with that of the Labour Opposition. Labour tabled a vote of censure against the proposed RAF expansion regretting that the Government 'should enter upon a policy of rearmament neither necessitated by any new commitment nor calculated to add to the security of the nation'.[5] Adherence to the system of collective security provided for in the Covenant of the League of Nations was, in the Opposition's view, all that was required.

That winter Stanley Baldwin, Lord President of the Council, gave the House of Commons further details of what Germany was doing unilaterally to revise the military clauses of Versailles, and he too did not seem unduly perturbed. She was, he said, 'in the course of expanding her long-service army of 100,000 men into a short-service peace-time army of 300,000'. He added strangely: 'That claim, if I remember aright, was made for her at the time she left the Disarmament Conference.' He did not add that it was one with which the British Government had been prepared to concur.[*]

He went on with simple frankness: 'I think it is correct to say that the Germans are engaged in creating an air force.'

He estimated this as consisting of between 600 and 1,000 military aircraft. Churchill disputed the figures as far too low and indeed Baldwin agreed the following year that at least as far as the rate of German expansion in the air was concerned he had been wrong. However to that first statement in December 1934 he added a masterly definition of the attitude in which the Government now faced what Germany was doing. He told the House:

> There is no ground at the moment for undue alarm and still less for panic. There is no immediate menace confronting us or anyone in Europe at this moment – no actual emergency. But we must look ahead, and there is ground for grave anxiety, and that is why we have been watching the situation for many months past and are watching it now, and shall continue to watch it.[6]

Today this anodyne assessment of Baldwin's seems to verge on the absurd. But at the time it seemed to most people, other than Churchill and his relatively few supporters, an example of the sober common sense they had come to expect from him. The danger which Germany might in future present was seen primarily in Britain as something which could be averted by freeing Germany from the grievances which made her a danger. In a much-

*See above, page 44.

applauded speech at the Royal Institute for International Affairs a fortnight before, the respected Empire elder statesman, General Smuts, had asked the question: 'How can the inferiority complex which is obsessing and I fear poisoning the mind of Germany be removed?' And he had answered it himself:

> There is only one way and that is to recognise her complete equality of status with her fellows and to do so frankly, freely and unreservedly ... While one understands and sympathises with French fears, one cannot but feel for Germany in the prison of inferiority in which she still remains sixteen years after the conclusion of the war. The continuance of the Versailles status is becoming an offence to the conscience of Europe and a danger to future peace ... Fair play, sportsmanship – indeed every standard of private and public life – calls for frank revision of the situation. Indeed ordinary prudence makes it imperative. Let us break these bonds and set the complexed-obsessed soul free in a decent human way and Europe will reap a rich reward in tranquillity, security and returning prosperity ...[7]

The Times called the speech 'perspicacious', 'wise' and 'imaginative'. Not long afterwards the paper itself proposed that the former Allies should give up the restrictive military clauses of Versailles voluntarily. For Germany herself to give them up unilaterally was not of course proper – however much everyone, including the British and French governments, might freely admit that this was what was happening without formal remonstrance. But there could be no objection to unilateral action the other way round. 'It is open to any beneficiary of a settlement to surrender the advantages he enjoys,' wrote *The Times*.[8]

The plebiscite prescribed by the Treaty of Versailles for the Saar region after fifteen years of French occupation was duly held in January 1935. It resulted, as everyone had expected it would, in an overwhelming vote for a return of that region to Germany. Both the expectation and the result made it easier still to see realisation of full equality of status for Germany as the chief desirable concern. There were, however, technical difficulties. As *The Times* said:

> There are obvious objections to a mere condonation of German infraction of the disarmament clauses of the Peace Treaty.

English commonsense may not react against it violently, but neither French national feeling nor French love of logic could agree to such a course . . .

On the other hand it argued:

German rearmament has become a widely acknowledged fact. It is moreover no static fact but one which becomes more formed as time passes . . .[9]

This was the same leading article which proposed voluntary unilateral abandonment by Britain and France of the Versailles military clauses.

Hitler's own reaction to his plebiscite victory in the Saar made an optimistic approach to the future even easier. This end to what he called 'so unhappy an injustice' would be, he hoped, a first and decisive step towards a gradual reconciliation of all who had fought against each other in the war. It would contribute towards 'an appeasement of European humanity'. And he added, with a convolutory sentence worthy of the British Foreign Office itself:

Great and inflexible as is our resolve to achieve and secure equal rights for Germany, we are just as ready not to withhold ourselves from those tasks which are necessary to produce a genuine solidarity of the nations in face of the present dangers and needs.[10]

If that was indeed his intention – and *The Times* at least saw no reason to doubt it[11] – then it seemed that Hitler would soon find himself in close accord with the British and French.

The French had acquired a new and more supple Foreign Minister to replace the intransigent Barthou*: Pierre Laval, a man who like Mussolini had begun political life as an extreme Socialist but had since moved to the right. Indicating what, in Britain, was seen as a more constructive French approach he came to London a week after the Saar plebiscite to exchange views on the direction in which the two countries might shape their policies in future. The basic question on the agenda was how to contrive a security scheme which could legitimise German rearmament. France's concern was

*Assassinated by Croat terrorists together with King Alexander of Yugoslavia in Marseilles on October 9, 1934.

to obtain categorical reassurance of Britain's continuing commitment under the Locarno Pact. With that assured, there were creative possibilities which both countries might pursue. The French saw Eastern Europe as the potentially dangerous area and with some reason in view of Hitler's long-proclaimed theoretical resolve to achieve self-determination for all Germans. They were particularly worried for the future of the small independent republic of Austria. In the previous year, 1934, an attempted internal Nazi *coup d'état* there had failed, though the Austrian leader Dollfuss had been murdered in the course of it and Hitler, not without some embarrassment and difficulty, had done his best to dissociate himself from involvement in the attempt.

The affair had caused much consternation in Italy whose 250,000 Germans in the South Tyrol awarded to her after the war were not without their own obvious claim to self-determination and thus union with other Germans. (Dollfuss's wife was actually staying with Mussolini when news of her husband's murder arrived.[12]) In January Laval had concluded with Mussolini an agreement by which, 'in consideration of the necessity to maintain the independence and integrity of Austria', France and Italy would consult together and with Austria, 'should this independence and integrity be menaced'. On the more immediate point at issue, the two countries also agreed that no country had the right unilaterally to modify its treaty obligations in the matter of armaments and that 'in the case of this eventuality also they should consult together'.[13]

The Anglo-French London conversations which immediately followed and whose purpose was reliably reported by lobby correspondents as being 'to advance together towards a general policy of appeasement and settlement' concluded on February 3 with an agreement which, had the later course of events proceeded as the participants hoped, would have made that day one of the historic dates of the decade.

The object of future policy was defined in the Anglo-French communiqué as being 'to promote the peace of the world in a spirit of most friendly confidence, and to remove those tendencies which, if unchecked, are calculated to lead to a race in armaments and an increase in the danger of war'. The British Government, the text continued, welcomed the Rome agreement of France and Italy and considered itself to be among those powers which would, as

56

provided there, 'consult together if the independence and integrity of Austria is threatened'. And while the communiqué agreed that Germany was not entitled by unilateral action to modify the obligations of the Peace Treaty it equally envisaged a replacement of those obligations by a general settlement freely negotiated. 'Nothing,' it added, 'nothing would contribute more to the restoration of confidence and the prospects of peace among nations.'[14] Nothing in other words was more important than a free negotiation of that rearmament whose unilaterally determined character they at present had to deplore. A further example of such necessarily delicate handling of logic was provided by a simultaneous formal proposal for an 'Air Pact' involving the air forces of the two Powers and that of Germany which theoretically did not exist.

In Berlin the new Anglo-French accord was generally welcomed. The opinion was that more consideration had been given to German feelings than at any time for years and that Britain had succeeded in persuading the French to accept a course which would lead to an end of the Versailles *Diktat*. The first official German response virtually confined itself to a welcome for the idea of an 'Air Pact'. Neville Chamberlain, welcoming in his turn this early favourable response, talked at Edgbaston in mid-February of 'a great advance towards the establishment of a sense of security in Europe' and 'the introduction of a new factor into the situation'.[15]

With Britain taking a leading role and Germany ready to exchange views in detailed talks, Europe indeed appeared to be on the threshold of something new.

A British visit to Berlin was arranged for Sir John Simon and his number two, Anthony Eden, at the beginning of March. Eden, it was announced, would go on afterwards to Moscow for further talks. And, although some French voices were said to be 'somewhat apprehensive' about the Berlin visit, the official French view was, in the light of the recent agreement, supportive.[16] From a British point of view the outlook for a settlement was brighter than at any time since Hitler became German Chancellor and indeed since the agreement with Stresemann at Locarno ten years before. The changing of the name of a street in Berlin from Stresemann-strasse to Saarlandstrasse a few weeks before did not seem a matter of significance.[17]

A series of events then occurred to alter the picture, disturbing at first the balance of immediate hopes and finally upsetting them altogether so that February 3, 1935 was to have after all only the most recondite place in the history books.

On March 4, with Simon and Eden about to visit Berlin, the Government issued a White Paper on Defence. Its external purpose was to supply a realistic back-up, but certainly no obstacle, to the negotiating process by which British foreign policy hoped to make a break-through. But it also had a domestic role. The Government had no problem getting anything through Parliament; it had one of the largest majorities of all time in the House of Commons. But a General Election was due at the end of 1935 and the mood of the electorate on national armaments was, it was thought, likely to be closer to that of the Opposition in the House than might be comfortable. (A so-called Peace Ballot held by the League of Nations Union a few months later was to reveal that over 25 percent of the nine million people who voted on the issue were opposed to the use of any military action against an aggressor.[*]) The electorate were unlikely to accept at face value Aneurin Bevan's claim that 'a socialist government in Great Britain . . . would change the whole face of international affairs'.[18] They might be equally reluctant to endorse immediately the view of Clement Attlee, deputising for the pacifist Labour leader George Lansbury, that whatever dangers Britain might have to guard against, national defence would be no help and they could only be dealt with 'by moving forward to a new world, a world of law, of the abolition of national arms . . . and a new economic system'.[19] More seductive was that ideal, to which indeed the opposition also subscribed, of international action solely through the 'collective security of the Covenant of the League of Nations'. The phrase became a popular moral refuge for all who wanted both to think themselves realistic and at the same time to remove themselves from the guilt and horror of modern war.

For the Government to justify even a limited amount of increased spending on national armaments it was necessary to convey some

[*]Questions and answers in the Peace Ballot published on June 27, 1935 can be found in J. Wheeler-Bennett, *Munich: Prologue to Tragedy*, p.249. Over 90 percent were in favour of economic and non-military sanctions against an aggressor; another 90 percent in favour of the abolition of all air forces by international agreement.

urgency. The White Paper singled out Germany for reproach, saying that His Majesty's Government had already drawn public attention to German rearmament without 'of course' thereby implying condonation of a breach of Versailles, and that this rearmament if continued at the present rate might produce a situation 'where peace would be in peril'. It criticised too the way in which German youth was being organised and trained and said that in consequence 'a substantial feeling of insecurity' was being generated.[20]

It was an indication of the extent to which Hitler was still largely improvising the details of his foreign policy that he chose to take offence. After all, the British were about to come to Berlin to discuss just how the revision of the military clauses of Versailles could now be respectably sanctioned. He might have been expected to disregard the White Paper. Instead he chose to let the British Foreign Office know that he was unable to see his visitors as arranged, having caught a cold which rendered him hoarse and in need of medical attention for the next fortnight. Immediately afterwards Germany announced officially that she now had an air force; it had actually come into existence, ran the announcement, on March 1.

This news was indeed no surprise to anyone, particularly those who in recent days had been watching German bombers and fighters flying demonstratively over the centre of Berlin. A more disturbing event, though again no real surprise, was the announcement a week later on March 16, 1935 that Germany was unilaterally giving legal sanction to the general rearmament which she had been carrying out for the past few years. In defiance of the Treaty of Versailles she was now going to introduce a conscript army, estimated at some half a million men.

The only surprise was in the timing. What made things difficult was that Hitler had thus formally taken that unilateral action which all along the Powers, however much they let it pass, had always made clear they could not condone formally without negotiation. The revision itself could hardly be a problem; negotiation had been on the point of formalising it.

For over two years now Britain and France had been agreeing German conscription in principle. The numbers were higher than the 200–300,000 which had been under discussion. But the increase was justified by the Germans as necessary to match a recent increase by the French of their own conscripts' length of service. What was really awkward was the obligation it now seemed to place on the Versailles Powers to slow down that process of assimilating Germany into a new European security settlement on which they were already advanced.

The Times, as might be expected, put the situation in a nutshell. This was, it wrote:

> . . . a grave and important event both for Germany and for the rest of Europe, even though its gravity is in some degree diminished by general expectation . . . There is something indeed to be said on general grounds for having the German cards on the table and for the principal parties in the forthcoming negotiations . . . knowing exactly where each other stands . . . But it is a flagrant violation of the Treaty which can hardly be passed over in silence.

The Times did however also articulate some sort of anxiety likely to assert itself increasingly with those who shared its views, if Hitler were to make more such moves.

'If,' it said, 'Herr Hitler's move is simply rather a crude method of asserting German equality no irreparable harm has been done . . . But it becomes of more urgent importance than ever to know from Herr Hitler himself whether Germany intends sincerely and whole-heartedly, to play her part in a collective system for security for Europe and to join with this in an equitable plan for the general limitation of armaments.'[21]

Certainly Simon and Eden were not going to be put off by the conscription announcement from making contact with Hitler personally. What might have been thought a slightly humiliating enquiry to the German Foreign Office to know if they would still be welcome received an affirmative reply. It had actually accompanied the official British note of protest over the action which was in any case mild, merely deploring the unilateral nature of the action as 'calculated seriously to increase uneasiness', and saying that the European settlement of which all were desirous 'cannot be facilitated by putting forward as a decision already-arrived-at strengths for military effectives greatly exceeding any before arrived at . . .'[22]

The last passage was of course tacit acknowledgement that the principle of conscription had been previously conceded.

The note immediately caused some disappointment in France quite apart from its relative mildness. The fact that it was sent independently rather than as part of a joint Anglo-French protest caused resentment, not unreasonable given the emphasis on joint initiative in the declaration of February 3; such separate action by the British could be seen to play into German hands by creating an impression of disunity. The French Ambassador in London called twice on Simon before he and Eden left for Berlin to express anxiety on the point.[23]

Laval, visibly upset, told the British Ambassador in Paris that he was 'gravely alarmed' at the prospect of Hitler's reaction to the knowledge that Britain had decided to go ahead with the visit to Berlin without previously consulting the French. He feared that 'it could only lead him before long to commit further acts of defiance'.[24] After all, without waiting for the talks, Hitler had simply appropriated one of the principal concessions the British had been ready to discuss with him, and yet they were prepared to go ahead with the talks just the same.

The Italians made a similar point. Mussolini himself was 'gravely concerned', also feeling that the British, in acting without consultation with Italy or France, would stimulate the Germans to further actions.[25]

Under such pressure Simon agreed to a preliminary meeting in Paris between Eden, Laval and the Italian Foreign Under Secretary for Affairs, Suvich, on March 23 before he and Eden went to Berlin the following day. But he rejected a strong request from Laval that the meeting should in fact be held in Northern Italy, where Mussolini himself was anxious to participate. He did however finally agree that a further meeting planned to discuss the Berlin talks when they were over should indeed take place there so that Mussolini could be present.[26]

Eden, arriving in Paris, must have had a fairly clear idea of what he was in for. The French note of protest to Germany which had now been delivered had been couched in far stronger terms than the British, and the French had referred Germany's action to the Council of the League of Nations under that Article 11 of the Covenant which concerned itself with 'any circumstances whatever affecting international relations which threaten peace'. *The Times* labelled this French move 'a profoundly regrettable decision'. The former Foreign Secretary, Sir Austen Chamberlain, wrote to *The Times* at once deploring the leader in which these words occurred. Next day he spoke to Unionists in Birmingham about 'the same old German spirit' being alive which had plunged Europe into the war, declaring that the cause of peace was best served 'if we make it plain that there are some things which England would not stand for and which would find her ready to resist'.[27]

In Paris Eden found both the Italians and the French seriously alarmed by what appeared to be happening, by the rapid pace of German rearmament and by the disappointingly mild British reaction to Germany's recent unilateral action. He wrote in his diary that the French were 'watchful, sad at us, and, beneath outward calm, profoundly disturbed'. If anything the Italians seemed more alarmed than the French. It was, according to Suvich, Mussolini's view that, if Germany were allowed to continue to violate one engagement after another, in a very short time she would endeavour to absorb Austria and that would mean war. It was essential, Mussolini thought, to 'take steps to immediately stop the rot', which was why a meeting in Northern Italy at the earliest possible moment was so important.[28]

Flandin, the French Prime Minister, told Eden almost as strongly of his urgent anxiety over the situation brought about by Germany's unilateral action and her rapidly increasing rearmament. Once the Berlin talks were over Britain, France and Italy would really have to make up their minds what their future course of action was going to be. What, for instance, he asked, was Britain going to do if Germany violated the demilitarised zone? This would be a violation of Locarno as well as of Versailles and French opinion might well demand an appeal to Britain from France under Locarno's terms. What would be Britain's response?[29]*

The question of the demilitarised zone came up at the official meeting. If, said Laval, it should get abroad that Great Britain and France would prove indifferent in the event of a violation of the

---

*A note on the Foreign Office document which recorded this conversation between Flandin and Eden reads '. . . H.M.G. will have to make up their minds on this and very quickly too. It is a most disagreeable necessity.' The note was initialled by Sir Robert Vansittart.

zone, it would not be long before a violation took place. The possibility of some Central European pact to guarantee Austrian independence was also discussed as was the Eastern pact to which it was assumed that Germany was likely to give an unenthusiastic response. Eden, for Britain, stressed that it was not his Government's role to tell Germany what sort of pact she should or should not adhere to.[30] The communiqué issued after the meeting was bland enough, speaking of 'complete unity of purpose', hardly surprising since the main purpose of the meeting had been to be able to issue just such a communiqué. But the difference of emphasis between, on the one hand, the French and Italian concern to ensure no more unilateral breaking of treaties and, on the other, the British concern to bring Germany back into an international equilibrium in Europe was not lost on observers, particularly the French.[31] *The Times* was prepared to express satisfaction insofar as the meeting meant that the other powers gave their seal of approval to the British visit to Berlin, but it thought it would have been even more satisfactory if the other powers had not regarded the preliminary assurance of this meeting necessary at all. 'It ought really to be possible,' it continued peevishly, 'for Great Britain to pursue a policy of her own without having to explain and justify every step, least of all to one particular group of countries . . .'[32]

Sir John Simon, speaking in the House of Commons just before his departure for Berlin had made clear enough what that policy was:

> The object of British foreign policy, he said, has been to help bring this great State [Germany] back into the councils and community of Europe on terms which are just to her and which are fair and secure for all, so that she with her great talents and resources may contribute with a full sense of equal status and dignity to the task which every good Europe who wants peace has got to share in, and that is the task of sustaining and strengthening general peace.[33]

CHAPTER NINE

APPEASEMENT IN BERLIN ON THE ROAD TO STRESA, MARCH 1935

THE TALKS BETWEEN HITLER, HIS FOREIGN SECRETARY VON Neurath, his Special Commissioner for Disarmament von Ribbentrop, Sir John Simon and Anthony Eden took place in Hitler's Chancellery in Berlin on March 25 and 26, 1935. The relative mildness of the British note of protest over the introduction of conscription and the simultaneous British request to know if the talks were to be held just the same conveyed to the Germans in advance that unpleasantness was unlikely. The Anglo-French communiqué of February 3 had already envisaged a new general settlement to replace the military restrictions of Versailles; thus, for all the disapproval for the unilateral nature of the action, the action itself was known to have approval in principle.

In fact the decision to introduce conscription was only referred to with a hint of reproach once during the talks when Sir John Simon reported at the beginning that he did not wish to discuss whether such unilateral acts were justified, only to say that they very greatly disturbed public opinion in England. That the French had reported it to the League of Nations was never mentioned at all.[1] The German Foreign Office had in any case just been informed by their Ambassador in London that Simon would 'leave no stone unturned to bring Germany into a system for safeguarding peace'. Eden, he said, had recently become cooler towards Germany and so should be given special attention in order to win him over again to a better appreciation of German affairs.[2]

Expressions of general sentiment came from both sides. The Germans stressed the sense of humiliation which derived from Versailles but at the same time the non-expansive character of National Socialism. The British emphasised their goodwill towards

Germany but at the same time their need to reassure British public opinion of Germany's good intentions. A number of important areas were then covered in the course of the two days. German opposition to any sort of Eastern mutual assistance pact on the lines of Locarno was made clear, though Hitler said he had no objection to straightforward non-aggression pacts. The British, while favouring some sort of mutual security system in the east along the lines hoped for by the French, usefully reminded Hitler that this was a matter with which 'His Majesty's Government were not of course directly concerned'.[3]

Simon similarly made clear that, while His Majesty's Government also favoured some sort of Central European pact to guarantee the integrity and independence of Austria, this was again not a matter which was of direct concern to them. 'His Majesty's Government,' he said, 'could not treat Austria in the same way as a country like Belgium which lay at their doors.' Their 'only desire was to see that part of Europe settle down'. The British saw interference by one side as being '*as objectionable as interference by the other*'.[4]*

Hitler himself only a few minutes before had explained that in his view there could be no question of German interference in Austria or of imposing union on her. With a free expression of popular Austrian will, such as was at present suppressed by the Austrian Government, there would be no need for this. The implication was obvious. The Germans reported what Simon had said as a 'proposal'† which Hitler could 'accept'. Their record of it was curt; 'Britain had not the same interest in Austria as, for example, in Belgium.'[5]

When talking of Germany's alleged unequal treatment by the League of Nations, Hitler, somewhat to the discomfort of the British, brought up forcefully the question of Germany's need for colonies. Otherwise the only really new initiative in the talks came from the British side. In the course of 1935 meetings were to take place about certain existing naval treaties between Britain and other powers, and an international Naval Conference was in the offing. Simon issued an invitation to Germany to come to London for informal talks about 'the requirements which Germany would wish to be discussed at a naval conference'.

*Author's italics.
†The British Foreign Office report used the word 'idea' instead of 'proposal'.

Now, the Versailles Treaty had laid down rigorous restrictions on the German navy. It was common knowledge that the Germans required these to be eased at least. They had mentioned a desirable figure of 35 percent of British naval strength to the British Ambassador in Berlin. The invitation to London was in all but name an invitation to discuss bilaterally with the British Government the revision of yet another aspect of Versailles. Simon's technical need to put on record that it was not such led him into the casuistry of saying that it was 'not an abandonment of existing treaty provisions . . . because it was for the future negotiation to reach a new agreement'.

The German claim to 35 percent of the British naval strength was, Simon now maintained, a figure so large as to make general agreement 'almost impossible'; but it was agreed in principle that such a meeting should be held in London. In case any suspicious interpretation might be placed upon it, Simon told the Germans confidentially that, if he found himself in England having to make a statement about it, he would say that it was in order to prepare for a naval conference which aimed for a new naval agreement in the future.[6]

The one surprise from the German side came when Hitler almost casually let drop the information that Germany now had air parity with Britain. Neither the British nor the German account of the talks record any British reaction to this.[7]

Near the end of the talks, Hitler stated categorically that 'to return to the League of Nations was the honest desire of the German people and their Government'. Germany could not, however, he added, do so until she was quite sure she would not have to leave again for lack of equal rights.[8]

Had the talks really taken anyone any further? Did they fortify or undermine that quest for international appeasement upon which British policy had been so long embarked? What deductions was Hitler likely to draw from them?

Sir John Simon expressed to Hitler a certain disappointment that they had not been able to get further in promoting the general European agreement which both sides wanted, but he felt that the British 'had gained very much by learning so frankly the point of view of the German Government'.[9] The official communiqué spoke of 'the frankest and friendliest spirit' in which respective points of view had been clarified and of the satisfaction of both parties over the usefulness of the talks.[10] To the House of Commons Simon reported that despite 'considerable divergence of opinion' the talks had been 'undoubtedly valuable'.[11] Perhaps the 'divergence' was emphasised to reassure the French.

Von Neurath issued a circular to all the principal German missions abroad saying that none of the points of difference which had emerged during the talks provided an insuperable obstacle to a general understanding and that the British Ministers, particularly Sir John Simon, had acquired a sincere admiration for Hitler. Hitler himself commented with satisfaction that, whereas Simon had probably come to Berlin believing him to be an ogre, he must now realise that he was like anybody else.[12]

The British Press on the other hand was in general sceptical about the meeting, noting the divergences expressed and concluding that Germany was not really interested in a new international security system but preferred to rely on her own strength. Only *The Times* remained faithful to its vision of future appeasement saying that there was 'nothing inherently unreasonable' in Germans wishing to abrogate the disarmament clauses of Versailles.[13] As Eden travelled on to Moscow, Warsaw and Prague in pursuit of the elusive Eastern pact which Britain wished to encourage but not embrace, *The Times* further commented approvingly that British foreign policy had lately become at once more detailed and more far-reaching. 'There is an end of what may be called, for want of a better term, the Versailles habit of mind which kept British statesmen in too narrow a groove.'[14]

However, on his thirty-six-hour train journey to Moscow, Eden, reviewing the talks in his mind, was beginning to have second thoughts and to question the lines along which British foreign policy was proceeding.[15] A year before he had genuinely believed that there was a possible basis for a new general European settlement. Now he found it 'exceedingly difficult' to maintain that there was one. Germany, he had seen at Berlin, was not really interested either in an Eastern or in a Central European pact. It seemed that her return to the League of Nations was to depend on, among other things, her re-acquisition of colonies. If there were no basis now for a general settlement, what then should the British Government's policy be? Was it right to continue to offer a hand to Hitler, or would he simply take more?

67

Britain had been playing the part of honest broker. Now, thought Eden, she had to recognise that she was a principal. In which case there was perhaps only one course of action to follow, namely to join with other League Powers in strongly reaffirming and upholding the principles of the Covenant. Perhaps, he mused, the spectacle of the Great Powers of the League collaborating more closely than ever was the only one which would keep Germany within bounds. It was a thought which was to lodge powerfully in his mind. Ironically it was to lose its way there under the pressure of quite different events about to upset the balance of international affairs.

Meanwhile, on the day on which Eden arrived in Moscow, Goering sent for the *Daily Mail* correspondent in Berlin, Ward Price, and asked him if he really thought that if France attacked Germany Britain would honour her pledge under the Locarno Pact and come to Germany's assistance. Ward Price told him he did not see how Britain could fail to do so but Goering cited a remark Eden had made to him privately in answer to the same question in the course of a Berlin dinner. Eden had replied in what he thought was appropriately light-hearted vein, that Britain had no soldiers but might put economic pressure on France.[16] However, behind Goering's present question there was, as the British Ambassador in Berlin correctly surmised, an ominous exploratory intent. 'If General [*sic*] Goering and Herr Hitler come to the conclusion,' he wrote, 'that Locarno is a dead letter it may lead them to re-occupy the demilitarised zone sooner than they would otherwise do.'[17]

In Moscow Eden had conversations with Stalin, Molotov and Litvinov. After mutual reassurances of collaboration and non-interference in each other's affairs in the spirit of the League of Nations, Stalin asked Eden whether he thought the European situation was more alarming than it had been in 1913. Eden said he would use the word 'anxious' rather than 'alarming'. But Stalin replied that he thought it was fundamentally worse because there were now two aggressors – Japan as well as Germany. On Germany, Eden noticed that Stalin was more appreciative than Litvinov of the German point of view but he thought that her recent actions were losing her sympathy and that the only way to deal with her was by some system of pacts which would make her realise that if she attacked any other nation she would have Europe against her. As for Britain, Stalin said that much would depend on her willingness to play her part in a collective system and he emphasised the dangers of hesitancy. Eden reminded him that in Britain public opinion had to be taken into account and that though as a result she sometimes might seem weak and vacillating this apparent weakness was in no way a cover for sinister designs at the expense of others. To which Stalin replied: 'Britain will have to think many times before she comes to a decision on such issues.' He spoke throughout in measured tones and displayed no emotion whatever except for an occasional chuckle or flash of wit.[18]

In further conversation with Litvinov Eden learned that in the Russian view 'the League at present did not provide any security at all' because action under Article 16 was only optional and that, without either making it compulsory or, alternatively, going for the conclusion of regional security pacts, 'the League could hardly continue to exist'.[19]

Earlier Litvinov had observed that the real point of difference in the attitude of the British and the Soviet Governments was that the former did not believe in the aggression of German policy. Eden said he thought it fairer to say that His Majesty's Government were not so convinced of it as were the Soviet Government, adding that they 'had hitherto wished not to believe badly of Germany's intentions'. The word 'hitherto' may have slipped in as a result of his thoughts in the train.

His reply expressed neatly the basic attitude from which British foreign policy was being conducted. Something of the doubt that had been growing in his own mind prompted him to ask Litvinov what he had already begun to ask himself. If, he said, Germany was saying – as indeed she was – that she must have full equality before returning to the League, should her terms be granted or would it be wrong to offer Germany a bribe for this purpose?

Litvinov's reply revealed the different approach to these matters of the Soviet Union. He said he thought that all states ought to have equal international status, but the only relevant issue was that Germany's present policy seemed based on aggression.[20] In fact of course no German aggression had as yet taken place, though German rearmament in defiance of Versailles could certainly be seen to show an aggressive attitude. But Litvinov's remark shows how it was possible at this stage for reasonable men confidently to anticipate German aggression in future.

From Moscow Eden went to Warsaw where he saw the aged President Marshal Pilsudski and gave him too some insight into British foreign policy but from a more traditional angle.

I told him for our part that we wished for nothing better than to leave Europe to her own troubles but that our experience was that the present troubles had an unhappy knack of involving our own country.

In conversations with the Polish Foreign Minister, Colonel Beck, Eden received the Poles' own version of a national self-centred approach. The Poles, Beck made clear, had no interest in any Eastern pact of mutual assistance which might antagonise one or the other of the two neighbours with whom Poland had potentially difficult relations: Germany and the Soviet Union.[21]

In Prague Eden found Beneš, the Czech Foreign Minister, in equally self-confident mood. Ideally he wanted both a Central European pact to guarantee the independence of Austria and some sort of Eastern pact. But if the latter proved impossible then the only alternative was a Franco-Soviet alliance. Above all something must be done. It would be disastrous, he said, to leave the Soviet Union in isolation, for then she would make an agreement with Germany at the expense of the others. He himself was not afraid of Germany. Even if an Austrian *Anschluss* were to be accepted by the Great Powers as a *fait accompli* he would make his terms with Germany. Czechs had after all been encircled by Germany for centuries. He did not think Germany wanted to take the Sudeten areas off Czechoslovakia, though he did qualify this by saying she wanted all or nothing. He thought she would in fact leave the Sudetens there to make trouble for the Czechs.[22]

Eden had a turbulent and physically upsetting flight back from Prague which left him with a strained heart. The shadow of doubt beginning to form in his mind over the soundness of British foreign policy may, or may not, have contributed to the short illness which prevented him both from reporting immediately to the Cabinet and attending the scheduled meeting in Northern Italy.

In the light of later knowledge the problem Eden was considering seems straightforward enough. But at the time it was a disturbing one. Pursuit of the principle on which British foreign policy had been based for years – the need to bring Germany to equality of status as part of a new order of peace in Europe – had created a situation which called the principle itself in question. By the time he had recovered sufficiently to send a short paper to the Cabinet to supplement his reports from the various capitals, he was able to say that he was not 'alarmist about the present European situation . . . but anxious because the attitude taken up by His Majesty's Government in the next few months may decide the future for years to come'.

He concluded:

> If we refuse to be scared or weakened by Germany's growing demands, if we resist the temptation to accept everything Germany asks for as a basis for discussion between us, if for a moment we can cease to be an honest broker and become the honest facer of truths, then I am confident there is no call to view the future with alarm. If on the other hand, we appear to the outside world to be weak and vacillating, if we allow *The Times* to continue to preach defeatism and to continue to be regarded as the organ of His Majesty's Government, then we shall encourage Germany's demands . . .[23]

His conviction was to prove stronger on paper than in action. Disastrously, such real strength as it carried was in any case about to be deflected in another direction. And, although the view of His Majesty's Government was to remain closer to that of *The Times* than to Eden's there was no question of him leaving the Government.

The meeting between Britain, France and Italy held at Stresa in Northern Italy from April 11 to 14, 1935 was intended to be the climax to the whole series of events which had begun optimistically with the Anglo-French declaration of February 3. The hope that that Agreement would lead eventually to a general European settlement had only been partially set back by the unilateral German decision to introduce conscription. Evidence of continuing optimism was revealed by the Stresa Conference's contact with Germany in the course of its proceedings to clarify her exact position over Eastern pacts. On the one hand it was as if she were regrettably an absentee from the Conference: on the other hand the Conference took place to decide what to do about her in future.

71

Some of the clearest apprehension about the future firmness of British foreign policy was to be found on the eve of the Stresa meeting in the Italian press controlled by Mussolini. The *Giornale d'Italia* noted with concern an increasing detachment of British policy from that of France and Italy. Other Italian papers called with some alarm for a 'united western front' against Germany with frequent reminders of the effects of hesitations and delays in July 1914.[24] Had the Italians had a sight of the briefing paper which the British Foreign Office sent to the Cabinet before Stresa they could have found still more reason for concern.

This dealt at some length with the principal problem with which Germany might present the Powers in the future: violation of the demilitarised zone of the Rhineland. Revealingly, the way in which the Foreign Office approached it was via the question: 'how are we going to deal with the questions which the French will ask us about it?'[25]

There were two procedures under which Britain's obligations under Locarno might be invoked in this event: one was by France bringing the violation to the notice of the League of Nations Council which would then decide if a breach of Locarno had indeed been committed. If so, Britain was pledged to 'come immediately to the assistance of France'. Here the Foreign Office helpfully pointed out that a) the nature of that assistance was not defined in the Treaty, and b) that of course a Council decision would require British agreement which could be withheld 'if we considered the facts were not sufficiently proved'. In the second form of procedure, however – that for a flagrant breach of Versailles – the options were less flexible: Britain was bound 'to come to the help of France' without any previous consideration by the Council, though once again it was pointed out that there was no specific definition of what that help was to be. In either case, wrote the Foreign Office, the French would ask at Stresa what action the British were likely to take in what circumstances. The briefing paper proposed a 'general line' with a somewhat devious ring to it, as follows:

Britain should publicly declare that she regarded our obligations under Locarno as binding 'according to its terms'. But there should be no specific reference to the demilitarised zone. 'We should avoid making any public declaration or giving any private assurance which defines exactly what we would do in a particular hypothetical case.'

If pressed by the French the significant difference between a minor infraction like the building of a small fortification in the Rhineland and a major infraction like the mobilisation of large forces should be pointed out, 'but it is surely most undesirable to be drawn into the discussion of these distinctions'. The final point made was one which in the light of the foregoing appears little short of hypocritical: 'We should remember throughout, and remind the French, that the main purpose of any pronouncement about the sanctity of Locarno at Stresa is to give the Germans notice that though they may have disregarded Treaty obligations about armaments, they had better be warned against disregarding Locarno.'[26]

Two other future possibilities were examined in this paper. On Austria there was a reminder that, while the integrity and independence of Austria was an object of British foreign policy, Britain had already made clear her wish to be excluded from any pact designed to preserve it. ('We cannot undertake special responsibilities of our own on the matter.') On the possibility of some eventual German aggression in the east which might bring the French treaties with Czechoslovakia and Poland into play and result in German invasion of France, Britain might have to take part in the conflict. '*But if we do take part it will be because we judge our vital interests to be gravely affected and not because the Treaty of Locarno requires us to do so.*'[27]*

Thus was emphasised the nature of that other basic principle which, twinned with the desirability of incorporating a Germany of equal status into Europe, was to dominate British foreign policy on the road to Munich. British interests alone would govern the need for British intervention in Europe and these were not considered vitally affected by anything that happened to the east of Germany – that direction in which Hitler had always said Germany's destiny lay. That France, in pursuit of her own security against Germany, should seek alliances on Germany's other frontiers was an unfortunate reality that had to be accepted. But on this matter too the Foreign Office paper had something to say: 'We must not express approval of any new engagements on the part of France in such terms as will increase our obligations under Locarno.'[28]

France was in fact known to be already engaged in the negotiation of a new straightforward mutually defensive pact with the Soviet

*Foreign Office italics.

Union which was to be signed in the month after Stresa. As for her relationship with Britain, this had come a long way from the wartime alliance of seventeen years before. The two countries, locked in a friendship which neither could avoid, were at the same time friends apart.

CHAPTER TEN

STRESA, BRITISH REVISION OF VERSAILLES AND THE ROAD TO THE RHINELAND, MARCH 1936

THE STRESA CONFERENCE DID NOT IN FACT EXPOSE ANY OF THE marked differences of emphasis between the three Powers in their attitude to Germany. It was accepted that, much as Britain wished the independence of Austria to be preserved, her interest in that country was 'secondary'. It was also accepted that she could not enter into any new commitments in any area; Sir John Simon had promised the House of Commons before leaving that she would not. The possible remilitarisation of the Rhineland was not discussed at much length, presumably because the resolution to be drafted for the League Council's censure of Germany's unilateral action on conscription was the more immediate issue. But such relative lack of concern for the Rhineland was surprising, not only because it had already been recognised as a likely problem for the future, but because the French presented the Conference with a detailed and convincing report about the military training, construction of fortifications and other proscribed activity already observable there.

The final draft of the resolution for the League decided that such unilateral repudiation of treaties, where it affected matters relating to the security and peace of Europe, should 'call into play all applicable measures on the part of Members of the League and within the framework of the Covenant', and that a committee be set up to propose ways of making collective security more effective, in particular by economic and financial sanctions. British intervention secured a milder version of the resolution than that originally proposed by the French. A final statement of 'solidarity' declared the three Powers to be completely agreed on opposition to any such unilateral repudiation which endangered the peace of Europe.

But, as in the Sherlock Holmes story, the most important thing about Stresa was something that never happened. Mussolini had already set in motion his own plans for an Italian revision of that part of the Versailles settlement which had conspicuously ignored Italian aspirations in the Mediterranean and Africa. His designs on Ethiopia, where Italian colonial aspirations had been active many years before, were widely known and new clashes had already taken place between Italian and Abyssinian troops in the ill-defined frontier areas between Ethiopia and Italian Somaliland. Any attack on Ethiopia itself and consequent embarrassment for the League of Nations of which both Ethiopia and Italy were members was at least likely. Simon took with him to Stresa a Foreign Office expert on the area who met a number of times with the Italian officials Mussolini had brought with him in his turn. But Ethiopia was never mentioned in all the four days of the Conference itself.[1]

Only one small hint of its presence in the background was for a moment discernible. After Simon had given the Conference a general report of his and Eden's visit to Berlin, Mussolini asked him whether Hitler's remarks about colonies had been a positive demand for their return or only a passing reference. He received what was for him the fairly reassuring reply that they had been used as an illustration of Germany's present inferiority status by contrast with, for instance, Japan.[2] That Germany might be in competition with Italy for space in the African sun was a further reason, in addition to concern about Austria, why Mussolini then wanted the three Powers to display a firm front towards her. When, at the end of the Conference, Ramsay MacDonald, the British Prime Minister who had accompanied Simon to Stresa in place of Eden, was asked by a correspondent whether Ethiopia had been discussed, he replied: 'My friend, your question is irrelevant,'[3] thus sounding a further reassuring note for Mussolini.

But as, throughout the rest of 1935, the Ethiopian affair moved towards crisis, its relevance to the European situation became painfully clear. For those anxious to prove that the notion of collective security through the League of Nations was more than an idealistic phrase, this remote situation in the African sun provided a less complex opportunity for firmness than the German problem. Eden was among those who were relieved to be able to embrace it. As Mussolini eventually launched his war against Ethiopia, this primitive and reactionary state which some thought unfit to be a member of the League of Nations in the first place became a symbol of weak and virtuous innocence oppressed by the rapacious strong. Economic sanctions of the sort intended in the Stresa resolution to act as a warning to Germany were applied in reality to Italy.

Stanley Baldwin replaced MacDonald as British Prime Minister in May 1935, knowing that around the end of the year he would have to call a General Election in which he stood to derive much benefit from the Government's support of the League stance against Italy. In the meantime he presided over the next major step in British policy towards Germany. It was one which succeeded in straining Anglo-French relations to near breaking point.

Eden, in his recent travels round Europe, had reported Germany's claim for a navy exceeding the Versailles restrictions to 35 percent of the strength of the British navy. He had also reported the British reply to the Germans that this was unacceptable. But nowhere did he mention that the Germans had at the same time been invited to London for preliminary talks. Similarly at Stresa the German claim was reported but no hint was given of possible negotiation. In fact Simon had said categorically on the first day of the Conference that on armaments 'there was no question of negotiations between Germany and the United Kingdom'.[4]

Just over a fortnight later the Germans gave notice that they were assembling parts for the construction of twelve submarines, an arm specifically prohibited to Germany by the Treaty of Versailles. When the matter was raised in the House of Commons, Simon asked not to be pressed on it.[5] Indeed the post-Stresa climate in Britain continued favourable to Germany despite the necessary reprimand on conscription delivered through the League. And an excuse for what was about to happen could be found in the fact that the French in any case were embarked on their own individual strategy and signed the Franco-Soviet Pact at the beginning of May.

On May 21 Hitler in a major speech rejected the League reprimand. But he did so in tones of moderation, justifying his unilateral revision of Versailles by saying that the other Powers had already invalidated it by their failure to disarm in accordance with the Treaty's terms. He pledged the German Government to 'scrupulously observe every treaty voluntarily concluded even

77

before their assumption of office'. This was a categorical reference to the Locarno Pact, and its confirmation of the demilitarised state of the Rhineland voluntarily agreed by Stresemann in 1925. Hitler further declared himself ready both to support the principle of collective security in Europe (provided the way was left open for 'evolutionary' treaty revision) and to subscribe to any future international agreement on the limitation or abolition of armaments.

This was, said *The Times*, 'reasonable, straightforward and constructive . . . a sincere and well-considered utterance, meaning precisely what it says' and its leader writer referred to 'the absurd criticism already heard from Paris, and even in some quarters in this country, that the Chancellor's proposals were too vague to be of value'.[6]

Hitler's was 'a striking declaration', said Baldwin in the House of Commons.[7] Before a massed Conservative audience in the Albert Hall a few days later he further addressed himself to the problems of the day in his own special style.

'Sometimes,' he admitted, 'we feel the French are difficult,' and he made a decent plain man's excuse for them: 'You put yourself in the position of a country twice invaded by her neighbours within the lifetime of many living,' he said. 'You would look at it differently . . .'

He faced the facts of history realistically. '. . . The French and ourselves have fought through the centuries, have fought in those very narrow seas,' but he concluded with a sort of double-edged reassurance: 'What was possible then is impossible today . . . However we may feel, however we may regard each other in the moment when each perhaps feels to the other as neighbours sometimes do, we know perfectly well we have got to be neighbours and we have got to be friends.'[8]

The *Frankfurter Zeitung* had little difficulty in deciphering this. 'All who are earnestly concerned to improve the European situation,' it wrote immediately after Baldwin's speech, 'will observe with satisfaction that the British Government have kicked the diplomatic ball in the right direction.'[9]

A week later Anglo-German naval talks began in London. Joachim von Ribbentrop made his first appearance there to represent the German side. It was soon reported that the talks were taking place 'in the frankest manner with an obvious desire on both sides to come to a friendly understanding'.[10]

They lasted a fortnight. Complete agreement was reached between Britain and Germany for a new German navy, the strength of which was to be 35 percent that of the British navy, the very figure which the British had been telling their former allies and others was unacceptable. The Germans were permitted to build an equal number of submarines to the British if they so wished, provided that the total ratio of all craft remained at 35 percent of the British strength. It was a bilaterally-agreed basic revision of the Treaty of Versailles. The French had not been previously notified. The Agreement was signed on the anniversary of the Battle of Waterloo, June 18.

The German News Agency proclaimed that a new chapter had been opened in the history of Britain and Germany and that it was now possible to say that the first great practical step had been taken for essential cooperation in Europe.[11] *The Times*, whose editor was a close friend of Baldwin's, while admitting that the Agreement 'obviously' infringed the Treaty of Versailles, saw nothing in it which need diminish the cordiality of relations with France and Italy. 'It has long been recognised in theory,' it commented with Olympian detachment, 'that the new order which it is hoped to set up in Europe could only be built on the equality of all nations; and it is really time to put the principle into practice.'[12] The Italians were disagreeably surprised. The Naval Agreement was rightly seen by them as a betrayal of the spirit of Stresa.[13] But it was the French who were really taken aback.

Eden had to fly to Paris to try to pacify them. There Laval told him that opinion ran high and complained that the Agreement not only infringed Versailles but also the Anglo-French communiqué of February 3 which had specifically undertaken to treat the whole question of security and armaments as an indivisible whole. Perplexed, he reminded Eden of the British statement at Stresa that the figure of 35 percent was unacceptable.

To this last point Eden made an extraordinary reply which he repeated with some pride in his memoirs a quarter of a century later. It had, he told Laval, been the original British intention to conduct only preliminary conversations with the German naval experts. But the Germans had refused to go on with the talks unless they got an answer on the figure of 35 percent. This 'offer', as Eden called it, was 'one which no government of the United Kingdom could possibly have refused'. After all, he said, Germany had hitherto been revising Versailles without asking anybody.[14]

Eden's increasing preoccupation with Ethiopia may have accounted for his reasoning, for he was not a man naturally given to cynicism. At any rate his mission had little immediate effect in calming the French. He notified London from Paris that nothing would modify the judgement there that a blow had been struck at the principle of solidarity behind the communiqué of February 3.[15]

Other members of the British Government were equally untroubled by what they had done in the Anglo-German Naval Agreement. Baldwin, at a public meeting in Yorkshire, even spoke out quite strongly, for a politician of his naturally assuaging character: 'I regret profoundly,' he said, 'observations of one or two members of the House of Commons that you cannot trust the Germans to keep their word.'[16]

His Chancellor of the Exchequer, Neville Chamberlain, speaking in the New Forest, strongly defended the Agreement, insisting that 'it was *not* a cunning attempt to divide us from our French friends' though, taking his cue from the Prime Minister's Albert Hall speech of a few weeks before, he added that it was 'perhaps not unnatural' that the French should show 'some anxiety, some resentment'.[17] Samuel Hoare, the new Foreign Secretary, in his first speech as such to the House of Commons was equally patronising. 'I am quite aware,' he said, 'that the logical and juridical mind of the French often sees things from an angle different from that of the empirical and the practical.'[18]

Ministers were in any case beginning to look towards the General Election and to draw the threads of British policy together on all counts into a presentable package. The Chancellor of the Exchequer, Neville Chamberlain, had to balance his own departmental concern for thrift with a wider concern for the nation's safety. Money had to be found for that limited increase in armaments whose budget the Labour and Liberal parties were continuing to oppose. 'Only if Britain is strong enough,' he proclaimed in Scotland in July, 'can she fulfil her mission as the peacemaker of Europe. Disarmament must follow, not precede the establishment of a sense of security. In that way only can she fulfil her mission –

80

the mission of peacemaker of Europe.'[19] And at the Mansion House in October and at the Conservative Party Conference two days later he returned to the same theme.

> To concentrate upon disarmament at the moment seems to me to be putting emphasis on the wrong point . . . if everybody is willing to disarm we shall be only too glad to disarm, but at the moment we must fill the gaps in our defences in order that we may make our country safe, that we may preserve our Empire and that we may faithfully fulfil our obligations to other nations . . .[20]

The criticism to which Chamberlain was later subjected for his own handling of the established policy of appeasement is sometimes unfair to him. The need for as much armed reinforcement of that policy as the electorate could be persuaded to accept was one he never shirked, however secondary it might be in his mind to that policy's main purpose.

In the shadow of the coming election and in the light of the knowledge of the Peace Ballot results earlier that summer, the necessary emphasis was placed by all members of the Government on the obligation to collective security under the Covenant of the League of Nations. But Chamberlain was already putting his own private edge to this attitude in the name of the Government. 'Unless and until the League has been proved incapable of fulfilling the function for which it was created,' he had said at the Mansion House, 'we intend to take our part – *though no more than our part* – in fulfilling our obligation under the Covenant.'[21]

And at Bournemouth he said: 'We are supporting the League because we believe that through the League we may be able to prevent war and establish peace by collective security. If the League cannot do that, then it is not going to fulfil the function that we expect of it. But we must be satisfied that it cannot do that before we abandon what seems at present the only hope of establishing a permanent peace in the world.'[22]

Baldwin won the General Election in November by an overwhelming majority of seats and even a majority in the popular vote. His Government tried to abandon hope in the League almost at once, seeking to solve the Ethiopian crisis bilaterally with France by an offer of territory to Italy at Ethiopia's expense. The subsequent public outcry caused the attempt to be abandoned and Sir Samuel

Hoare, who had by then replaced Simon as Foreign Secretary and had agreed the plan with the French Minister, Laval, had to resign to save the Government's face. Britain then back-tracked and, disconcerting the French, again headed the League opposition to Italy. Details of the Ethiopian crisis are not relevant to the story of Munich but its domination of international affairs for so many months in 1935 and early 1936 are a not insignificant feature in the prologue to it.

In the first place, Italy became separated from 'the Stresa front' and that Conference was consigned to a backwater of history along with the Geneva Conference on Disarmament. Unexpected opposition to Italy's African venture, particularly from Britain, sent her in search of sympathy from the other Power intent on adjusting the post-war settlement to its own liking, Hitler's German Reich.

Secondly, differences of emphasis in foreign affairs between Britain and France increased. France saw Italy as potential support, through the Locarno Pact, for security against Germany; she disliked having to antagonise her. Thus though dutifully subscribing to the principle of collective League action against Italy she did so with misgivings in the absence of any further British commitment to French security than the Locarno Pact. In some quarters in France there was traditional suspicion that Britain was perfidiously exploiting the Ethiopian affair in her own Imperial interests. The risk to the British Mediterranean fleet from possible Italian reprisal, while necessitating French concern, did not easily command immediate help in the event of war.

Finally absorption in the Ethiopian crisis deflected British foreign policy dangerously away from the more difficult and central problem of Germany, which waited in the shadows.

The British Ambassador in Berlin, Sir Eric Phipps, reported steadily on the continuing German organisation of what he called 'this enormous military machine'. He quoted a German lady from a garrison town who said that if war came she did not think she would see much difference, 'except that I might be woken at night by bombs instead of these endless squadrons of low flying machines'. Phipps himself commented 'that military expansion will be followed by territorial expansion goes without saying, though Germans in private conversation often say it'. He concluded this report of November 1935: 'It will be seen that the present Ethiopian

Gustav Stresemann, 1925

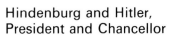

Hindenburg and Hitler,
President and Chancellor

Members of the Council of the League of Nations, 1926. Beneš
in the centre, Briand on his right, Austen Chamberlain on his left.

Mussolini's men at the Disarmament Conference in Geneva,
1932. In the centre, Balbo, Minister for Air; to his left, Grandi,
the Foreign Minister and Graziani, Minister for War.

Beneš and Laval at the Quai d'Orsay in 1934

Eden and Laval, 1935

Anschluss, March 1938

imbroglio is mere child's play compared to the problem that will in some not very distant future confront His Majesty's Government.'[23]

The German General and Commander-in-Chief von Blomberg had told Phipps that, if Germany were not allowed to expand, 'the kettle would some day burst'.[24] A British Foreign Office official, commenting on Phipps's despatch, asked if the transfer of colonies, one of the German claims, was really going to stop the kettle from boiling again 'and eventually bursting on the East where the kettle's sides seem extremely weak?' He went on to say that it was difficult to hope that the sort of economic sanctions the League was applying against Italy could be effectively applied to Germany.[25]

The application of League collective security to problems other than Italy was one to which Sir Samuel Hoare had given his mind shortly before he betrayed the principle in the plan with Laval which brought about his downfall as Foreign Secretary. At a time when, in the aftermath of the Anglo-German Naval Agreement, relations between France and Britain were at their worst for many years, he had tried to reassure the French Ambassador in London that to suggest or insinuate that British full acceptance of the obligations of League membership was confined to the Italo-Ethiopian dispute 'would be a complete misunderstanding . . . an underestimate of British good faith and an imputation on British sincerity'. But he immediately qualified this with a wily distinction, pointing out that under Article 16 of the Covenant procedure appropriate to a positive act of unprovoked aggression was not applicable to a negative act of mere failure to fulfil the terms of a treaty. 'In regard to treaty obligations,' he said, 'it is pertinent to recall that . . . elasticity is a part of security and that every member of the League must recognise, as the Covenant itself recognises, that the world is not static.'[26]

Elasticity, in other words, would be applied by the British Government to the Rhineland, remilitarisation of which would of course be a breach not only of Versailles but of the Locarno Treaty.

The French had already noted many signs of forthcoming military activity in the zone. The need to prepare a coherent response in advance of German action there nagged at both Governments, and they in turn found in it cause to nag each other. Phipps reported from Berlin in the middle of December 1935 that the raising of the matter by the Germans was 'only a question of time'. The Foreign Office itself complained that no consideration had been given to the question. No one, they said, either in Paris or in London had 'any clear ideas to what attitude ought to be taken if we were suddenly presented (as we may be at any moment) with a serious infringement'.[27]

In the course of a meeting between Phipps and Hitler a few days earlier the German Foreign Secretary von Neurath had said that if, as was being discussed, Locarno was to be extended to cover aerial as well as ground attack, the Germans would have to remilitarise the Rhineland to have their aircraft as close to the frontier as the French. Hitler had thereupon complacently observed that he could in fact have easily remilitarised the zone when introducing conscription in March without provoking war but had chosen to respect Locarno. Phipps commented in his despatch, 'I fear that the zone will be re-occupied whenever a favourable excuse presents itself.'[28]

On January 16, 1936 the French informed the Foreign Office that in their view the demilitarised zone had now to be regarded as one of the questions of the hour. Internally a Foreign Office paper analysed the question as being whether the zone would be reoccupied by agreement or in the brusque and unilateral manner used to introduce conscription the previous March. One 'escape', as the Foreign Office put it, which might make agreement possible, was to be found in a re-writing of Locarno to include aerial attack in such a way as quietly to omit all reference to a demilitarised zone.[29] (A breach of Versailles itself was thus tacitly acknowledged as a matter of no significance.)

Eden, who had replaced Hoare as Foreign Secretary, submitted a paper to the Cabinet on January 29 summing up the present realities of the German situation and, in the light of them, the possible future direction of British policy. He assessed Hitler's own foreign policy objective as being the destruction of the peace settlement and the re-establishment of Germany as the dominant power in Europe. Like Chamberlain, he stressed the need to hasten and complete British rearmament 'to be ready for all eventualities'. But he also stressed the need to consider how possible it was to find a *modus vivendi* with Germany'. The Baldwin Cabinet, having heard his views, 'agreed that the question of British policy towards

Germany should be taken up when Mr Eden was ready'.[30] He was still much absorbed in the Italo-Ethiopian affair.

Flandin, who had recently become French Foreign Minister, had had a conversation with Eden, in the course of which the French position emerged as both concerned and imprecise. Flandin had actually asked Eden what he thought the attitude of the French Government to a remilitarisation of the Rhineland ought to be. Eden merely repeated German assurances and said it seemed unlikely that they would take any precipitate action in the near future. When he followed this up with questions to Flandin about how much importance the French really attached to the zone, and whether they might not use it as some bargaining counter while it lasted, Flandin replied that these were just the subjects which he thought the two Governments should consider and about which they should then consult.

Flandin did however contribute one realistic note. Germany, he said, was not likely to rest content with the continued existence of the demilitarised zone if she contemplated any aggressive action elsewhere. 'For example,' he said, 'suppose that Germany intended to attack Czechoslovakia, the existence of the demilitarised zone would leave a gap in her defences which would make her very vulnerable.'[31]

France of course had a long-standing mutually defensive treaty with Czechoslovakia, concluded in 1924. Eden had long ago made clear that Britain was not interested in commitments to those parts of Europe with which she was not intimately concerned. Locarno was the limit of British European commitment. He was however, on January 27, 1936, resolute in saying, at least to the German Foreign Minister, that His Majesty's Government would on no acccount do anything to weaken or injure Locarno. They regarded it, he said, as being of the greatest value in the preservation of peace in Europe.[32]

At a Foreign Office meeting over which Eden presided on February 3, it was agreed that it was desirable to negotiate with Germany provided material for negotiation could be found. The demilitarised zone was suggested, and it was asked whether the French would always have to be consulted in the course of such negotiations. Eden said he thought they should be consulted simultaneously with the Germans.[33]

A week later, while again stressing the need to rearm, he argued in favour of starting negotiations with Germany and 'on balance' of making concessions to her provided this action was not such as 'stimulates the appetite it is intended to satisfy'. The abandonment of the demilitarised zone was again put forward as one of the offers that might be made. Baldwin appointed a committee to examine the whole question.[34]

Meanwhile Eden urged the British Ambassador in Paris not to enter into any discussion with the French about possible violation of the zone because the question was 'highly delicate and complicated'.[35] He said the re-occupation of the zone could not be entirely discounted though it was not necessarily imminent. The Germans might well use the now-pending ratification of the Franco-Soviet Pact as an excuse. He argued with shrewd casuistry that though a violation of the zone would indeed constitute an act of unprovoked aggression under the terms of both Versailles and Locarno it would not be obligatory for Britain immediately to give France military assistance if France then attacked Germany – which, he said, France was anyway unlikely to do if she knew that Britain would not support her.[36]

The Franco-Soviet Pact, signed in Moscow nearly a year before, still had to be ratified by the French Assembly who were about to vote on it. Increasingly bitter differences between Left and Right in France were already seriously influencing foreign policy. The Right, who had always spoken out most strongly for the French need for security against Germany, was now increasingly concerned at the prospect of an internal menace from a possible left wing Popular Front government which might include communists. It now looked with concern at the alliance with the Soviets. The Pact was however ratified by the Chamber of Deputies on February 27 by 353 to 164, and only on that day did the French Cabinet consider formally for the first time what to do if the Germans moved into the Rhineland.

The French military leaders, grossly overestimating the existing German forces, recommended only defensive measures; mobilisation would first be necessary if the offensive were to be taken. The French Cabinet decided, and five days later informed Eden, that France would not take any isolated action but would act only in accord with the co-signatories of Locarno. After the months of prevarication on the matter this could not mean anything but that German action would not be opposed. To complete the picture of

86

self-delusion in which the whole problem had been faced, or rather not faced, the French Government having taken this decision said that, awaiting the opinion of the co-signatories, they reserved the right 'to take all measures, including those of military character'.[37]

On the morning of Saturday, March 7, the Germans crossed the Rhine with three battalions.*

Having failed to decide what to do, except in the most negative terms, the French did nothing but cancel some military leave. The British, who had for months been seeking for a way out of their obligations should the French do anything, were relieved though anxious for a few days that they might do something after all.

Eden immediately sent for the French Ambassador who found him curiously unmoved. While expressing formal disapproval of what the Germans had done, Eden showed 'the unexpressed relief that follows a misfortune long feared'. His attitude was 'that of a man who looks for the advantages that can be drawn from a new situation . . .'[38] He urged the French 'to do nothing to make the situation more difficult'.

As in the year before, Hitler tied his unilateral action to a set of reasonable-sounding proposals. He offered to replace Locarno with a twenty-five-year non-aggression pact beween Germany, France and Belgium which Britain and Italy would guarantee. He talked of Germany's return to the League of Nations.

As the year before, all that had really happened was that Hitler had taken, without waiting, what the British had been preparing to offer him anyway. Now, after a decent interval they could start again where they had left off.

Eden had predicted that, if the Germans moved, the French would make belligerent noises but in the end do nothing. His forecast proved correct. The French Prime Minister, Sarraut, spoke with emotional patriotism of the insult delivered to France by the assumption that differences within the country could be exploited to prepare her subjection.

'They forget,' he said, 'once more that in every grave hour in our history such disunion gives way to the immediate union of French energies . . . Our cause is just and strong. In defending it we are

---

*Jodl's figure given after the war. The German Foreign Office notified Britain immediately after the event of a higher figure, but it is possible that this would have been an exaggeration for purposes of bluff.

conscious of defending at once our destiny and an essential element of European peace.' And he pronounced a stirring rallying cry: 'We are not disposed to allow Strasbourg to come within the range of German guns.'[39]

It already was. It would remain so. After the cautiously defensive nature of the military briefing given to the French Cabinet by the Commander-in-Chief, General Gamelin, this traditional talk of a nation on the brink of war had only theatrical impact. It was no less than French pride demanded, but also no more.

Eden, after first attending a Cabinet meeting and addressing the House of Commons, flew to Paris two days later with the Lord President of the Council, Lord Halifax, to make sure that the French did nothing foolish. He opened his speech there by saying that he was 'glad to hear from M. Flandin that there was no intention to try to reach decisions at the present meeting'.[40]

Flandin himself was one of the French Ministers most seriously prepared to contemplate action – if not military action, then economic sanctions – against Germany. But, in the light of the running failure of economic sanctions against Italy and divergences among the French themselves, it did not prove difficult for the British gradually to defuse tension until all response became merely a matter of further words. They were often bitter words between French and British.

Within ten days of the German move Flandin was telling Eden that the British, in their self-appointed if understandable role as mediator, 'had gone too far'. They seemed to be virtually treating France and Germany as if they were equally guilty. The crisis had resulted in 'a misfortune for Anglo-French relations'. He was afraid that Laval, who had always said it was useless to rely on England, would become more influential.[41] René Massigli of the French Embassy in London told the Foreign Office that France and Britain were heading for catastrophe. '*Des conclusions terribles*' and '*calamité*' were some of the words he used.[42] Eden continued imperturbably on the course he thought right. On the same day as he listened to Flandin's protest he assured the Germans that 'His Majesty's Government are doing and will continue to do their utmost to find means of bringing about a peaceful and satisfactory settlement of present difficulties.'[43] As Massigli said, to begin immediate negotiations with a Power that had just torn up a perfectly good and valid treaty, as it had done several times before, savoured of *opéra bouffe*.[44]

On first hearing the news of the German move, Eden and Baldwin had decided, in line with Cabinet and Foreign Office reasoning of recent months, that there would be no support in Britain for any military action by the French. The British Press bore them out. Though Eden had told the German Ambassador that the effect on British opinions of Germany's unilateral action would be deplorable, it was hardly seen to be so. The Press, like the Foreign Secretary himself, while reproving the incorrect manner in which the leap over such an awkward and long-dreaded problem had been made, expressed a general sense of relief at the chance to move forward to safer ground. There was nothing special to *The Times* about the heading to its leader on the subject: 'A Chance to Rebuild'. Eden himself echoed the phrase in the House of Commons next day, speaking of 'a manifest duty to rebuild' and 'the transition from a bad past to a better future'.[45]

The Liberal *News Chronicle* struck the same note. Speaking of 'Herr Hitler's symbolic occupation' it wrote:

> Accompanied as it is by an offer of terms which hold out the possibility of rebuilding good international relations, it will not be regarded by a single Englishman as constituting sufficient ground for supporting French punitive measures against Germany.

'Certainly the people of this country will not stand for such a war,' wrote the Labour *Daily Herald*, and the Conservative *Scotsman*: 'Nothing should be done that might result in making the European crisis more delicate than it is already.' 'The real task,' wrote the *Liverpool Post*, 'is to see whether this deplorable happening may not be used to yield some good.'

The Beaverbrook Press went much further. The *Evening Standard* said that Britain had awoken from a 'nightmare. She finds herself blessedly free from Locarno.' 'What does it mean to us?' asked the *Daily Express*. 'Do not think in mournful numbers of the fears of the French. There will be no war and if there were we should not be involved.'[46]

Baldwin prided himself on an instinctive rapport with the average Englishman's thinking. He could sometimes give this a peculiar twist of his own, thus transforming what in other circumstances might seem hypocrisy into a convincing appearance of plain dealing. He reminded the Cabinet that when Locarno was signed in 1925 the commitment to France it contained could be accepted without undue risk because France at the time was strong and Germany weak. But things were different now. The Germans had rearmed and, since British public opinion had to be taken into account, it had been difficult not to be left at a disadvantage. 'All that is perfectly well known to the French Government, and it seems very unfriendly of them to put us in the present dilemma. People will take a long time to forget it.'[47] The word 'dilemma' flattered the British conscience. The British Government were not facing a dilemma at all, only the embarrassment of having to make clear that they did not consider there to be one.

Eden's memorandum to the Cabinet on the day before he met Flandin in Paris had admitted in a convoluted phrase that the German action had not been one 'which we were not prepared ultimately to contemplate'. Far from thinking that in the new situation further contemplation of that sort was out of order, he said that such negotiations were now 'inevitable' and that 'owing to Germany's material strength and power of mischief in Europe it is in our interest to conclude with her as far-reaching and enduring a settlement as possible while Hitler is still in the mood.'[48] The sort of doubts which had begun to trouble him a year before on his journey across Europe after the Berlin talks seemed to have been dissipated in the Ethiopian misadventure.

Thus was officially prescribed and sealed with approval the principle that the already-established policy of European appeasement should continue regardless of setbacks. It was a principle that led inexorably to Munich.

In fact Eden spelt out in this memorandum the very formula that provided the structure for the Munich Agreement. Under the heading 'Future Policy of His Majesty's Government' he said that since it was now evident that Hitler might always repudiate a treaty simply because it suited him to do so it was necessary to distinguish between agreements with him which were a) advantageous and safe, b) unimportant but expedient, and c) dangerous. The first category covered those agreements which gave immediate and more or less lasting relief from present international tension; the second, those which were useful for the temporary improvement of international relations but which were not of vital importance to Britain; and the third, those involving serious mutual restrictions or concessions which Germany might in certain circumstances well repudiate. Shades of all three of these categories figured in the Munich Agreement.[49]

A further straw in the wind that was to become a whirlwind appeared at the end of the month. In a skilled and lucid speech on the Rhineland crisis in the House of Commons on March 26, Eden managed to extract credit both for sticking by the principle of Locarno and not entirely doing so at the same time. He was having to deal both with the views of those who wanted more direct British participation in the affairs of Europe and those who wanted less. Addressing the latter, to whom he gave the reassurance that Locarno was in no way inconsistent with the Covenant of the League of Nations but complementary, he used a prophetic phrase:

> They may be thinking of another situation when, owing to obligations elsewhere, our neighbours may become involved in conflict and may call for help in a quarrel that is not ours.

In such a case, he said, the people of Britain were determined that this should not happen. Which, he added, was the view of the Government. 'We agree with it entirely.' Britain would stand firm in support of the Covenant of the League '. . . but we do not add, nor will we add, one jot to those obligations, except in the area already covered by Locarno.'[50]

Neville Chamberlain, still Chancellor of the Exchequer, who wound up this debate for the Government, was asked outright at one point in his speech what would be the attitude of the Government in the event of unprovoked aggression by Hitler against Czechoslovakia or Poland. He replied that Britain would then be bound by her obligations under the Covenant of the League of Nations which she would be ready to fulfil in company with her fellow members of the League.[51]

Chamberlain had given his personal emphasis to the future of British foreign policy only a few days before in a message to the Birmingham Unionist Association. 'The Government have,' he said, 'as their principal object the maintenance of peace and the bringing together of France and Germany into relations of better understanding and goodwill than have existed in the past. For these purposes we shall spare no effort.'[52]

He was saying no more than what the Foreign Secretary was proud to say. 'I assure the House,' Eden said towards the end of his speech in the Commons on March 26, 1936, 'that it is the appeasement of Europe as a whole that we have constantly before us.'[53]

There seemed, then, nothing shaming about the word at all.

PART 2

CHAPTER ELEVEN

AFTER THE RHINELAND

THE FAILURE OF BRITAIN AND FRANCE TO TAKE ANY EFFECTIVE action over the German remilitarisation of the Rhineland in March 1936 is often looked back upon as the moment when the chance of 'stopping Hitler' was lost. Inasmuch as we know now that the German General Staff were apprehensive about the operation and were prepared quickly to withdraw if the French took action, there is theoretical substance in the argument. The German Commander-in-Chief, von Blomberg, was seen white-faced and twitching behind the scenes on the morning of March 7 as Hitler delivered news of what was happening to a cheering Reichstag.[1] The first belligerent-sounding reaction from the French made Blomberg hesitate; Hitler remained firm. Hitler himself, looking back later over greater triumphs, said that the forty-eight hours after the march into the Rhineland had been the most nerve-racking of his life.[2] Certainly his later successes all proceeded from his success at this stage; each further stage was easier for him as a result of it. Similarly each further attempt to bring his advances to a halt by allowing him to proceed was more ill-judged. But appeasement was a policy to which such conscientious and conclusive commitment had been made that any alternative policy seemed impossible. It was from this point onwards that appeasement became an entanglement gradually revealed itself as a trap.

On the other hand the retrospective view that this was the moment at which the British and French might jointly have acted against him is not a historical one. There was never any chance that such action would be taken. The British and French were far apart, keeping as much of an eye on each other as on Hitler. British policy had been conceived too long in terms of negotiation with Hitler, and

95

not opposition to him. French policy, made uncertain partly by such British emphasis and partly by the country's own internal political divisions, was defensive, not aggressive. The moment that should have been never was.

Subsequent events ensured that both countries, instead of looking critically at the positions they had reached, settled into these more firmly. Within a month of the march into the Rhineland Eden was telling Ribbentrop that 'our object in the present difficult situation is the same as it has been from the first: to seek to get negotiations going about a final settlement.' He wanted Ribbentrop to take away from their meeting 'the definite assurance which I would ask him to give to the Chancellor [Hitler] on behalf of His Majesty's Government, that we would do the utmost in our power to secure from the troubled conditions of the present time a European settlement'.[3]

The French continued to make stronger noises from a still inconclusive stance. What guarantee was there, they asked the British Government, that the new system of security to replace that which Germany had thought fit to destroy on March 7 would be preserved?[4] On the other hand, with some ambivalence of spirit, they also said that they could not disregard the British view that possibilities for conciliation still existed and that 'they would not wish to lay themselves open to the reproach of having shut the door to the hope of a final settlement before the British Government had convinced themselves of the uselessness of pursuing the present attempt at conciliation.'[5] Insofar as they themselves were prepared to be positive they recommended action through the League of Nations, with, if necessary (if, for instance, the Germans began to build massive fortifications in the re-occupied zone), the application against Germany of sanctions such as those being applied against Italy. At which Eden observed to them that Germany had not yet invaded France.[6]

Clutching thus at the Covenant of the League of Nations when in doubt was proving an increasingly illusory gesture. It had been of no assistance when the Japanese invaded Manchuria in 1931 or when their invasion of China was extended in 1935. It was of very small assistance now to Ethiopia. With Italian military victory and formal proclamation of Mussolini's African Roman Empire in the summer of 1936, sanctions themselves had to be decently abandoned. The

British Chancellor of the Exchequer, Neville Chamberlain, who had already hinted at the recent General Election that the League might not prove to be the rock which its supporters liked to consider it, declared that it would be 'the very midsummer of madness' to keep sanctions going.[7] Within a few weeks a further set of quite different events diverted British and French foreign policy into still other areas and placed appeasement temporarily on the sidelines.

In May 1936 a General Election in France had returned a left-wing Popular Front Government to power under the Socialist Léon Blum. In foreign affairs Liberals and Socialists in France as in Britain invested their idealism in the convenient formula of the League. The increasingly rickety nature of that structure served rather to emphasise in their minds the need for it to be reinforced than to impress them with its uselessness. In any case the main emphasis of the new French Government's mind was not on foreign affairs at all but on Socialist policy at home and the domestic difficulties this entailed. In addition to which a quite new factor now engaged the minds of all concerned with European affairs: a civil war in Spain.

There, a democratically-elected but unstable left-wing Republican Government was suddenly threatened by a serious right-wing revolt pioneered by a General from Spanish Morocco, Francisco Franco. The military help which Franco immediately sought and obtained from the two European countries also crusading against Communism, Germany and Italy, was countered by military help supplied to the Spanish Government by the Soviet Union. The intervention of all three states was determined by calculated individual objectives of their own.

Hitler immediately saw an opportunity not only to support another active European opponent of Communism but also to test some of his newly-developed military equipment, particularly that of the Luftwaffe, in conditions of modern war. Three-engined Junkers 52 aircraft helped transport Franco's Moroccan troops to the mainland, but Heinkel 51 fighters were soon discovered to be inferior to the Russian Ilyushin 15s and 16s. They were replaced by the new Messerschmidt 109s which shot them out of the skies at a time when in Britain the first Hurricanes and Spitfires were only undergoing their early trials. Although there were never more than about 6,000 German personnel in Spain at any one time, regular turnover ensured that many more than that number received training in modern war.

For Mussolini the investment in Spain of personal Fascist prestige was combined with a natural strategic interest in acquiring a Fascist ally in the Mediterranean. His contribution was mainly in the form of ground troops, numbering nearly 50,000, some of whom failed to justify his pride in them when they suffered a major defeat at the battle of Guadalajara in 1937.

A characteristic impenetrability of motive accompanied Stalin's interest in Spain. An early phase seemed to correspond with a wish to test the strategic waters in terms of the Communist International (the Comintern) and an effective European Popular Front. Later a reduction of enthusiasm synchronised with Franco's gradual progress and the gathering likelihood of Republican defeat. The switch to the second phase was eventually signalled by the liquidation of many individuals who had participated loyally in the first.

Military pressure on the Spanish Republican Government quickly sent it looking for help towards France. But Léon Blum and his successors were too enmeshed in their own domestic political turmoil to be able to do much more than allow an International Brigade of Communist, Socialist and Liberal idealists from many European countries and the United States to enter Spain across the Pyrenees. 'Non-intervention' was to become the official policy of Britain, France and the League of Nations, implemented to little effect though proclaimed with a pious idealism which only served further to expose the inadequacy of the League's mechanism.

For much of the rest of 1936 and 1937 the international spotlight was thus focussed elsewhere than on the central European problem, while intermittently, long after the re-occupation of the Rhineland, desultory talks between British, French and sometimes the Belgians continued about the possible summoning of a Four Power Conference to which Germany and Italy would come to help regulate 'conciliation' and promote European appeasement.

From time to time people asked themselves in what direction Germany, confident on the basis of its Rhineland achievement and busy testing the efficacy of its new weapons in Spain, would turn next, if appeasement failed to materialise. The message of *Mein*

Kampf, with its clear indication of German expansion eastwards, had been studied by diplomats all over the world, not least in France and Britain. The book had been written in 1924 when Hitler was an insignificant factor in German politics. Now, twelve years later, he had acquired not only total power in Germany but stature as a European statesman. It was not unreasonable to assume that his ambitions were no longer so simplistic and that they would have had to adjust themselves from literary semi-fantasies to the pragmatic realities of political life. Hitler had, in his first three years of power, moved as relatively cautiously on the international scene as previously on the domestic stage of the Weimar Republic. On the other hand, in these years it had become clear to him that European countries were as ready to collaborate in their own defeat as had been his political opponents in the democratic system of Weimar. The way was clearing for the materialisation of his ambitions abroad just as it had done earlier at home. Years later his Propaganda Minister Goebbels was proud to point out the exact analogy.[8]

The fact remained however that *Mein Kampf* could by no means necessarily be taken as a reliable guide to his moves at the time. The British Ambassador to Berlin, Sir Eric Phipps, no friend to National Socialism, hesitated to do so. Blomberg had told him that it was unfair to take the foreign affairs passages of the book literally and Phipps admitted that Hitler himself had said it was sometimes necessary to bow to the inevitable and deviate from one's course. Phipps reckoned that it was not impossible that though Hitler's ultimate goal, as specified in *Mein Kampf*, might remain the same he might equally be genuine in offering to keep the peace for twenty-five years. Phipps recounted how the Czech Minister in Berlin, Mastny, after dinner at Goering's house one evening had seen a book there bound in a fine sixteenth-century cover which Goering described to him as his bible. On picking it up Mastny had found that the binding covered *Mein Kampf*. When he expressed surprise at Goering's description of this as his bible Goering looked embarrassed. But two days later Goering went out of his way to say to Mastny that *Mein Kampf* was only his bible for domestic and not for external affairs.[9]

Certainly Hitler's priority in his first three years of power had been to consolidate that power both internally and externally. By the end of March 1936 such consolidation had been achieved. His greatest external success of all had been not so much the two practical coups of conscription and the remilitarisation of the Rhineland but in keeping British foreign policy aligned on appeasement in spite of them. In this respect the Anglo-German Naval Agreement of June 1935 must be seen as of equal significance with the other two events. The sustained wish of the British to pursue negotiation even after the Rhineland action put Hitler on a diplomatic plateau from which for the first time he could comfortably take stock of his next move. Even before the Rhineland Phipps in Berlin had seen Austria and Czechoslovakia as the direction in which Hitler would soon be looking. Now, the removal of the Rhineland as a weak spot in Germany's defences made it all the more tempting, since the value of the French alliance to the Czechs had been greatly reduced.

For all the protestations about the need to preserve Austrian independence, Britain in particular had already made clear that this was of secondary interest to her. Provided force were not used, Hitler could apply the principle of self-determination reasonably to justify a union or *Anschluss*. A look at the map revealed the immediate strategic advantages to Germany. With Austria part of the German Reich Czech defences in the Sudetenland would have their flank turned. What then were Hitler's thoughts about Czechoslovakia?

Phipps had said that although there was German talk of wanting only 'full cultural autonomy' for the Sudeten Germans he was by no means certain that their complete Nazification was not the aim. 'But,' he added, 'in any case, it is primarily a matter for M. Beneš and does not concern His Majesty's Government directly.'[10] Goering, whom Phipps saw at this time, was expressing the view that Austria would one day join Germany of her own free will, adding, perhaps significantly, that the oppression of the Sudeten Germans in Czechoslovakia was intolerable and could not go on indefinitely.[11]

Czech reaction to the remilitarisation of the Rhineland had been sharp. Beneš at once drew British attention both to the fact that a German-Czech arbitration treaty which had been twinned with Locarno was, with the German destruction of Locarno, automatically invalidated and to the fact that the Franco-Czech treaty was now 'appreciably weakened'.[12] The French Commander-in-Chief himself emphasised this latter point to the British Military Attaché in Paris, pointing out how with the Germans now planning to construct major fortifications in the Rhineland (what was to become Hitler's West Wall) the French 'would find their way barred and be unable to bring the instant reinforcement to their Central European Allies which is so vital'. In which case it is difficult not to wonder why Gamelin himself had been so signally lacking in instant response to German occupation of the zone. Years of unsure French policy, debilitated by negative British support, had settled a sort of defensive rot over the French military mind. While Gamelin reasonably saw some hope if the Czechs built strong fortifications along their German frontier to help them resist an initial blow, his further development of strategy in saying that this would give 'French action' time to take effect rang rather hollow. Time, he said, would be of the essence and in this at least he was right.[13] The Czechs too were well aware of the fact and began at once the construction of a massive series of fortifications in the Sudetenland for the defence of their state.

Logically, it was to Austria that Hitler turned first. As long ago as his meeting with the then British Foreign Secretary Simon and his League of Nations Minister Eden in Berlin in March 1935, Hitler had made his view on Austria clear and they had not demurred. It was, he had suggested, just a matter of waiting. Austria would naturally become part of Germany once the Austrian people were freely allowed to express their wish for union, though this was a condition which the ruling Austrian Government under its Chancellor, Kurt von Schuschnigg, would not permit, repressive as it was of opposition National Socialists and other good Germans.

Britain's 'secondary' interest in Austria had been made plain in Berlin and again at Stresa. Ramsay MacDonald had there remarked, unperturbed, that Hitler's view of Austria was that since the fruit above his head was ripening he did not need to shake the tree. It was Mussolini, the man who had moved his troops to the Brenner Pass at the time of the attempted Austrian Nazi coup in 1934, who commented sharply that, the day on which the fruit fell, Germany would in fact have 80 million inhabitants.[14] Since then the estrangement between Britain and Italy over Ethiopian sanctions had tempered Mussolini's anxiety about Austria. He felt an increasing affinity to Hitler as a fellow object of censure by the

League of Nations. The sensation was to be augmented by further togetherness in their intervention on Franco's side in the Spanish Civil War.

Not long after the occupation of the Rhineland Hitler made his first preparations for shaking the Austrian tree. In an agreement signed with Austria in July 1936 he promised non-intervention in Austrian affairs but in a secret clause obtained the concession that the pan-German 'National Opposition' should be allowed a share in political responsibility. Germany continued to intervene with an increasing supply of funds and propaganda to Austrian Nazis. In January 1937 Hitler sent Goering to Rome to sound out Mussolini about Austria in the light of the new German-Italian relationship. He found him still sensitive on the issue but greatly reassured to be told that no German action on the Austrian question would be taken without consulting him.[15] German intervention in support of Austrian Nazis continually increased despite the July agreement. Schuschnigg on the other hand did his best to honour it, for all the German protests that he was not doing so. In the summer a prominent Austrian Nazi sympathiser, Artur Seyss-Inquart, was appointed an official state councillor. Any student of Hitler's tactics before and after he had come to power could have foretold what would soon happen.

In September 1937 Mussolini visited Berlin, to be much impressed by German military might as displayed after the continuing rapid German rearmament. He was flattered to hear Hitler announce that between National Socialism and Fascism there now existed not only a community of views but also a community of action.[16] In November when Ribbentrop went to Rome to formalise a Rome-Tokyo-Berlin axis with the addition of Italy's signature to the Anti-Comintern Pact Mussolini told him that Austria was no longer of such importance to Italy. Her interests had now switched to the Mediterranean and her new colonial empire. France, he told Ribbentrop, now knew that, if there were a crisis over Austria, Italy would do nothing.[17]

This particular part of the road to Austria was thus clear for Hitler. He can never have had much doubt about difficulties that might be caused for him on it by Britain. But, should he have had any, his mind was to be set at rest that November by a visitor in the form of the British Lord President of the Council, Lord

102

Halifax, who brought reassurance about more dangerous ground as well.

The schemed pattern of progress apparently discernible in Hitler's moves of the 1930s can be misleading. It suggests a meticulousness of calculation that in fact was not there. Four bold moves in four years were actually made within ten days of the same date in March each year, yet in none was the timing precisely planned. What is indisputable is that Hitler's mind was fixed unwaveringly on one goal: restoration to the German people of that great German Reich to which race and destiny had called them but of which recent history and evil men had defrauded them. Equally established was the geographical direction in which the living space for that goal was to be found. Above all, Germany must move eastwards. Yet to achieve his unalterable objectives he was prepared to bide his time, or strike, or just not make up his mind, as circumstances of the moment seemed to require. Opportunities were to be seized, made, waited for or even delayed. What mattered was that when a decision was taken it should carry the strength of will-power that was behind the aspiration to the final goal itself.

Thus Hitler was at the same time both an improviser and not an improviser, an opportunist and not an opportunist. For all his proclaimed intentions his opponents had continual difficulty in making up their minds about what he was doing or how to deal with him. He had neither a plan for war nor no plan for war. Personally attracted to the single-mindedness which martial qualities require, his own inclination was for the inevitability of battle. But this had to be balanced against the knowledge that the people whom he led favoured peace. Always he had the advantage over the other statesmen of Europe that while they operated within a concept of the *status quo*, with some room for flexibility, for him the *status quo* did not exist.

Four days after assuming power in 1933, on February 3, he had made his plans for the future clear to the German army he had inherited. His aim, after consolidating power domestically, was, he told his generals, 'Perhaps – and no doubt preferably – to conquer new living space in the east and Germanise it ruthlessly'. The most dangerous period, he added, was that immediately before them, the period of rearmament. 'Then we shall see if France has

103

statesmen. If she does, she will not grant us time but will jump on us.'[18]

But France had not jumped. With final acceptance of his move into the Rhineland the first major phase in his progress towards the ultimate German goal had been completed. Materially and psychologically it was a triumph. The Olympic Games held in Berlin in the summer of 1936 provided a symbolic public relations celebration of the achievement. Few could recognise that it also marked the beginning of a new phase altogether.

By November 19, 1937 when Halifax went to see him at Berchtesgaden, Hitler's mind had already been concerned for some time with the shape this new phase was to take. Even so, while the general outlines were forming, the details were far from exactly calculated.

On November 5 he had held a four-hour meeting with his top ranking military, naval and air force chiefs.[*] Basing his thoughts now on 'thorough deliberations and the experiences of four and a half years of power' he expanded frankly on options likely to present themselves while in pursuit of the objective of eastern 'living space'. Germany's problem, he said, could in the long run only be solved by force and this was never without attendant risk. If no suitable opportunities appeared earlier he would have to act by 1943–5 because the superiority of German military technology would then be at its peak and would thereafter decline. Meanwhile, should internal divisions in France render her incapable of fighting a war against Germany, 'the time for action against the Czechs' would have come. Czechoslovakia should also be 'overthrown' at once should France and Britain become involved, as he thought possible, in a Mediterranean war with Italy in the wake of the Spanish Civil War. Britain and France too, he thought, had already tacitly written off the Czechs and their interference in either that or the Austrian question could be discounted. If such a Mediterranean war were to develop, Hitler said, he was resolved to take advantage of it whenever it happened, even as early as 1938.[19]

The immediate practical effect of this conference on Germany's War Minister, von Blomberg, was to hurry him into making plans

[*]This is sometimes known as the 'Hossbach' conference because Hitler's adjutant, Colonel Friedrich Hossbach, who was present, made notes at it, of which a transcript provides the only surviving written source of what was said.

for a contingency which in certain circumstances might thus be no more than two months away. Two theoretical contingency plans for the German armed forces had already been drawn up by him that summer. In a preamble to these he had correctly estimated that in the 'politically fluid world situation' the Wehrmacht must be ready for war 'a) to counter-attack at any time, and b) to make possible the military exploitation of favourable circumstances should they arise'. But both were at this time ostensibly defensive plans. The first, known as 'Case Red', dealt with a surprise attack by the French in the west. The second, 'Case Green', involved 'a surprise German operation against Czechoslovakia in order to parry the imminent attack of a superior enemy coalition'.[20] Now, after the 'Hossbach' conference, he had to give Case Green urgent priority over Case Red and adapt it to a much more openly aggressive contingency if necessary. On the other hand, in line with an appreciation of Hitler's principle of flexibility in the face of opportunity, Blomberg also directed that it might well have to be postponed for some years.

A fortnight later Halifax arrived at Berchtesgaden. He had come with the special blessing of the new British Prime Minister, Neville Chamberlain, who had succeeded Baldwin when that homespun figure merged into retirement in May 1937.

CHAPTER TWELVE

HALIFAX GOES A-HUNTING

CHAMBERLAIN, THE STRONGEST MEMBER OF THE CABINET FROM the days when Ramsay MacDonald had been Prime Minister, was the natural, able and hard-working successor to the lackadaisical Baldwin. Lloyd George's jibing summary of him as 'not a bad Lord Mayor of Birmingham in a lean year' was quite a way wide of the mark.[1] He had in fact been a good and caring Lord Mayor of Birmingham in the middle of the Great War. A considerate but determined Chairman of Committees, he lacked the charisma and major political clout of his famous father, Joe, who had broken the mould of English politics in the previous century, and the intellectual flair of his elder brother Austen, the Foreign Secretary who had negotiated Locarno with Stresemann. But he was no fool nor was he quite the dry stick which his somewhat old-fashioned and arid exterior could suggest. A lover of crocuses and Beethoven quartets, he was an expansive diarist and, like his letters, the entries reveal a human if conventional soul addressing the ups and downs of life with normal feeling.[2] In politics, pertinacity and a certain ability to strike adeptly if undramatically in a manner not unrelated to his favourite sport of fly-fishing had earned him the respect and confidence of many colleagues. Insular, even parochial, in a style symbolised by the umbrella he frequently carried, he now took the stage as international statesman in a role no British Prime Minister had played since Lloyd George. But he was a curious match for Hitler. Indeed he was no match for him at all.

His eventual failure on the international scene is sometimes put down to his lack of knowledge or experience of foreign affairs. But, if he was certainly to some extent an amateur in the field of diplomacy, the policy to which he subscribed was one bequeathed him by professionals – Simon, Hoare and Eden. Moreover as Chancellor of the Exchequer for more than five years he had kept a wary enough eye on the subject partly because of the demands it placed on national defence and thus the economy, and partly because a quiet ambition to become Prime Minister alerted him to its increasing priority. He appears in history as appeasement's 'fall guy' only because, inheriting the policy as an enlightened one to which he felt sympathetic and to which he now contributed a personal enthusiasm of his own, he was too long temperamentally disinclined to recognise that it could turn to ashes while he espoused it.

Such an attitude may seem to characterise a man lacking in realism, but this too is a simplistic view. Chamberlain's diary entries long before he became Prime Minister reveal him as loathing the callous brutality of Nazism, and as seeing, as early as 1934, the need for a strong air force to deter a Germany potentially aggressive against Britain.[3] His public speeches even before the election of 1935, in which the Covenant of the League of Nations required paramount respect, conveyed clear doubts about that Covenant's effectiveness. 'Munich' itself was to be nothing if not an attempt at a realistic treatment of Czechoslovakia's problems. He was just operating in a different dimension of realism from that of his opponent.

The extent to which British foreign policy in the middle of 1937 concerned itself with other matters than those on which Hitler's mind was concentrating is well illustrated by a telephone conversation on the international situation which the Foreign Secretary Eden held with Chamberlain on September 1, 1937. The Far East, Spain, the Mediterranean and Abyssinia were referred to in advance of the following week's Cabinet meeting but there was no mention of Austria or Czechoslovakia or indeed of Germany itself.[4]

Yet there was at that time no shortage of indications that Central Europe would soon dominate the scene. It is true that when the new British Ambassador to Berlin, Sir Neville Henderson, had seen Goering in July to try to obtain from him, on Eden's instructions, what really stood in the way of greater Anglo-German understanding, Goering had told him to expect 'no more surprises for several years'. But, quite apart from the inherent signal that there were thus surprises to come, Goering immediately followed it with the remark that there were three and a half million Germans in Czechoslovakia asking, 'Would the latter ever give them up without a struggle?' and adding that 'Germany could not eternally listen unmoved to their complaints.' Austria and the *Sudetendeutschen* were not, he said, vital questions for Britain as they were for Germany. In making this last remark he may with reason have assumed that he was preaching to the converted, for Henderson himself had earlier obsequiously drawn his attention to the way in which Britain had displayed a 'considerable sense of comprehension of Germany's standpoint' and 'firmness . . . in her intervention at the time of the re-occupation of the Rhineland'.[5]

Henderson's predecessor, Sir Eric Phipps, in his valedictory despatch to the Foreign Office in July had listed the aims of Germany as being 'the absorption of Austria and other Germanic peoples (e.g. the German fringe of Czechoslovakia)' and 'expansion in the east as well as recovery of colonies', and Henderson, before taking over his post, reminded the Foreign Office of this, suggesting that 'none of these need injure purely British national interests'.[6] It was of course this latter consideration, hinted at openly at least since Eden's statement of June 1934[*] and implicitly long before, which certainly diminished much sense of urgency in Britain's concern for the area, a concern which was restricted to the need to see that such alterations as were to take place should be made without violence. On the other hand there were indications that violence in the last resort was a method which the Germans were in no way excluding.

In August the British Military Attaché in Berlin had reported that Germany had already reached a stage when she was for all practical purposes unassailable. And while he reckoned that 1940 would be the year when German troops would best be in a position to carry offensive action outside their own frontier he reported that the German General Staff were viewing with disfavour the Czech construction of fortifications on their Sudeten frontier and suggested that 'a suitable political situation may cause Herr Hitler to take action sooner than the state of his rearmament might appear to justify.'[7] In which case the priority of British foreign policy was likely to be the defusing of any such political situation so as to

[*]See above, page 33.

render violence unnecessary. This prior aim would be given precedence over any intrinsic judgements about the situation itself.

A certain confidence that it was along these lines that he could effectively act was already forming in Chamberlain's mind. Though Henderson reported a further conversation with Goering in which the latter said both that an Austrian *Anschluss* was a matter of course and inevitable and that once the Germans had entered Austria the Czechs would be obliged to do something for their German subjects or lose them, Chamberlain was able to write to President Roosevelt at the end of September that the situation in Europe was 'less menacing than it has appeared for some months past' and that there were various circumstances 'to ease the tension and to encourage the friends of peace'. It was only of the situation in the Far East that he wrote: 'At any moment some incident may arise with repercussions which cannot even be guessed at.'[8]

The Czechs themselves were less happy about the way things looked that autumn. When the founder of the Czech state Thomas Masaryk, who had retired from the Presidency of Czechoslovakia two years before, died in September, the French Prime Minister, Léon Blum, who attended his funeral in Prague, brought back an urgent message from Masaryk's successor Beneš that Germany was contemplating some action soon in both Austria and Czechoslovakia.[9]

Inevitably the French too, bound by treaty to defend Czechoslovakia against aggression, were becoming anxious on their own account. Early in October the Czechs sent their Foreign Minister to Paris to ask the French point blank whether in the event of Germany moving against Czechoslovakia, perhaps under the pretext of restoring order in the Sudeten areas, they could count on French military support. Delbos, the French Foreign Minister, replied that 'Czechoslovakia could always rely upon France loyally honouring her engagements under treaty between the two countries', but immediately prevaricated by saying that moves of the sort hypothetically envisaged 'might conceivably not be covered by treaty and must be considered as and when they occurred'. He promised that the French Government would 'consider the matter carefully'. Delbos in fact admitted to the British Ambassador in Paris Eric Phipps (previously in Berlin) that, in any clear case of German movements against Czechoslovakia, France would have to go to her assistance 'unless she were content to become a second-rate power'.[10] However, Krofta, the Czech Foreign Minister, returned from his visit to Paris without illusions. He told the British envoy in Prague that when an emergency came France would in fact support Czechoslovakia against aggression if – and only if – she felt it in her own interest to give such support.

Beneš himself maintained an outward show of optimism. He told the editor of the British weekly, the *Spectator*, that he did not anticipate that Germany would be ready for aggression for two years, but in fact anxiety had been, as the British envoy in Prague put it, 'widespread and chronic in Czechoslovakia ever since Germany had re-occupied the Rhineland'.[11]

The Czechs of course also had a treaty of mutual assistance with the Soviet Union but the Russians were only obliged to implement it if the French implemented their treaty with Czechoslovakia too. The attitude of the French to whatever might happen would obviously be crucial. The British were concerned above all for some long-term understanding with Germany and not primarily interested in what happened to Czechoslovakia. The attitude the French were likely to adopt was not, in the Government's currently confident mood, particularly a matter for anxiety.

Eden addressed the problem cagily when the French Ambassador to London came to see him on October 8, 1937. The Ambassador reported how struck Blum, his Prime Minister, had been, on returning from Masaryk's funeral, by the Czechs' present grave preoccupation with their situation; hitherto they had been almost blindly optimistic. He put to Eden the same sort of hypothesis which the Czechs themselves had put to the French. If, for instance, there were trouble between Czechs and Germans in the Sudetenland and Germany intervened in some way, perhaps with irregular forces, it would be difficult for France to deny that her Treaty obligation came into force. What then would be the attitude of the British Government? The Ambassador revealed the incipient prevarication in the minds of both parties when he added immediately that he did not suppose that Eden could tell him. 'I replied,' wrote Eden in his report of this conversation, 'that His Excellency was right in that supposition. It would certainly not be possible for me to forecast now our attitude in such hypothetical circumstances.' He added that the French Ambassador had clearly expected this reply.[12] Of such mettle were composed the two most formidable Powers whom Hitler was now preparing to confront.

A few days later Eden received a telegram from the British Embassy in Berlin to the effect that though Hitler did not yet appear to have made up his mind about Austria and Czechoslovakia it seemed clear that the Germans were 'determined sooner or later to take Austria and regions in neighbouring countries where the majority of the inhabitants are German, and that the German Government is counting on Britain not to march'. Sir Orme Sargent, the Assistant Under-Secretary at the Foreign Office, minuted this telegram to the effect that the matter was better expressed the other way round, namely that the only thing that was restraining Hitler was uncertainty as to what Britain's attitude would be. Hitler was in fact to make clear at the 'Hossbach' conference in less than three weeks' time that he was in little doubt about this and his view was to receive confirmation from Halifax, when he went to see him at Berchtesgaden ('Berchtergarten [*sic*] – or whatever the place is,' wrote Halifax in a letter to Chamberlain) that November.[13]

The visit had originated in an invitation from Goering as Reich Game Warden to an International Sporting Exhibition in Berlin. In accepting it Halifax expressed a hope, which Eden approved with some reservation, of making contact with the German leadership and perhaps even Hitler himself. Eden's concern was sensibly that Halifax should not be seen to be soliciting a meeting with Hitler. He wanted no impression to be given of a British overture which somehow side-stepped the French. He had it recorded too that Halifax would at the meeting 'confine himself to warning comment on Austria and Czechoslovakia', and that he had impressed on Henderson the need to do everything possible to discourage German initiative in the two states.[14] At the same time even Eden had a rather less certain approach to the immediate future than appears from the account in his memoirs written a quarter of a century later.

On the one hand, alerted by the prospect of Halifax's visit to the dangers of Britain's lack of policy in the event of German moves in Austria and/or Czechoslovakia, he told Henderson constantly to bear in mind that Germany should have 'no encouragement whatsoever' for believing that Britain would contemplate any

111

settlement in Eastern and Central Europe at the expense of the political independence of the nations there.[15] But he also sent to Halifax on the eve of his departure a Foreign Office paper prepared for him by William Strang which was far from specific about what Britain would actually do if such moves took place. An Austrian *Anschluss* would not be condoned if 'achieved by force against the will of the inhabitants'. But, as to incorporation of the Sudeten Germans of Czechoslovakia within the Reich, all that could be said was that Britain could not undertake not to intervene 'in any steps taken by Germany' to this end: such an undertaking would be in conflict with her obligations under the Covenant of the League. Moreover ambivalence entered into even this degree of firmness. For, having first enunciated those League obligations in a somewhat negative form ('The United Kingdom cannot bind itself to take no action in the event of Germany committing an act of aggression against a member of the League'), the paper proceeded to qualify even this commitment with the sentence: 'This is not to say that in the circumstances suggested His Majesty's Government would necessarily intervene by force of arms against Germany.' Later still, this was said more straightforwardly. In the case of any territorial change in Central and Eastern Europe: ' . . . we are not (though we do not publicly say so) prepared to intervene by force of arms to prevent it.'[16]

But, if Eden can be faulted for more ambivalence than he later remembered, it is to his credit that at least some doubts about British policy were at work in his mind however contradictorily formulated. They were however still not sufficient to make him leave the Government and when he did resign three months later it was on a different issue.

It was Chamberlain who above all was enthusiastic about the prospect of Halifax's meeting with Hitler. When at an early stage Sir Robert Vansittart, Permanent Under-Secretary at the Foreign Office, had argued strongly against it, on the grounds that Halifax would be asked awkward questions, Chamberlain had been 'really horrified' at the thought of 'another opportunity to be thrown away' and had insisted that the project went ahead.[17] And later, when there seemed some doubt as to whether the meeting could be arranged without giving the impression of undue anxiety for it, he stressed that he was in fact 'most anxious' that it should take place.[18] In a speech at the Lord Mayor's Banquet on November 9 he had said how he wanted relations with the Rome-Berlin axis to be based upon mutual friendship and understanding, adding that he thought such understanding could be more hopefully pursued by 'informal discussion'.[19] The idea of some personal contact between Hitler and a British politician was not in fact a new one. A proposition for an informal top level meeting had been put forward and actually welcomed by Hitler in the spring of 1936 when Baldwin was Prime Minister. Baldwin himself had been rather taken with the idea but in the manner of so much that he embraced had quietly let it slip away.[20]

Halifax arrived in Berlin on November 17 and, after visits on that and the next day to the Hunting Exhibition where he found himself an object of considerable interest to the German public, he moved on to Berchtesgaden. The meeting got off to an inauspicious start when Halifax failed to recognise his host on the steps of the house and mistook him momentarily for a footman. Once he was inside it was quickly established that it was the British who had called the meeting. Hitler signalled to Halifax to begin and to say what he wanted to discuss.

Halifax started strangely, averring in an introductory aside that British public opinion was perhaps less offended by Nazi treatment of the Jews than by the treatment of the Church. But in general he spoke in the tone which had run through British foreign policy for more than four years. 'A genuine settlement by means of which quiet and security might be established in Europe' was what he was after, in the hope of coaxing Germany back into the League of Nations. Among those questions which he told Hitler fell into 'the category of possible alterations in the European order which might be destined to come with the passage of time' he listed Austria and Czechoslovakia. He expressed Britain's interest in these matters as being that 'methods should be avoided which might cause far-reaching disturbances'.

Hitler himself could hardly have expressed his objective better. Admittedly the words are as reported by Paul Schmidt, Hitler's interpreter, but Halifax's own account was virtually identical. Among 'questions arising out of the Versailles settlement which seemed to us capable of causing trouble', he said, he had instanced Austria and Czechoslovakia. 'On all these matters,' he went on, 'we were not necessarily concerned to stand for the *status quo* as today, but we were concerned to avoid such treatment of them as would be likely to cause trouble. If reasonable settlements could be reached with the free assent and goodwill of those primarily concerned we certainly had no desire to block.' Halifax reiterated the theme when he met Goering the next day, telling him at one point that Britain 'did not wish and never had wished to stand strictly on the present state of the world' and at another, as regards what Germany might consider her special spheres of influence, that Britain 'had no desire to intrude into matters that were not primarily our concern'. All this seemed quite a long way from the injunction to confine himself to *warning* comments on Austria and Czechoslovakia which Eden had understood to be Halifax's brief.

Hitler at the Berchtesgaden meeting had made a philosophical analysis of the problems confronting Europe. He contended that there were only two alternatives once it was accepted that the *status quo* was subject to change, namely: the free play of forces which meant war, or settlement by 'higher reason'. It was imperative, he said, to find the latter course though in that case 'one must clearly realise that this higher reason must lead to approximately similar results to those which had followed from the working of free forces.' In other words, commented Eden (but a quarter of a century later), 'would we be good enough to give what otherwise he would be compelled to take'. In Cabinet at the time he expressed 'great satisfaction with the way the Lord President had dealt with each point in his conversations with the Chancellor'.[21]

But it was Chamberlain who was really pleased. He wrote almost at once to his sister that the meeting with Hitler had been 'from my point of view a great success because it achieved its object, that of creating an atmosphere in which it was possible to discuss with Germany the practical questions involved in a European settlement'. And he added: 'I don't see why we shouldn't say to Germany, give us satisfactory assurances that you won't use force to deal with the Austrians and Czechoslovakians and we will give you similar assurances that we won't use force to prevent the changes you want if you can get them by peaceful means.'[22]

A few days after Halifax's return the new French Prime Minister Chautemps and his Foreign Minister Delbos came to London to hear what had happened. Chautemps noted from Halifax's report

114

Chamberlain and Neville Henderson, British Ambassador to Germany, at Bad Godesberg, September 22, 1938

Sir John Simon, Foreign Minister in 1935

Nazi Iconography

Halifax (centre left) waves Chamberlain off to Munich

Ribbentrop welcomes Chamberlain to Munich

The signing of the Agreement: Chamberlain and Hitler

that in a conversation he had had with Field Marshal von Blomberg after seeing Hitler Blomberg had seemed to suggest that Central Europe and particularly Czechoslovakia were likely to be the crucial area in the future (Blomberg was of course working in secret on Case Green at the time). This led inevitably to the awkward matter of France's treaty obligation and once again Delbos endeavoured to draw some sort of fine line between disruptive German action which would not constitute aggression and more positive action as a result of which treaty action would be unavoidable. Whereupon Chamberlain said outright that there was a strong feeling in Britain that 'we ought not to be entangled in war over Czechoslovakia'. He said the public would welcome anything that could be done to bring about a settlement in Central and Eastern Europe. But he did not think it would be possible to mobilise opinion in England in support of forcible intervention against Germany on behalf of Czechoslovakia. People did not think the Sudetens were getting fair treatment from the Czechs.

Delbos took this remarkably mildly, saying he quite understood the Prime Minister's preoccupation, but added in the circumlocutory manner which all such further discussion of policy seemed to induce that, since the French had treaty obligations towards Czechoslovakia which might, if the worst came to the worst, have to be implemented, it would be 'a keen disappointment' to the French Government and French opinion if Britain felt she was being drawn too far in the direction of intervention. To which Eden replied that there was no question of asking France to reconsider her obligations, or of Britain asking her not to carry them out. But there was a feeling that the Czechs were not doing enough for Sudeten grievances. The right course was to get the Czechs to do something about this and then Britain and France could approach Berlin. Two days of meetings concluded with a decision to insist on Beneš examining concessions to be made to the Sudeten Germans.[23]

Subconsciously, the statesmen of Britain and France were setting the stage for the Munich Conference ten months in advance. But for the moment this was all theoretical. Meanwhile Hitler shook the Austrian tree.

CHAPTER THIRTEEN

AUSTRIA

THE FORMER FRENCH PRIME MINISTER AND FOREIGN MINISTER Flandin, now in opposition, bet the British Ambassador to Berlin in the middle of December 1937 a dozen oysters that the Austrian situation would be 'liquidated' within three months.[1] He was to win with two days to spare.

Hitler, from the position he had secured with the Agreement of July 1936, was increasing pressure on the Austrian Chancellor, Schuschnigg, to promote pan-Germanism. Von Papen, the German Ambassador in Vienna, criticised the Government for not properly aligning itself with German goals. The German Reich, he said, was embarked on a movement of the greatest historical significance; in this process, Germany had to demand more than passive assistance from Austria; she had to demand that Austria with heart and soul support this struggle of the German world for its existence.[2]

Money from Germany poured into Austrian pro-Nazi organisations, in spite of the commitment to non-interference in Austrian domestic affairs. Seyss-Inquart's influence increased. At the beginning of February 1938 other pan-German Austrians were given important positions in the state in the hope of easing the pressure. This was merely augmented in consequence. It became more and more difficult for the Austrian Chancellor, Schuschnigg, and his own Fatherland Front with its specifically Austrian patriotism, to maintain the reality of independent Austrian freedom of action.

Hitler was the one who was free to act. As always, up to the last moment he kept his options open. He knew that Mussolini's tacit support was now virtually assured. He knew too from his recent conversation with Halifax that he could continue to assume relative detachment from Britain, and thus by implication France. Indeed he invited Schuschnigg to Berchtesgaden to tell him this: 'I see eye to eye with Mussolini . . . And England? England will not move one finger for Austria.'[3]

After threats of military action, he then presented Schuschnigg with a number of demands including the appointment of Seyss-Inquart as Minister of the Interior, a general amnesty for all Austrian Nazis, close linking of the German and Austrian armed forces and an undertaking not to outlaw National Socialism in Austria. As before, Hitler was, in return, prepared to agree to non-interference in Austrian affairs by German Nazi agencies.

Schuschnigg protested at the peremptory nature of the demands: they were incompatible with Austrian sovereignty. Hitler made further threats. He demanded an instant signature which Schuschnigg pointed out would not in any case constitutionally bind the Austrian state without confirmation from the Austrian President, Miklas. After achieving marginal adjustment of some of the demands though not of Seyss-Inquart's appointment as Minister of the Interior in charge of security, Schuschnigg signed and Hitler gave him three days in which to get Miklas's agreement. German land and air manoeuvres were in progress near the Austrian border. Miklas in any case could hardly have repudiated Schuschnigg's signature without making Austria seem even weaker. He signed too.

Against an increasing groundswell of enthusiastic Nazi activity in Austria Hitler watched to see how the situation would evolve. He made a speech to the Reichstag in which, disconcertingly for both Austria and Czechoslovakia, he spoke of 'ten million Germans . . . subjected to continuous suffering because of their sympathy and solidarity with the whole German race' and of their 'right of racial self-determination'. But he did not move. It was Schuschnigg who moved first.

Schuschnigg took his own and Austria's life in his hands and organised a sudden plebiscite to be held within four days of its announcement. The voters were asked to says 'Yes' or 'No' to an apparently simple statement: 'For a free and German Austria, an independent and social Austria, a Christian and United Austria; for peace and employment and for the equality of all who stand for their people and their nation.'

The skilful wording presented an immediate threat to Hitler's evolutionary tactics. These had already done much to undermine the Austrian state. They would be effectively stymied by a positive 'Yes' vote for independence.

Hitler acted at once. It was the sort of situation in which his gift for opportunistic development of a long-conceived general plan excelled. Although no detailed military scheme yet existed for a march into Austria, the German High Command was given forty-eight hours in which to deploy the necessary troops to prevent the plebiscite. But Hitler still kept his options open. He sent Schuschnigg an ultimatum to cancel the plebiscite.

On the morning of Friday, March 11, two days before the plebiscite was due, Schuschnigg heard that the Germans had closed the frontier. He gave in and cancelled the plebiscite.

German demands immediately increased. Schuschnigg must resign and Seyss-Inquart be made Austrian Chancellor. Schuschnigg again gave in and agreed to resign. But Miklas, the President, stood firm, refusing to appoint Seyss-Inquart in his place. Seyss-Inquart as Minister of the Interior then announced over the radio that he was taking full executive power. A telegram allegedly from him, but in fact written and even spuriously time-stamped in Berlin, was 'received', asking for German troops to march in and 'restore order'. As the American historian Telford Taylor puts it: 'Shortly before dawn on Saturday, March 12, 1938, for the first time since the First World War, German troops crossed their own frontiers to occupy another country.'[4]

A British newspaper correspondent, who had just arrived from Paris expecting to cover Schuschnigg's plebiscite, drove out to a point just north of Innsbruck to watch the German troops pouring in; motor cyclists at first with rifles on their backs, then troops in trucks, then field guns and anti-tank guns and then a column of infantry marching in threes with a band at their head. 'It was a lovely spring morning,' he recounts. 'The snow was still lying across the fields; the mountains behind Innsbruck were a tremendously dramatic backdrop. I suppose because it was spring time and one was getting into the avalanche period, the thought I had was: what I'm seeing now is the first boulder in some great landslide, or the first chunk of snow coming down and something terrible and terrific and powerful is being let loose.'[5]

On the following day, on which Schuschnigg's plebiscite should have taken place, Hitler, delighted by the enthusiasm with which both he and his troops had been welcomed, decided finally on the formal *Anschluss* or annexation of the seven million Germans in Austria to the German Reich. Two days later, in the plane flying back to Berlin, he was seen to lean across the gangway to his new Commander in Chief of the Wehrmacht, Keitel, holding a sketch map of the changed Reich frontiers from a newspaper. Placing his left forefinger and thumb round the frontiers of Czechoslovakia now half encompassed by the Reich, he squeezed them slowly together and winked.[6]

What had been the British and French reaction to these developments?

The attitude of the British Government had remained throughout pivoted on Halifax's November visit to Hitler. In Chamberlain's mind and thus that of his Cabinet this visit had become established as a diplomatic landmark. Chamberlain, enthusiastic about it at the time, had seen it as the starting point from which his own particularly personal commitment to the policy of appeasement was to proceed.[7] He was, as Henderson found on a visit to London in January 1938, 'determined not to allow the Halifax visit to remain without a sequel' and a month later, with the pressure on Austria, Eden himself was talking of 'the work which we have been doing here since Lord Halifax's conversation with the Chancellor'.[8] Eden was then within a few days of resignation over a question of tactics in talks with the Italians, aggravated by a sense of personal incompatibility with his Prime Minister which had lately been much on the increase. But his resignation was quite unconnected with any considerations of policy towards Germany. Indeed, one of Eden's very last memoranda as Foreign Secretary had concerned itself with the 'German contribution to general appeasement', an objective which he defined as creating 'an increased sense of international security and enhanced prospects of the preservation of peace'.[9] However the effect of his resignation and of Halifax's appointment in his place was to concentrate the conduct of that policy in the hands of Chamberlain.

The British attitude to the situation in Austria and Czechoslovakia had been made clear: provided force was not used, changes of the sort Germany might want there could be accepted. Eden himself, still just in office when Schuschnigg was forced to sign the Berchtesgaden agreement, admitted that it was the British Government's impression that this agreement did indeed 'detract from the independence of Austria'.[10] But in fact Britain's principal concern at that moment, expressed by both Eden and Chamberlain, turned out to be not that but whether the Germans should think that they had tried to persuade Schuschnigg not to sign it. Both the German Foreign Secretary von Neurath and Hitler himself reproached Henderson for daring this. Henderson replied in an injured tone that he thought this 'most unlikely . . . Great Britain,' he said, 'would be the last to hinder a peaceful and satisfactory solution of the continued state of tension in Central Europe.' When Chamberlain heard of the German reproach, he expostulated: 'I hope we should leave them in no doubt of our indignation over their false accusation.'[11]

The British Ambassador to Vienna, Sir Michael Palairet, had reported that Austrians were constantly telling him that England was Austria's last hope. But England's only concern had been that the independence of Austria should not interfere with the more ambitious goal of a general European settlement.[12]

The French had viewed the events with a different form of realism. They were more concerned with difficulties they saw coming for themselves over Czechoslovakia than with the virtues of appeasement, though appeasement was a policy with which they otherwise concurred. At the time of Schuschnigg's return from Berchtesgaden they would have preferred Britain and France to speak out lest Germany should believe that the governments of London and Paris were prepared to let things go further still. 'This,' the French said, 'would be opening the way to new initiatives, doubtless of a still more serious nature.' What would happen when ultimatums started going to Czechoslovakia? France had recently reminded Britain of the obligation she herself was under towards Czechoslovakia. What was likely to happen to appeasement if an ultimatum were rejected and the Czechs were determined to resist? They urged, in their memorandum, combined action – which they did not specify – on the part of Great Britain and France before it was too late.[13] A Foreign Office annotation on the document ran: 'This is a rather typical French production. They put up proposals which go well beyond what they themselves are willing (or in a position) to perform, and will place the responsibility for the inaction upon us.'[14]

The gibe contained some truth but was itself dishonest, skating over the fact that the British were positively in favour of no action. In fact the French memorandum did, in passing, spell out a realistic if unpalatable alternative. 'The Western Powers,' it said, 'should not deceive themselves as to the credit which they will retain in Central Europe and elsewhere if Germany's next ultimatums are accepted.'

Halifax's response to such heart-searchings had remained calm. 'I still maintain,' he wrote as late as February 25, '. . . that any joint warning or protest in Berlin by His Majesty's Government and the French Government on the question of Austria is to be deprecated.'[15]

Two days later he went so far as to instruct Henderson to say that the British Government 'cannot conceal from themselves that recent events [i.e. at Berchtesgaden] have aroused apprehension in many quarters, which must inevitably render more difficult the negotiations of a general settlement'.[16] The instruction was a substitute for the earlier one sent by Eden about the British having the 'impression' that the events had done something to 'detract' from the independence of Austria.

Presented with the news of the *fait accompli* on March 11 while he and Chamberlain were giving a farewell luncheon to Ribbentrop at the conclusion of the latter's ambassadorship to London, Halifax did for a moment appear to be ruffled. But he had regained his calm before Ribbentrop left. As for Chamberlain, his attitude was summed up by his concluding remark to the Cabinet when it met in emergency session on March 12: 'At any rate, that question is now out of the way.'[17] As previously at the time of the introduction of German conscription and the occupation of the Rhineland, what was chiefly deplored in public were the methods by which Hitler had achieved his aim.

But what was to be said in public about the likely Government attitude when such methods were applied, as they were soon bound to be, to the Sudeten problem in Czechoslovakia? A position had first to be agreed in the Foreign Policy Committee of the Cabinet.

There was no doubt whatever in the minds of both Chamberlain and Halifax what this should be. The Austrian crisis did not invalidate the policy of appeasement, it merely demonstrated the need to accomplish it more completely before the European situation got out of control altogether. After several days of debate dominated by Chamberlain and Halifax, it was decided that there could be no question of Britain entering into any new commitments in Europe towards either Czechoslovakia or France. Britain and France would persuade the Czechs to make the necessary concessions to satisfy the Germans. Britain 'would use any influence we might have with Germany to induce her to take up a reasonable attitude'. Chamberlain stressed that if Germany could get what she wanted by peaceable methods there was no reason to suppose that she would reject such a procedure in favour of one based on violence. He noted that 'throughout the Austrian adventure Herr Hitler had studiously refrained from saying, or doing, anything to provoke us. It indicated a desire to keep on good terms with us.' He admitted that at first Britain should merely say that her objective in Czechoslovakia was some measure of local autonomy for the Sudeten Germans.[18]

Chamberlain was more candid in a letter he wrote to his sister on March 20 in which he said the map showed Britain could do nothing to save Czechoslovakia from being overrun by the Germans if they wanted to. To commit Britain to helping her would simply be a pretext for a war against Germany which he saw no prospect of Britain being able to win in reasonable time. He said he was prepared to approach Hitler personally and say to him: 'The best thing you can do is tell us exactly what you want for your Sudeten Germans. If it is reasonable we will urge the Czechs to accept and if they do, you must give assurances that you will let them alone in the future.'[19]

It was almost exactly what he was to say when he did to go see Hitler at Berchtesgaden six months later.

For the time being, however, the British public were not made fully acquainted with what was in his mind. To a House of Commons naturally anxious to know what in the light of the Austrian events the Government's attitude was going to be to Hitler's growing demands on Czechoslovakia, he made a masterly speech on March 24. Without giving away his intentions, he managed to please for a moment both those who thought that Britain ought to be firm and those fearful of her making any further European commitments. He again made clear that the Government's overall aim in international affairs was 'the maintenance and preservation of peace and the establishment of a sense of confidence that peace will in fact be maintained'. He made it equally clear that Britain was giving no guarantees to Czechoslovakia nor any further guarantees than already existed in Locarno to France. But having said that he added that the Government could not pretend that, where peace and war were concerned, legal obligations alone were involved; if war broke out it would be unlikely to be confined to those who had assumed such obligations. It was 'well within the bounds of probability' that the pressure of events would involve other countries than those who were parties to the original dispute, particularly in the case of countries which had such long associations of friendship as Britain and France.[20]

What he left out of this speech was the information that Britain, knowing France's anxious dilemma over Czechoslovakia, was going to help her put pressure on the Czechs to get her out of it. The events of the next six months were to be like the erratic burning of a fuse laid to what, it was hoped, would be a controlled explosion.

CHAPTER FOURTEEN

CZECHOSLOVAKIA II: 1933–8

IN CZECHOSLOVAKIA THE YEAR 1938 HAD BEGUN, FOR CZECHS, IN a certain spirit of optimism. Beneš had said at Christmas that it would be a year of negotiation. This suggested that the state would successfully deal with the alleged civic grievances of its more than three million Sudeten Germans in such a way as to placate Germany's anxieties. That the Sudeten Germans, for all their full democratic representation in the constitutional machinery of the state, had long had legitimate minor grievances was something neither President Beneš nor the Prime Minister Hodza sought to deny. They periodically stressed to the German Minister in Prague their determination to see them removed as far as possible.

At the heart of much of the sense of grievance was that chauvinistic attitude of Czech civil servants and police in the Sudetenland which was the psychological inheritance of three hundred years of Austro-German rule so recently reversed. Germans were under-represented in the civil service in proportion to their share of the country's population. Resentment at this reversal of dominating roles aggravated other Sudeten complaints. These often centred on education. Since the introduction of a new state law banning private education, Germans in Sudeten areas sometimes found their children forced into schools where teaching took place only in Czech. There were other language complaints such as an inadequate right to use German as a first language in all official transactions. Recently a more immediate material issue had made its appearance. The building of Czechoslovakia's vast new network of fortifications was proceeding in the heart of the Sudetenland. A National Defence Law of 1936, the year in which the work had started, gave the state power to acquire land in the

124

interests of security and for the same reason to refuse residential permits and labour permits in such areas. These powers inevitably affected Germans, some of them Reich-Germans and some Czechoslovak Germans, but all, in the increasingly nationalistic climate of the time, were Germans whose primary consideration was not the security of the Czechoslovak state.

By and large, though, the Czech claim that, in contrast with other minorities in the world, the Sudeten Germans were fairly treated as integral components of the state was not unreasonable. But the external factor of a powerful, successful and thus, to most Sudetens, natural and attractive alternative state to which they could turn from the old racial and cultural tensions of the constructed state in which they lived had transformed the nature of Czechoslovakia's domestic minority problems. These had been something potentially difficult. Since the arrival of Hitler they had become potentially dangerous.

On the other hand the very power and presence of this outside state to which, if they so wished, Sudeten Germans could now look for change and emotional fulfilment presented problems to the leader of the party which had spoken for them in Czechoslovakia since 1935. Konrad Henlein's own political theories, as far as they went, had vague philosophical affinities with Hitler's National Socialism; but in personality he was just the racially conscious gymnastic instructor he had always been by profession rather than a professional politician. Indeed he had been chosen as leader of the new Sudeten German Party in 1935 principally because he was the sort of popular and even, to some of his small-time followers, charismatic figure round whom Sudeten Germans of many different points of view could quite easily rally. He had no great political skills and his political leadership was necessarily un-focussed because what bound his party together was not politics but race. Consciousness of German blood and pride in German racial heritage were its inspiration. But what the inspiration was to lead to, in a state not motivated by this inspiration, was difficult to determine.

With hindsight, identification with German National Socialism appears the obvious course for the party to have pursued. But this, with its inherent separation, would in fact have led to immediate suppression by the Czech authorities. Moreover, probably until the beginning of 1938 it would hardly have been acceptable to the general membership which contained far too disparate a collection of different Sudeten views to be so straightforwardly satisfied. Certainly many dedicated Hitlerite National Socialists were now in the party ranks, for the Czechs had banned the Czech Nazi Party. But together with such radical extremists Henlein also had to keep happy political moderates prepared to opt for some degree of autonomy within the Czech state and other traditionally-minded Germans who had always preferred to think in terms of German cultural purity rather than political goals, and, before the *Anschluss*, had often retained a nostalgic glance towards Vienna rather than Berlin.

If Henlein had been a Hitler he could perhaps have imposed a viable finite political will upon his membership but he had none of Hitler's political flair. Nor would Hitler have wanted him to have it. Hitler wanted Henlein to remain as long as possible an unpredictable factor in Czechoslovakia. He himself wanted to decide what role the Sudetens were to play when the time came.

Henlein was as a result in an extraordinary position. At the Czech parliamentary General Election of 1935 his party had won a larger share of the popular vote than any other party in Czechoslovakia; it held the second largest number of seats in the Prague parliament. Yet this was not really the arena in which in the following years his political energies were concentrated. These were required to deal with the strains and stresses within the party itself due partly to the personal rivalries and conflict of ambitions inevitable in any expanding human organisation with unforeseeable prospects, and partly to the increasing pressure from radical extremists impatient with the party's need to keep its activities within the law. This was a political climate in which it was possible for Germans to be imprisoned by a Czech court for the seditious cry of '*Heil Hitler!*'[1] Such occurrences both emphasised the need to be politically circumspect and at the same time fanned the flames of German indignation into further extremism. But Henlein's chief difficulty was simply an uncertainty, which lasted until after the Austrian *Anschluss*, about the precise scope of the Third Reich's interest in his Sudeten Party and its place in Hitler's wider scheme of things.

A number of different Reich agencies concerned with the affairs of ethnic Germans outside the Reich had involved themselves with the Sudeten German Party's affairs over the years. Their own internal rivalries had further complicated Henlein's uncertainties. Money from Germany had certainly been available and had played a useful part in the sweeping electoral victory of 1935. But, in accordance with Hitler's policy of not committing himself to courses of action before deciding that it was opportune to do so, there had been no political lead from Germany, only the occasional reminder that local German ethnic interests must be subordinate to and wait upon the demands of Reich foreign policy.

During the autumn of 1937 radical extremist elements in the party were increasingly asserting their influence. They acted independently of any direction from the Reich and sometimes required restraint from the German Minister in Prague himself. But they were not without orchestrated support from Goebbels's press, particularly when one of them, the parliamentary deputy Karl Herman Frank, was involved in a brawl with a Czech policeman who hit him with a truncheon and put him under arrest. Henlein, knowing that the sole justification for his position was to keep the party united, eventually decided that the radical line was the one to take if unity and his own position were to be preserved.

On November 19, 1937 he sent a long document personally to Hitler outlining in great detail the disadvantages and injustices inflicted on the Sudetens by 'the Czech dictators and people' since the Führer's seizure of power. For the first time he committed himself unreservedly to the statement that 'at heart the Party desires nothing more ardently than the incorporation of Sudeten German territory, nay, of the whole Bohemian, Moravian and Silesian area within the Reich.' He stressed an urgent need to discuss with the leaders of the Reich the road the party was to take next.[2]

He received no reply, not even an acknowledgement from Hitler, for over four months.

The Czech Government adjusted themselves with outward calm to the unpleasant change in their circumstances brought about by the *Anschluss*. They had a new vulnerability now on their southern border where no serious fortifications had been built. But Beneš was able to remain reasonably confident that he could preserve the state's territorial integrity. This confidence proceeded not so much from the inevitable German assurances that the Czech frontiers would be scrupulously respected as from a combined assessment of Chamberlain's delphic utterance in Parliament on March 24 with an appropriately more definite re-statement of their treaty obligations which came from the French. Less than a week after the completion of the *Anschluss* further reassurance came in a statement from the Soviet Union that it would, in accordance with the treaty Beneš had signed in Moscow in 1935, come to Czechoslovakia's aid provided the French did.

The *Anschluss* had led to enthusiastic expectation in some sections of the Sudeten German Party that they themselves were now about to be taken into the Reich. The Czechs felt confident to be able to deal with this by gestures of conciliation towards their German minority. This was, after all, what was now recommended by Britain and France as an implied condition of continued support. Whether the gestures would be enough or would have to be extended lay in the future field of practical politics.

The first immediate gesture announced by the Prime Minister Hodza as early as March 28 was in fact no more than the promise of a statute properly to codify for the first time the full set of rights conferred by the Czechoslovak state on its minorities. But it was at least accompanied by the admission that 'our minorities policy still suffers from a certain lack of proportion.' 'Czechoslovakia,' Hodza continued, 'has been, and is, large-minded and generous towards the Germans on major issues, but dilatory in minor details . . .'[3]

Within a day the Czechs were confronted with an outright demand from the Sudeten Party for autonomy, a notion which they dismissed as incompatible with the integrity of the state. Given the worm-like geographical shape of the German-populated regions round long frontiers of the state it was indeed reasonable enough to regard these as unsuitable for conventional federal status. But forces inimical to reason were at work in the Sudetenland. An almost irrepressible local dynamic was now under way there. There was also now a factor at work there of which the Czechs were unaware. For on March 28, the very day on which Hodza made his speech about the minorities statute, Henlein himself was in Germany seeing Hitler for the first time.

Four months after Henlein's impassioned plea to which no reply had been received, Hitler was preparing to use him at last, though still in such a way as to be able to keep his options open. But now for the first time Henlein came under Hitler's orders as an instrument of German policy. His instructions were Machiavellian: 'demands should be made that are unacceptable to the Czechs'.[4] Thus neatly was it made impossible from the start for Beneš to win within the context which the British Cabinet decision had just set him.

Beneš's elaborate attempts over the next six months to accommodate himself and his country to the various pressures now put upon them can only be watched from the historical vantage point of fifty years later with a painful sense of dramatic irony. We know now that they were doomed to futility from the start and, for all their ingenuity, irrelevant.

Henlein went back to a Sudetenland where the excitement was soon such that as party leader he hardly had control of it any more. In an all-important speech at Karlsbad on April 24 he made a detailed and formal demand for wide-reaching autonomy on eight specific points. The last was such as virtually to deny the sovereignty of the Czechoslovak state. This demand spoke of: 'Full freedom to profess German nationality and the German political philosophy.' Much of the rest of the speech consisted of an attack on the whole concept of the Czechoslovak Republic as established in 1918. He now openly professed National Socialism. At times he sounded almost like Hitler himself. 'We do not want war,' he declared, 'either at home or abroad, but we can no longer tolerate a situation which for us means war in peace . . .'[5]

Even though the Czechs did not officially know that Henlein was now acting under Hitler's instructions to demand more than could be satisfied, it was clear that that was what he was doing.

The other factor of which the Czechs were ignorant, and at which even in their most pessimistic appraisal they could hardly yet have guessed, was something of which the British public were equally ignorant, namely, that Chamberlain's mind was already made up to give the Germans the Sudetenland rather than allow the problem to lead to war. On May 7, after the Czechs had responded to Henlein's Karlsbad demands with an offer of negotiations, the British and French envoys to Prague, Newton and de Lacroix, called on the Czech Foreign Mininster, Krofta. But the full significance of what lay behind their words cannot have been apparent. They expressed to him the hope of their Governments that Czechoslovakia would go to the furthest possible limits compatible with the integrity of the state, in order to solve the Sudeten problem.[6]

On the same day Neville Henderson handed in a personal memorandum to the head of the German Foreign Office's European Department. His Majesty's Government, it said, was urging the Czechs to seek without delay a solution to the Sudeten problem 'on comprehensive lines' and it hoped that the German Government too would be 'ready to use their influence to promote a settlement'.[7]

A further communication from Henderson's office to the German Foreign Office three days later conveyed the assurance that if the Germans would tell the British 'confidentially' what solution they were striving for the British 'would exert such pressure in Prague that the Czechoslovak government would be forced to accept the German wishes'.[8]

Henlein himself now left on a short trip to London which he had visited the previous year, noticeably impressing a number of people with his inoffensive geniality and moderation. This time he was acting under instructions and, with tension mounting in the Sudetenland, his instructions were further to mollify British opinion by presenting himself once again as a moderate autonomist. At the same time he was to make it plain that his visit was informal and that he had no connection with Berlin.[9] It says much for his persuasive gym instructor's manner that his mission was again a quiet public relations success. None of those he met seem to have read the full text of his Karlsbad speech which was then less than a week old.

He appeared in front of the newsreel camera seated round a small coffee table with two minor Foreign Office officials.

'We've ordered you some coffee, Herr Henlein. I hope that's all right?'

There was a pause.

'No, thank you very much. I've already had coffee.'

He went back to Berlin to report to Hitler. Hitler was as yet in no hurry to settle the Czech question. He had just told General Jodl exactly that; Austria had to be digested first.[10] When he had seen Henlein at the end of March he had merely talked of the 'not too distant future' and there is no reason to think that when Henlein reported to him on his return from London, as he did, Hitler told him anything different. A German Foreign Office official had recorded in his diary on May 13 that Hitler was 'thinking of dealing with the Sudeten German problem before the year was out', and on May 20 Keitel presented for signature the draft directive he had drawn up for him on the basis of earlier discussion of Case Green. This began: 'It is not my intention to smash Czechoslovakia by military action in the immediate future.'[11] But for once Hitler was not to be master of events. Something was to happen which within ten days would cause him drastically to change his mind.

A municipal election campaign had been in progress in the Sudetenland and had led to a number of violent incidents which received full anti-Czech treatment in the German press. The local Sudeten situation continued to manifest its own dynamic, and excitement was at fever pitch as Sudeten Party leaders yelled to enthusiastic audiences that their time of suffering under the Czech tyranny was about to end. The day was coming![12] They were going home to a Fatherland in the Reich! As the frenzied cheers echoed round the election halls with arms raised deliriously in Nazi salutes it hardly looked as if the Sudeten German Party were any longer much interested in remaining a constitutional component of the Czechoslovak state. There seemed a real danger that the Sudeten Germans might precipitate a crisis and force Hitler's hand. Popular rumour held that a German invasion was imminent. The local Czech authorities became apprehensive, tending to act first and ask questions afterwards. Two Sudeten German motor cyclists were shot. Whether to resolve the tension or because he genuinely believed what he gave as the reason for his action, Beneš now took the initiative. There were continuing intelligence reports of German troop movements towards the Czechoslovak borders. Beneš ordered a partial mobilisation, calling up reserves for the fortifications in the Sudetenland. Since, in spite of the reports about troop movements, no German attack was in fact under way this 'May crisis' quickly blew over but not without important psychological results. For it looked to the outside world as if the firmness of the Czechs, confident of British and French support, had made Hitler back down.

In the first place the May crisis put heart into the Czech people. It also provided a useful rehearsal for British Government attitudes in a moment when the possibility of German aggression against Czechoslovakia had to be taken seriously. Henderson in Berlin delivered two messages from Lord Halifax reminding the German Government of how difficult it would be for Britain to remain aloof if France had to fulfil her treaty obligations. And this, when he got to hear of it, may have put some heart into Beneš. What, however, Beneš would not have heard of was the emergency Cabinet meeting of which Duff Cooper, one of the Ministers present, reported ironically that 'the general feeling seemed to be that great, brutal Czechoslovakia was bullying poor peaceful little Germany.' Nor did he know of Halifax's warning to the French that Britain was not bound to join forever with them if they went to the help of Czechoslovakia. There was some psychological effect of the May crisis on Chamberlain too. Preening himself up to a point on the incorrect belief that it was the British messages to Berlin which had made the Germans hold back, he had to face the further conclusion that Hitler would now feel he had lost prestige as a result of the whole incident. This was a worry, illuminating, as he commented, 'the difficulties on the way of the peacemaker'.[13]

Here at least Chamberlain was right, for the greatest psychological effect of all was on Hitler. He is described by Ribbentrop's assistant as being 'furious';[14] he had appeared as having backed away when in fact he had not yet been meaning to move at all.

On May 30 he dramatically changed the directive for Case Green, the operation against Czechoslovakia drafted only ten days before. It now began: 'It is my unalterable decision to smash Czechoslovakia by military action in the near future.'[15]

This of course was not known to the world. Indeed the tensions in Czechoslovakia seemed temporarily to have eased. Some prospect of negotiation between Henlein and the Czech Government on the new Nationality Statute, approved just before the May crisis, even appeared possible though this of course fell far short of the Karlsbad demands. The Czech municipal elections passed off peacefully with Henlein's party winning more than 90 percent of the popular vote in the Sudetenland. Nevertheless Sudeten morale experienced something of an anti-climax as the crisis dissolved without anything new happening.

Chamberlain now made clear to the House of Commons that the Government's representations were being addressed primarily to the Czechs rather than to the Germans. The Czechs were told of 'the need of taking every precaution for avoidance of incidents and of making every possible effort to reach a comprehensive and lasting settlement' with the Sudeten Party. The Germans were asked by His Majesty's Government to 'cooperate with them in facilitating agreement'. The Czechs said they appreciated His Majesty's Government's interest. The Germans said they fully shared His Majesty's Government's desire to see negotiations succeed.[16]

The summer passed in what can now be seen as a haze of pointless political activity in Czechoslovakia. At the time, however, it seemed that the difficult and frustrating negotiations which took place between Benes's government and Henlein's Sudeten Party – observed from the wings by British and French and, from opposite wings, by the Soviet Union – were an all-important, even critical attempt to solve one of the last international problems left in Europe from the Treaty of Versailles. The Germans watched.

The two essential factors in the negotiations of which one participant had no knowledge – Henlein's commitment to Hitler and Hitler's own commitment to action – were of course unknown to the British and French, and presumably the Russians too. However, even had it been known that Beneš was struggling in a trap, it would have made little difference. Chamberlain himself had decided since March that it would be right to let Hitler have the Sudetenland if he wanted it – something else Beneš did not know, however strongly the British and French envoys in Prague urged him to offer Henlein concessions. The position of the French, who had been over to London in some state of concern at the time of the May crisis, has since been well summarised by a member of the British Foreign Office of that day. 'While the French obviously had to keep on saying to us: "well, don't forget we have our alliance to Czechoslovakia", they were really rather pleased that a strong-minded Chamberlain, who had not got any alliance with Czechoslovakia, was so to speak finding ways by which they would not be called upon to honour their engagement.'[17] The new Prime Minister, Daladier, was reported as saying to his *chef de Cabinet*: 'I shall do anything to avoid war, because we will lose it.'[18]

In these circumstances, speeches made by Czech statesmen at different stages of the negotiations have a pathetic ring. Beneš, for instance, speaking in Prague on June 30 expressed his confidence that 'within a very short time, within the next few days or weeks, we shall solve our nationalities problems . . . in a just and reasonable manner . . . We shall strengthen the whole structure of our state by a well-conceived nationalities, social and cultural policy, and we shall emerge from the present crisis stronger than before.'[19] A Czech Government communiqué in the middle of July attested to 'evidence of a certain reasonableness' in the Sudeten Party approach.[20] And at the end of August when the Czechs were about to announce their reluctant acceptance of most of Henlein's Karlsbad demands for autonomy Hodza, the Prime Minister, preferring to use 'self-administration' rather than 'autonomy . . . an ambiguous term', could still look hopefully to the future, confident that the integrity of the Czechoslovak state could be preserved.[21]

But by this time an extraneous figure had arrived on the scene. He came from Britain. He had in fact been instrumental in getting the Czechs to accept most of the Karlsbad points. This was Lord Runciman, a former British Cabinet Minister, appointed by Chamberlain without previously consulting the Czechs but with their subsequent acquiescence, to 'mediate' if possible between Henlein and the Czech Government.

Runciman's role was also 'to inform public opinion generally as to the real facts of the case' and possibly make proposals for its resolution. 'Hitherto,' Chamberlain told the House of Commons, 'we have ourselves abstained from making suggestions as to the particular method of trying to solve this Czechoslovakia question, although of course in this country we have had a certain amount of experience of the difficulty of trying to provide for local government without endangering the stability of the state.'[22]

This analogy with the problems of Birmingham City Council may have struck a reassuringly parochial note for members of the House of Commons, but it was, as has been remarked, a peculiarly patronising thing to do 'to send somebody into somebody else's country to negotiate between the Government of that country and one of its citizens who was in dispute with that government'.[23] To the British Foreign Secretary Lord Halifax, though, Runciman was on a 'patriotic' mission. Runciman had told him, when his function was explained to him: 'I quite understand; you are setting me adrift in a small boat in mid-Atlantic.' To which Halifax had replied: 'That is exactly the position.'[24] But it was not the position at all.

Runciman was being sent on a 'patriotic' mission to help enforce upon the Czechs a solution of the type which the British Government required for European appeasement. When on September 2 Henlein went to see Hitler at Berchtesgaden, the German communiqué which reported the meeting said that it had been 'at Lord Runciman's desire' that Henlein had explained to the Führer the stage in the negotiations reached by the Prague Government and that complete unanimity was reached in reviewing the situation.[25] When on September 7 the Czechs drafted their 'Fourth Plan' to meet the Sudeten demands – virtually full acceptance now of Henlein's Karlsbad points – they emphasised that it had been drafted 'personally and on repeated pressure from Lord Runciman'. Beneš simultaneously stressed that to apply these eight points was in fact 'utterly absurd' because the eighth point – that of identifying with the Third Reich's world outlook – would establish for one section of the population a totalitarian régime within the democratic Czechoslovak Republic. He was, however, accepting it because he had been pressed to do so by the Western democracies. But he added that he expected his offer to be rejected, thus suggesting that he may by now have had some idea of the game Henlein was playing.[26] His offer was indeed rejected.

Runciman's report to Chamberlain when it came was a fairly balanced assessment of the situation in Czechoslovakia as he had found it but his unequivocal conclusion was that the Sudetenland should be ceded to Germany. He placed responsibility for the breakdown of negotiations between Czechs and the Sudetens directly on Henlein and his party whose supporters, he said, urged extreme and unconstitutional action. But he recognised that, although by now the largest party in the country's Parliament, its racial isolation doomed it to be a permanent minority there, thus providing some of its members with an excuse for their unconstitutional approach. He found a number of the local grievances from which Sudetens claimed to suffer 'mainly justified'. These included the 'tactlessness, lack of understanding' and 'petty intolerance' of Czech and non-German-speaking officials and police, the encouragement of Czech infiltration into German areas, and the discrimination against German firms, workers and people in need of social welfare. He had done his best to promote a solution of these problems within the framework of the Czech state but even so felt that could such a settlement have been arrived at it would prove 'temporary, not lasting'. If some cession of territory thus became inevitable as he believed it to be, 'it should be done promptly and without procrastination'.

Very properly, Runciman also addressed himself to what he called 'the question of the integrity and security of the Czechoslovak Republic, especially in relation to her immediate neighbours'. But curiously he did not do so in the sense in which, given his other conclusions, one might have expected. He was after all recommending that Czechoslovakia should lose 'without procrastination' the vast network of underground fortifications constructed in the Sudeten areas in the past two years together with important industries integrated into her economy, including the Skoda arms works. But he made no mention of all this. What concerned him – perhaps because he did at least recognise that the country was now vulnerable – was that for her own safety Czechoslovakia should not annoy Germany any more. And he went so far as to make recommendations about the way she should conduct both her domestic and foreign policy in future. Those 'parties and persons in Czechoslovakia' who deliberately encouraged a policy antagonistic to Czechoslovakia's neighbours should be prevented, if necessary by law, from doing so. (This presumably included refugees from Nazi Germany – Jews, Social Democrats and Communists.) She should also 'remodel her foreign relations' so that in no circumstances would her obligations to other states involve her in an attack on Germany. (This presumably involved abandonment of her French and Soviet alliances.) He closed his report with an appreciation of the courtesy shown him by Dr Beneš, Dr Hodza and the very many people in all ranks of life whose country he was now proposing should lose its heavily defended frontier areas to a hostile neighbour 'at once'.[27]

Runciman's report to Chamberlain was dated September 21, 1938. By then events had far outrun any strict relevance his 'patriotic mission' might have borne to the situation in Czechoslovakia. But, insofar as his conclusions provided up-to-date justification for Chamberlain's own long-held attitude to the Sudetenland, it must have been helpful in giving him confidence for the highly personal style of diplomacy on which he was by now embarked.

CHAPTER FIFTEEN

CZECH CRISIS

THROUGHOUT THE SUMMER HITLER'S DETERMINATION TO 'SMASH Czechoslovakia in the near future' never wavered. Only some of his Generals became anxious, even apprehensive about what his decision might mean for Germany. He ordered and personally supervised a crash building programme for the west wall on the French frontier. He attended and made his Generals attend a demonstration of artillery assault against exact replicas of Czech fortifications in the east. After this display in August he reminded them of the first seven steps he had already taken on the road to his great ideological goal of living-space for a greater German Reich: foundation of the party, its accession to power, withdrawal from the League of Nations, rearmament, conscription, the Rhineland, Austria and now: 'However the situation may develop, Czechoslovakia has got to be eliminated before anything else.'[1]

Believing as he had always done that war was an inevitable and indeed a healthy feature of a nation's natural growth he seemed increasingly to be looking to the prospect of war as something desirable in itself. A war was something which the new Germany would almost certainly have to experience sooner or later, and it was perhaps time for it to undergo a first taste.

'Chips down,' wrote one General after hearing the August address, 'Führer convinced Britain and France won't intervene.' But he added in the next sentence: 'Beck [Chief of the General Staff] opposite opinion, gloomy mood.'[2]

Beck's opposition had by then developed beyond gloom. A General who had no feelings of sentiment whatever for the Czechs – one colleague described him as specifically 'yearning for the destruction of Czechoslovakia' – he was nevertheless utterly

138

convinced that for Germany to be taken by Hitler into a war now would in the long run be fatal to her. Hoping in the first place to persuade Hitler himself to this view, he had become reconciled to the need to persuade other Generals to act with him in a show of solidarity in order to get Hitler to change his mind. From there Beck had moved to contemplation of some sort of military *coup d'état*.

The exact form this was to take evolved gradually. At first there had been some idea of liberating the Führer himself from the influence of SS and Party, a concept which made direct action more easily reconcilable with the oath of loyalty to him. But the need to accept that it might not be possible to persuade Hitler to be liberated meant that further action had to be envisaged. Beck and others of the same opinion became convinced that they must 'go to the limit' if necessary. From these beginnings the first resistance plot against Hitler from within the German army came into being.[3]

Other strands in an incipient opposition were already at work within the German Foreign Office and among former political figures, both Conservatives and trade unionists of the pre-Hitler era. But it was the military conspirators who were obviously crucial to any success, and their preparations for substituting one apparatus of power in Germany for another were by the first week in September quite far advanced, at least on paper. Beck had by this time resigned and been replaced by a General equally convinced that Hitler was taking Germany on a criminal path to disaster, Franz Halder.

Halder, who considered the death of Hitler necessary to success, thought it important that this should be contrived so as to absolve the army from any apparent responsibility. Others, including Beck, thought Hitler should be taken alive and brought to trial, some suggesting that he should thereafter be declared insane by a panel of doctors for whom a chairman had already been found. Still others including younger officers, more ideologically motivated than the Generals, planned to shoot him on their own initiative at the moment of arrest.[4]

The one condition for successful action which all the conspirators pre-supposed was that Britain and France should stand firmly by Czechoslovakia, thus precipitating the crisis which would make it necessary to remove Hitler and save Germany from war.

Contacts were made with London both through the German Foreign Office and by an emissary of the Generals themselves to stress the crucial importance of such diplomatic support for their plans. The German chargé d'affaires in London, Theo Kordt, a party to the plot, went to see Halifax, the Foreign Secretary, at No. 10 Downing Street, entering furtively by the garden gate. He told Halifax that, if everyone could be convinced that a German attack on Czechoslovakia would mean war with Britain, then if Hitler continued with his policy the German army leaders would intervene against him. Kordt actually left Downing Street – again by the garden gate – under the impression that his point had been taken and that an unequivocal British message to this effect would be delivered.[5]

But the firmest message that was ever sent by the British to Germany over the whole period of the summer, and which had been delivered in one form at the time of the supposed May crisis, was a repetition of what Chamberlain had told the House of Commons on March 24 after the Austrian *Anschluss*, namely that, if the Germans attacked Czechoslovakia, then France would have to fulfil her obligations and in that case 'His Majesty's Government could not guarantee that they would not be forced by circumstances to become involved also'.[6]

Now, with unmistakable signs of another crisis mounting, Halifax instructed the Ambassador in Berlin, Henderson, to deliver a similar message again, along marginally firmer lines. Having first stressed that Britain and indeed Lord Runciman had been exercising 'the strongest pressure' on the Czechs 'to make the concessions necessary to produce a strong just solution', he repeated that if France became involved 'it seems to His Majesty's Government inevitable that the sequence of events must result in a general conflict from which Great Britain could not stand aside'.[7]

But even this was now too much for Henderson. He telegraphed the Foreign Secretary at once to say that it would be 'the most fatal thing' to deliver such a message and the instruction was rescinded. 'I have made the British position as clear as daylight, to the people who count,' said Henderson, speaking more truth than he realised. Anything like the message of the May crisis, he said, would 'drive Herr Hitler straight off the deep end'.[8] This was hardly the sort of language to suit the German army conspirators.

140

Chamberlain's own reasoning for discounting most of a plea made as urgently as Kordt's a few weeks earlier on behalf of the German Generals by a Conservative landowner, von Kleist-Schmenzin, was that this man was 'violently anti-Hitler' and, in London, reminded him of 'the Jacobites at the court of France in King William's time'.[9]

The signals coming out of Britain throughout the whole of that summer had been virtually all one way. They had been concerned primarily with 'pressure' to be put, not on Hitler but on Beneš, to get him to make concessions to the Sudetens – concessions which we now know Henlein was pledged to Hitler never to find acceptable. The word 'pressure' figured constantly in telegrams passing backwards and forwards between London and Paris and London and Prague. In May the British Ambassador in Paris expressed the hope to the French Foreign Minister Bonnet that 'very firm and persistent pressure would be brought to bear upon M. Beneš by the French Government'.[10] In Bonnet himself the British had a willing listener for he was eager to reassure them that he 'would readily put any pressure on the Czechoslovak Government that you might think at any moment desirable in order to ensure a peaceful solution of the Sudeten question . . . Moreover,' he added, 'if Czechoslovakia were really unreasonable the French Government might well declare that France considered herself released from her bond.'[11]

Less compliant members of the French Government, however, might themselves require a certain amount of discreet pressure. The Prime Minister, Daladier, for instance had disclosed in the recent post-*Anschluss* consultations in London that had he been in power at the time of Hitler's re-occupation of the Rhineland he would have opposed it by force if necessary.[12] Possibly it was with him in mind rather than Bonnet that Halifax, picking up Bonnet's last remark, offered the French themselves direct advice about how to conduct their foreign relations. On May 31 (the day after Hitler had taken his irrevocable decision to crush Czechoslovakia in the near future, though Halifax was not to know this) he suggested to the French that the time had now come for them to give Beneš a warning that 'if through any fault of his the present opportunity for a settlement is missed, the French Government would be driven to reconsider their position *vis-à-vis* Czechoslovakia.'[13]

141

Certainly, for all Bonnet's support, the need for pressure on the French themselves surfaced from time to time. In mid-June the French Ambassador in London pointed out that Beneš had complied on every occasion with the advice given him from Paris and London and that there could be no complaint against him. In these circumstances, he said, the French Government were inclined to doubt the wisdom of keeping up strong pressure on Beneš, 'particularly in view of our complete failure to produce any corresponding effect in Berlin'. The British in return stressed only the danger that 'Dr Beneš might lose sight of the urgency'.[14] This implied assumption that Britain, periodically glad to stress that it had no commitment in Czechoslovakia, was better placed to judge the urgency of a situation affecting Czechoslovakia than the Czechoslovak Government itself was typical of the prevailing British attitude. The 'urgency' to which the statement referred was not primarily that of Czechoslovakia but that facing a British Empire neither willing nor equipped to be dragged into a major war.

The pattern of the British approach to the Sudeten crisis had really been sketched out by Halifax the previous November and put into words in April 1938. Ideally, he then wrote to Henderson in Berlin, in relations with Germany Britain should hope for 'something not wholly unlike the general settlement we have always worked for'. Otherwise, he went on: 'I think the only thing we can do is to prevent our relations with them getting any worse than we can avoid, and do the best we can at Prague to get Beneš to accept the settlement that Henlein would accept.'[15]

The detailed nature of the settlement which the British and French were urging on Beneš became rather more specific as the summer wore on and his offers to Henlein proved progressively insufficient. Early in June phrases such as 'the importance of not only going to the limit of what was possible but doing something for the immediate future . . .' were delivered to Beneš by the British envoy in Prague, Basil Newton. He followed this up with the remark that at any rate the vast majority of the Germans in the country who resided near the frontier could hardly be kept permanently as they were against their will.[16] At other times interference was more pragmatic as when Halifax told Newton to warn the Czech Government not to call up 70,000 reservists before they were due in the autumn, for fear of 'prejudicing the present position by hasty action'.[17]

The May crisis which seemed (however incorrectly) to have been successfully deflated as a result of Beneš's firm action in calling up reservists had undoubtedly given both himself and the Czechoslovak nation confidence. Acutely aware of the need to keep British and French satisfied of his sincerity for compromise, he became over-confident in his ability to do so, and was not fully to appreciate until too late how tenuous France's sense of obligation was in danger of becoming under British pressure and the strain of her own domestic tensions.

It was not until the end of July that the three Bills which were to constitute Beneš's grand new Nationalities Statute dealing with language and administrative reform throughout the state were offered to Henlein – due inevitably to founder in the latter's rhetoric and obstruction, like subsequent plans extracted under the pressure of the Runciman mission. Two days after the first details of the July Nationalities Statute were announced Henlein spoke at Breslau in Germany of the Sudetens taking their duties to the state in which they lived seriously but at the same time remaining 'German national citizens serving voluntarily under the laws of the German nation'.[18]

By this time British diplomatic pressure, about to be so strongly reinforced by Runciman, was already suggesting the possibility of definite cession of territory to Germany by means of a plebiscite. And though Halifax, who brought the subject up with Jan Masaryk, the Czech envoy in London and son of the state's founder, admitted that an analogy with the Saar plebiscite of 1935 which had returned that territory from France to Germany was false, yet in a manner very typical of his style of argument he said British opinion would make this analogy and would therefore dismiss objections to a plebiscite with the feeling that it provided 'a better way out than any other'. Continuing such tautological sleight of hand Halifax went on: 'If the Czechoslovak Government felt, as they no doubt did, the gravest objection to the plebiscite proposal, it was another argument for reinforcing the necessity of reaching a solution by negotiation.'[19] In Halifax's mind such solution by negotiation might of course result in a plebiscite.

The signs were already there for all to see, but the Czech nation seemed determined not to see them. Though violent 'incidents' occurred in the Sudetenland from time to time and the German press made the most of them (sometimes taking names from the telephone book at random to publicise them as martyrs to Czech brutality)[20] the Czechs' own national pride was buoyant, confident in their own strength and that of their allies.

The American writer and journalist, Martha Gellhorn, has described the scene in Czechoslovakia at the time: 'there was no flag-waving, jumping about saying isn't war lovely, but absolute solid determination. Everybody was ready – everybody knew they were going to fight and expected their allies to be with them.'[21]

A young Czech girl, Mirka Kunstantova, was one of many thousands of children who went to camp that summer. She still remembers the songs they sang, songs that were part of their lives and gave them hope, faith and optimism 'and showed that strength was in people to resist the evil which we saw in Fascism'. 'We'll march in millions' went one such song, 'and all of us against the wind.'[22]

In the first week of July the *Sokol*, the jubilant Czech gymnastic festival founded in the middle of the last century as an assertion of Czech national identity under German-Austrian rule, was in full swing. But it was in the first week of July too that the British Foreign Secretary wrote to Bonnet criticising even him for not pressing Beneš hard enough.

'While naturally not wishing to express any opinion as to the policy of the French Government in the matter of their treaty obligations to Czechoslovakia . . .' Halifax began. He then proceeded to do just that. It was vital, he said, that Beneš should realise with what difficulties the French could 'hardly fail to be faced if called upon to fulfil those obligations in circumstances where it could be argued that Czechoslovakia had failed to make, or had delayed until too late, her full contribution to the cause of peace'. The French, he said, seemed to be suggesting that the main reason for concessions was to satisfy British public opinion and keep alive 'the hopes on which joint Franco-British action in favour of Czechoslovakia is based'.[23] He said he was not quite clear what that phrase 'joint Franco-British' action meant. He hoped Beneš might not read more into it than was warranted.

Jiri Mucha, the son of the Czech painter Alfons Mucha, returned to Prague that summer from abroad. He found the country in a state of euphoria. 'People didn't know what was going

144

on. People really believed that everybody was on their side and that they would be able to say no to Hitler and the other big powers would help them... When I saw this euphoria I was terribly depressed. I knew that these people were on the crest of the wave and that the fall would be terrible.'[24]

Runciman, diligently pursuing his mission the following month, seeing German Counts, Sudeten Party members – though not until the end of his mission Henlein – and Beneš over and over again to counsel autonomy, had something of the same feeling as Mucha.

'Where are we going?' he asked in a sort of realistic despair. '... It is a pathetic side of the present crisis that the common people here, and, I am told, elsewhere are looking to me and my mission as the only hope for an established peace. Alas, they do not realise how weak are our sanctions, and I dread the moment when they find that nothing can save them. It will be a terrible disillusionment for them.'[25]

Although his mission was theoretically independent of the Foreign Office he was writing to the British Foreign Secretary at the time. Only a few days before, Halifax himself had faced those sanctions with equal realism, defining the British 'line' as '... perpetually telling Beneš of what we might *not* do in the event of trouble: and tactfully reminding the Germans of what we *might*[*] do.' John Buchan, the writer of political adventure fiction, had given him the phrase.[26]

Beneš, unlike the general public, was all too well aware of the evasive nature of British and French support but continued to display a confidence which was more real than bluff. Much as Henderson in Berlin, Halifax in London and Newton in Prague might regard his laborious preparation of concessions as evidence of dilatory stubbornness – 'It is heartrending,' wrote Henderson, 'to watch him playing Germany's game, thinking that he is gaining time when he is losing it' – he was at the same time doing something more realistic than what Henderson called 'gambling on British lives being squandered for Czechs'.[27] He was gambling on the very uncertainty which pervaded the British and French attitudes having in the end the deterrent effect Halifax himself half hoped for. It was not nearly so satisfactory as the outspoken threat of positive action

*Italics in original document.

he had wanted but it was something, and it carried with it the chance that if it failed circumstances might still precipitate Britain and France into positive action after all.

Moreover Beneš had certain sanctions of his own. Yugoslavia and Rumania, the countries which with Czechoslovakia had long ago formed the Little Entente, principally to defend themselves against Hungary's claims on their Hungarian minorities, were still his allies though what was to prove the last meeting of the alliance in August 1938 had emphasised differences in attitude to Germany as well as common interests against Hungary. Nevertheless the Germans thought it worth warning both Yugoslav and Rumanian representatives at this meeting of the danger of the Sudeten problem.[28]

More formidable, on paper at least, was Beneš's alliance with the Soviet Union, pledged to come to his support once the Franco-Czech treaty had been implemented. Categorical statements were made by the Soviet Foreign Minister Litvinov at the end of August and again early in September that if Germany attacked Czechoslovakia and France were engaged then the Soviet Union too would fulfil her obligations.[29] Considerable doubt, however, hung over the reality of this statement.

In the first place the inscrutable nature of Stalin's personality meant that some uncertainty was present in all his apparent commitments to policy. It was, for instance, Bonnet the French Foreign Minister's view that Russia's one wish was 'to stir up a general war in the troubled waters of which she will fish'.[30] William Bullitt, the US Ambassador in Paris, was of a similar opinion, maintaining that Russia wanted to provoke 'a general conflagration in which she herself will play but little part but after which she will arise like a phoenix, but out of all of our ashes, and bring about a world revolution'.[31]

Secondly and more clearly discernible was what Stalin, in his recent sweeping political purges, had done to the fighting ability of the Red Army. It could still look impressive enough on Red Square but the trial and execution of Marshal Tukachevsky and two of the other four Soviet Marshals, with many top ranking Generals, for treason and espionage had devastated its leadership. Most of the divisional commanders had been liquidated or jailed. As the Russians today concede: 'The army was beheaded by this action.'[32]

Daladier signs Hitler's visitors' book.
Goering observes.

The piece of paper

We, the German Führer and Chancellor and the
British Prime Minister, have had a further
meeting today and are agreed in recognising that
the question of Anglo-German relations is of the
first importance for the two countries and for
Europe.

We regard the agreement signed last night
and the Anglo-German Naval Agreement as symbolic
of the desire of our two peoples never to go to
war with one another again.

We are resolved that the method of
consultation shall be the method adopted to deal
with any other questions that may concern our two
countries, and we are determined to continue our
efforts to remove possible sources of difference
and thus to contribute to assure the peace of
Europe.

Adolf Hitler

Neville Chamberlain

September 30, 1938.

The four signatories

The departure from Munich

Chamberlain's triumph

'Peace with honour'

Hitler in the Sudetenland, October 1938

German troops in Prague, March 1939

In April 1938 the British Military Attaché in Moscow estimated that 65 percent of all higher-ranking officers had been purged and that this had had a disastrous effect on the morale and efficiency of the Red Army. His conclusion was that it might be equal to a defensive war within the Soviet Union but not much more.[33] Which, since Stalin knew well enough what he had done, gives some plausibility to William Bullitt's assessment of the Soviet Union's likely role in any war developing from the Sudeten crisis.

A third factor which reduced the apparent value of Soviet help was the lack of any common frontier between Czechoslovakia and the Soviet Union across which help could arrive. Both Poland and Rumania refused to grant right of transit to Red Army troops and the only help that could have come would have had to do so by air. There were conflicting reports as to whether or not Rumania, across whose air space lay the shortest route, was even prepared to allow the Red Air Force to use it. Hitler who had most reason to be worried about Soviet intervention, should it become a reality, seems not to have taken the possibility seriously.

Hitler alone of all the chief participants on the diplomatic scene was in possession of the vital piece of information: the date on which the Wehrmacht would move against Czechoslovakia, namely October 1, the day laid down in the orders for Case Green. But certain public signs of forthcoming action were available. At the beginning of August the Germans had started calling up some classes of reservists nominally as a preliminary for autumn training. The process continued and what could have been accepted as a test mobilisation began to look something like mobilisation itself.[34] The British Military Attaché in Berlin received information from an army officer once a Nazi but now opposed to Hitler, to the effect that, at a meeting attended by all commanding Generals of the Wehrmacht at Doberitz in the middle of August, Hitler had definitely announced his intention of attacking Czechoslovakia towards the end of September. The last stage of mobilisation was to be completed on September 15. Russia was not worth considering.[35]

One date which, it could be safely said, would have some effect on the Sudeten situation was September 12, the day on which Hitler himself was due to speak at the great Nazi Party rally at Nuremberg.

Tension mounted in the Sudetenland as the day approached. Incidents involving Czech police and Sudeten Germans or Czech and German civilians increased and were increasingly played up by the Nazi press. One such incident was used by the Sudetens as an excuse for immediately breaking off negotiations after Beneš's final offer to accept Henlein's Karlsbad points. On the same day, September 7, the world got its first clear public indication of the way in which the situation might be resolved. For some of those who had had little inkling of what was happening behind the scenes it came as a shock. *The Times*, often thought to represent the opinion of the British Government, ran a leader in typical circuitous terms:

> . . . if the Sudetens now ask for more than the Czech Government are apparently ready to give . . . it can only be inferred that the Germans are going beyond the mere removal of their disabilities and do not find themselves at ease within the Czechoslovak Republic. In that case it might be worthwhile for the Czechoslovak Government to consider whether they should exclude altogether the project, which has found favour in some quarters, of making Czechoslovakia a more homogeneous state by the secession of that fringe of alien populations who are contiguous to the nation to which they are united by race . . .

Both the French and Czech Governments immediately urged the British Government to dissociate itself from this view. It did so. The article was not indeed as many believed inspired by the Government but was the responsibility of the Editor of *The Times*, Geoffrey Dawson. However Dawson was a close personal friend of Chamberlain and Halifax. Lunching with Halifax on the day after the article appeared he reported the Foreign Secretary as not dissenting 'privately from the suggestion that any solution, even the secession of the German minorities, should be brought into free negotiation at Prague'.[36]

At Nuremberg on September 10 Goering set the tone for Hitler's speech two days later:

> One small section of Europeans is to-day tormenting other Europeans, namely the minorities entrusted to its care . . . We know what is going on down there. We know how it is that that little fragment of a nation down there – goodness knows where it

148

hails from – should persistently oppress and interfere with a highly civilised people . . . We have no desire to harm anyone but neither will we any longer tolerate the harm done to our German brothers . . . Let all the nations remember that Versailles banished peace from the world. To-day its contemptible creators stand helpless before the miserable makeshift work of their hands . . . The Lord sent us the Führer not that we might perish but that we might rise again . . .[37]

Hitler himself on September 12 spoke of 'a great part of our people . . . delivered up to shameless ill-treatment without any apparent means of self-defence . . . The misery of the Sudeten Germans is indescribable. It is sought to annihilate them. As human beings they are oppressed and scandalously treated in an intolerable fashion. When three and a half million members of a people which numbers eighty millions may not sing a song they like because it does not please the Czechs, or when they are terrorised and ill-treated because they use a form of greeting which the Czechs dislike . . . when they are hunted and harried like wild-fowl for every expression of their national sentiment . . . I can only say . . . that if these tortured creatures can of themselves find no justice they will get it from us . . . It was a short-sighted arrangement which the statesmen of Versailles devised for themselves when they called into being that monstrous formation Czechoslovakia.'[38]

Chamberlain, addressing Parliament sixteen days later, said that the effect of this speech had been to leave the situation unchanged with a slight diminution of tension.[39] It seems a strange judgement in view of what immediately happened in the Sudetenland.

The reflection of the floodlights of Nuremberg could be seen in the sky across the border. The Sudeten Germans put radios in the windows of their houses and turned up the volume as loudly as possible to broadcast Hitler's speech. Some put lighted candles in their windows saying that when they had burned down the Czechoslovak Republic would be finished.[40] Germans massed in town centres, sometimes armed, singing 'Deutschland über Alles'. There were violent clashes between them and the Czech forces of law and order during the night with fatal casualties on both sides. Something that looked very like a planned uprising seemed to have occurred though in fact it was no more than a spontaneous outbreak

149

of sporadic violence in which a tension building for weeks had been released by the impact of Hitler's speech.

The Czechs declared martial law in a number of districts on the border. Henlein and his deputy Karl Hermann Frank sent an ultimatum to the Czech Government to withdraw martial law at once. The Government rejected the ultimatum and restored order so successfully that by September 17 the German chargé d'affaires in Prague was reporting that the Czech Government was master of the situation.[41] The Czech national resolve was much strengthened.

The official casualty list of the abortive 'uprising' included 27 deaths, of whom 11 were Sudeten Germans and 13 members of the Czech police or army.[42] Henlein had fled to Germany whence he issued a defiant statement that all negotiations with the Czechs were now at an end and that the Sudeten demand was now incorporation within the Reich. But the morale of the Sudetens was shaken. Their leaders had left them. The Czechs were in control. And there was no sign of the Führer of the Reich making any move to incorporate them.

A surprise move of a different sort had, however, been made by somebody else. It was to bring about the same result in the end. Very late on September 13 while the Czechs were still restoring control in the Sudetenland a telegram sent from London at 11 p.m. was received by the German Foreign Ministry through the British Ambassador in Berlin. It was from Neville Chamberlain who 'in view of the increasingly critical situation' proposed to come over to Germany by air the next day 'to try to find a peaceful solution.'[43]

CHAPTER SIXTEEN

BERCHTESGADEN

CHAMBERLAIN'S DRAMATIC IDEA OF MAKING DIRECT PERSONAL contact with Hitler had been in the back of his mind for some time. He seems first to have put it forward as a concrete suggestion in conversation with the official who had become his most valued personal adviser, Sir Horace Wilson, on August 28.[1] Wilson, a civil servant, technically Chief Industrial Adviser to the Government, provided a welcome source of able administrative support independent of the Foreign Office, someone most necessary to a Prime Minister with his own vision of the way to conduct foreign affairs. Chamberlain's plan, which became known in jargon oddly military for a mission of peace as 'Plan Z', had next been communicated to Henderson on his recall to London at the end of the month. But it was a sign of Chamberlain's confidence in his ability to handle the developing crisis in his own way that he did not mention the idea even to Halifax until after a meeting for which the Cabinet were recalled from holiday on August 30.

Ostensibly this meeting had been to inform the Cabinet of latest developments but its real purpose was to ensure for Chamberlain continued Cabinet support for the policy of pressure on Prague without undue pressure on Hitler. Only the First Lord of the Admiralty, Duff Cooper, and the President of the Board of Trade, Oliver Stanley, argued strongly that the present policy should be replaced by a firmer attitude towards Hitler, but Chamberlain's hold over his Cabinet was such that they did not press their objections.[2]

When he did tell his Foreign Secretary about Plan Z it 'rather took Halifax's breath away', but he came round to it. Chamberlain himself still hoped that it might not be necessary but he kept it in

151

mind since Henderson had thought 'it might save the situation at the eleventh hour'.[3] The rest of the Inner Cabinet, though not the full Cabinet, were next told and approved in principle.

The dramatic events in Czechoslovakia on the occasion of Hitler's Nuremberg speech on September 12 and the possibility that for all the pursuit of careful policy Britain might be about to be dragged into a war she did not want at the heels of an unsure and ambivalent France decided Chamberlain for action. At a meeting of the Inner Cabinet on September 13, the day after the speech, it was decided that they would have 'great reluctance in involving this country in war, if the alternative was a plebiscite [in the Sudeten areas of Czechoslovakia], provided that a plebiscite on fair and reasonable terms could be obtained'. With a plebiscite and what that inevitably entailed for Czechoslovakia in mind they authorised Chamberlain to approach Hitler.[4] The 11 p.m. message on September 13 was sent to Henderson in Berlin for delivery to Hitler 'at the earliest possible moment'. It ran: 'In view of increasingly critical situation I propose to come over at once to see you with a view to trying to find a peaceful solution. I propose to come across by air and am ready to start tomorrow. Please indicate earliest time at which you can see me and suggest place of meeting.'[5]

The full Cabinet were told the next day. When they met no reply had yet come from Hitler. Some Ministers felt anxious lest Chamberlain should in fact be rebuffed. He admitted to them that he had at one time thought of leaving for Germany actually before saying that he was coming. But whatever Hitler replied the die was cast. The information that the British Government was now prepared to accept as a solution a plebiscite with its inevitable transfer of much Sudeten territory to Germany had been given to German press correspondents the night before.[6]

It was not until half-past three on that afternoon that a message came back from Hitler to say that he would 'naturally be pleased' to receive Chamberlain. His immediate response had been to think of going to see Chamberlain himself in order to spare the Prime Minister the journey at his age. He then considered a rendezvous on his yacht, the *Grille*, at Kiel.[7] Finally, however, he arranged the meeting for his mountain house at Berchtesgaden. This suited Chamberlain. As he wrote to his sister, if Hitler had

152

come to see him 'it would have deprived my coup of much of its dramatic force'.[8]

There was a clear sense of personal excitement about what he was doing. Hitler, he wrote happily afterwards, had been 'struck all of a heap' at the news of his proposal. It was an enjoyable thought that this would 'appeal to the Hitlerian mentality and . . . might be agreeable to his vanity'.[9]

It was indeed an unprecedented step he was taking. He was going to see Hitler face to face to settle the whole dispute peacefully. Much of his life had been spent resolving difficult problems in such face to face meetings, and the special challenge of this one supplied him with remarkable physical and mental stamina for the next two weeks.

'My policy has always been to try and assure peace,' he told the newsreel camera waiting for him with cheering crowds at Heston airport before he set off. 'And Herr Hitler's ready acceptance encourages me to hope that my visit will not be without success.'

To the German chargé d'affaires who was there to congratulate him on his decision he made a point of speaking expressly of 'the Führer'.[10]

He admitted later to a few 'sinking feelings' as the aircraft flew over London but arrived at Munich airport confident and cheerful with hat and umbrella to be met by Ribbentrop. He was taken thence first by train and then by car up the mountain road to Berchtesgaden.[11]

The Berghof, Hitler's spacious mountain house at Berchtesgaden which once looked out so impressively over the majestic valley below, is today quite invisible from the road. Allied bombs gutted the building in the last month of World War II and the standing remains were blown up in the early 1950s in an attempt to efface ineffaceable memories. But the dank cavernous stumps of the foundations still haunt the depths of the wood which in thirty-five years has grown over them like the forest in some fairy tale of evil. A man who was a child when Hitler lived there talking of a thousand-year Reich will find for you the insignificant lay-by – the sort of place in which road-menders dump their equipment – from which a track leads up through the trees towards the ruins. An official sign says merely that there is no access and that the path is dangerous.

Here once rose the broad drive up which the Mercedes in which Chamberlain climbed to be met in front of the imposing steps by young SS men running forward to open the doors even before the car had stopped.

Today, when historic newsreels leave only an impression of the slightly incongruous if not ridiculous figure of Chamberlain caught up in scenes which we now know to have been eventually followed by world disaster, it is too easy to see him only as some misplaced dupe. Certainly there were those who saw him as such at the time though what time has erased from the newsreels is the formidable quality which made it necessary for such opponents to dislike or even hate him. But many millions of people in many different countries saw in him only a man not necessarily of 'courageous genius' as the newsreel commentator labelled him but a man with the quiet strength to save the world from an even more horrible version of the nightmare it had been through only twenty years before.

Nor was he a dupe in the sense that he did not realise what he was doing. He knew exactly what he was doing and over the next two weeks successfully accomplished exactly what he had set out to do. That this did not in the long run lead to the permanent result he had hoped for – that final appeasement of Europe in the era after Versailles for which British foreign policy had striven so long – must be assessed as his eventual failure. But this failure was a possibility he consciously took in his stride and it did not rule out the desirability of temporary success. He knew that there was a chance that the man with whom he was dealing might not turn out to be dealing within the same conventions as himself and, though he certainly underrated that chance, he had no doubt that he was right to take it.

In the short term, in his eyes, it proved worth taking. There was to be no war that autumn. The future was a matter for the next deal. Only in the sense that he was unable to see that the only methods he knew how to use were in the long run wholly inappropriate to Hitler did he dupe himself. It was the combination of a certain prim arrogance of his own and Hitler's intuitive manipulatory skills that led him to do so.

Whether, even in the short term, he carried into this part of the deal the sort of values and moral considerations which the British people like to feel are upheld for them by their representatives as well as their interests is a different question. Certainly Britain had no formal

154

moral obligations to Czechoslovakia other than those generally incorporated within the Covenant of the League of Nations. The Ethiopian crisis of two years before had demonstrated how impractical was the morality that idealistic document enshrined. On the other hand, Britain with France had responsibility for Versailles, and Versailles had created Czechoslovakia twenty years before, giving a proud people of seven millions in the centre of Europe a country and a dignity of which they felt they had been deprived for three hundred years. Britain and France therefore both had a certain basic moral responsibility for Czechoslovakia and for its sense of dignity.

In France's case this was amplified by a formal undertaking in the shape of the 1924 treaty by which she was pledged to come to Czechoslovakia's aid if Czechoslovakia were the object of aggression. This treaty was in itself part of a defensive system for France to whom Britain had her own formal obligation under the Locarno Pact, in addition to those natural ties of mutual self-interest which had already bound the two countries together in one major European war. For all the differences of temperament, these interests were likely to remain close for the foreseeable future. Thus a further affinity to Czechoslovakia existed for Britain through the mutual alliance with France.

That Britain should now be not only putting pressure on the Czechs to accept fundamental changes to the structure of their state which they were reluctant to accept, but also putting pressure on France to reconsider her obligations unless the Czechs did as they were told, was, from the point of view of honour, at least a questionable stance. To any such questioning Chamberlain's natural response was first that what was being proposed was an adjustment to Czechoslovakia to enable her to survive at all and secondly that there was an overriding moral consideration superior to any sense of responsibility to Czechoslovakia, namely that of saving the world from another war which would be even more horrible than the last. Whether or not this was the only way of enabling Czechoslovakia to survive in the circumstances and whether or not this was the only way of saving the world from war are practical questions not strictly on the moral plane. Chamberlain was fully entitled to answer these in the light of his own judgement. Whether his judgement on such points was sound is a matter to be examined separately. But, even accepting, for the sake of argument, its soundness, questions about the honour and the style of the course on which Chamberlain was now embarked behind the backs of the Czechs are awkwardly insistent. Nor can they be dispelled by the further plea that in the very long run Chamberlain's only real concern was the future safety and well-being of the British Empire.

At least the first moments of Chamberlain's arrival at Berchtesgaden were more satisfactory than his Foreign Secretary's had been the previous November. He recognised Hitler on the steps at once, though he afterwards described him as 'the commonest little dog' he had ever seen.[12] A short greeting was exchanged through the interpreter Paul Schmidt and the party walked up the steps and into the Berghof in silence. They sat for a while in the room with the great window overlooking the valley towards Salzburg, making desultory conversation while they drank tea. Chamberlain himself led the small talk. He found Hitler shy and unrelaxed. There was a suggestion at one point that Hitler might come to England sometime. But he said he would be received with demonstrations of disapproval and, when Chamberlain said 'Well, perhaps it would be wise to choose the moment,' he allowed himself the shadow of a smile. Then rather abruptly he asked what procedure Chamberlain would like to follow and, on being told *tête-à-tête*, took him upstairs with no one but the interpreter. Chamberlain noted observantly the various details of the place, particularly the nudes on the walls, and counted the furniture and the bottles of mineral water ('which he didn't offer me') in the bare room where they sat down and talked. They talked for three hours.[13]

Months before, Chamberlain had rehearsed in a letter to his sister what he would say when he met Hitler: 'The best thing you can do is to tell us exactly what you want for your Sudeten Germans. If it is reasonable we will urge the Czechs to accept ...'[14] And this is virtually what he now did. Given his acceptance of the principle of a plebiscite for the Sudetenland before he set out for Germany it was unlikely that his idea of 'reasonable' would cause problems. As he was to put it a few days later: 'On principle I didn't care two hoots whether the Sudeten

Germans were in the Reich or out of it, but I saw immense practical difficulties.'[15]

It was not the principle of giving away the frontier areas of Czechoslovakia to Germany, but how to deal with the practical difficulties of conceding this principle that formed the substance of all three meetings Chamberlain had with Hitler, culminating in the Munich Conference itself.

At this first meeting Hitler successfully manoeuvred Chamberlain into conceding the principle in the terms in which Hitler defined it. It was after Chamberlain had suggested that, even on the assumption that all areas with an 80 percent German population should be handed over, there would remain practical problems requiring population transfers for the 20 percent Czechs and the equivalent German minorities in mainly Czech areas, that Hitler became impatient and insisted that all areas with more than a 50 percent German population must come into the Reich. He said the present situation with 300 Sudeten Germans already killed by the Czechs was intolerable and that he was prepared to risk war rather than let it continue.

Chamberlain, not bothering to rebut the detail of Germans killed (Runciman was to tell him that he reckoned the total dead by this time on both sides had been no more than 70, while the Foreign Office put it lower still), protested that if Hitler's mind was made up in this way then his journey had hardly been necessary. But Hitler then sprang his trap. He calmed down and said that provided the British Government would accept the idea of secession in principle there was still a chance of peace. Chamberlain said that for himself he did accept this principle and thereby tacitly accepted Hitler's version of the principle, namely that 50 percent or more was the figure for transfer of German population.[16]

Inasmuch as some sort of negotiation could be said to have taken place Chamberlain had just agreed to the transfer of almost twice the amount of Czech territory he had been prepared to concede at the start. If in his Birmingham days he had allowed himself to be so neatly out-manoeuvred he would hardly have become the successful business man he did. But then here at Berchtesgaden he had given away nothing for himself. He 'didn't care two hoots' about Sudeten Germans going into the Reich. He was negotiating for peace and it seemed that he had got it.

Hitler, making the one reservation that the German military machine was of course already wound up and that in such circumstances it was not easy to stop it, nevertheless said he would do his best to keep it in check. What Chamberlain did not know was that Hitler's Chiefs of Staff, working night and day on preparations for the implementation of Case Green, were telling him that it could not possibly be put into action before the deadline of October 1. Only that very morning, meeting in Berlin, they had addressed themselves to the question: 'What could be done if the Führer wants us to advance the date due to the rapid development of the situation?' Jodl himself had answered: 'It cannot be done.'[17]

Both parties to the Berchtesgaden talks could feel that they had got what they wanted and given nothing away at all. Chamberlain left saying that, having agreed for himself the principle that the Sudetenland should be ceded, he must now consult his Cabinet and the French. Hitler agreed that they should meet again in a few days' time and proposed that to save the Prime Minister such a long journey next time he should come halfway to meet him. The site was to be Godesberg on the Rhine.

Chamberlain's task was now to clear with the Cabinet the principle he had agreed and then, more difficult, persuade the French to agree it and to join with Britain in trying to enforce its acceptance on the Czechs. To get the Czechs to agree would be the most difficult task of all. But he gave no indication that it was a task which in any way embarrassed him.

CHAPTER SEVENTEEN

PRESSURE ON THE CZECHS

CHAMBERLAIN ARRIVED BACK AT HESTON LATE IN THE AFTERNOON of Friday, September 16, to be greeted by Halifax and other Ministers and a crowd of several hundred people waiting outside the airport to give him an ovation. He told the German chargé d'affaires, Kordt, who was also there, how pleased he had been by the reception he had had from the German public. 'They were very kind. I had a great time.' He announced that he hoped to be seeing Hitler again in a few days and that Hitler had offered to come 'halfway', adding puckishly, 'He wishes to spare an old man another long journey.'[1]

He was feeling anything but a tired old man and the crowds knew it and loved it, but they gave Hitler a round of applause for his courtesy. No one of course had as yet any idea what, if anything, had been decided at Berchtesgaden. From what Chamberlain said it sounded as if the news might be good. He drove off at once to break it to the Cabinet.

To them he emphasised more than once that he had been 'just in time' to prevent Hitler from marching.[2] Goering himself appeared to confirm this the next morning when he told Henderson that, but for Chamberlain's visit, 'Hitler would already have given instructions to his army to protect the lives and property of Sudetens across the frontier.' Goering either did not know or pretended not to know that the Wehrmacht had just said it could not possibly move before the pre-arranged date of October 1.[3] But the British Cabinet did not know either and could share the Prime Minister's conviction that he had saved Europe from war at the last minute. The question was: had it been at too high a price?

The question seems only to have been in the minds of those few

159

members of the Cabinet whom Chamberlain had successfully silenced before he set off for Germany; he had little difficulty in silencing them now. Only one Minister, the Lord Privy Seal, Lord de la Warr, spoke of honour. He was prepared to accept that the Sudeten areas should go to Czechoslovakia on the principle of self-determination, but he thought that to hold a plebiscite immediately and under German control was 'unfair to the Czechs and dishonourable to ourselves after all that we have done in the last six months'. He thought that, unless Britain stood firm, 'whenever Hitler threatened the world we should have to concede what he asked for'. He was prepared to face war now. Duff Cooper backed Chamberlain because he was in favour of gaining time 'until the Nazis fell'. Halifax, while pronouncing nobly that he 'would fight for the great moralities which knew no geographical boundaries', at least made clear that whatever these might be they were not for him at stake in Czechoslovakia.[4]

From the Cabinet Chamberlain thus got the free hand he wanted for his coming meeting with Hitler at Godesberg. But what would the French have to say with their moral obligations extending at least as far as the geographical boundaries of Czechoslovakia? They were told nothing about what had happened at Berchtesgaden for more than twenty-four hours but were then invited over to a meeting in London on the following day, September 18. As for the Czechs they were given no information at all. Just before the Anglo-French meeting they sent a telegram to London to say they were considering mobilising and asking for advice. They received a reply, advising them not to mobilise. But that, for the present, was all.[5]

While talks between British and French went on that afternoon, Jan Masaryk, the Czechoslovak Minister in London, sent Halifax a message. It said his Government was taking for granted that no decision would be taken without their being consulted. It added that the Czechs 'could not take any responsibility for decisions taken without them'.[6] But such a decision had already been taken at Berchtesgaden. Halifax and Chamberlain were at that moment getting the French to agree to it without consulting the Czechs in any way.

Daladier, when Chamberlain had met him at Croydon airport that morning, had repeated what he had said publicly in France the night before, namely that he was certain the Prime Minister's action had

160

met with universal approbation throughout the world.[7] This remark was some indication of the confusion in which the French and particularly Daladier already approached the matter; Daladier had as yet no idea whether he approved Chamberlain's action or not since he had not yet heard what Chamberlain had done.

In Downing Street he listened as Chamberlain went carefully over the ground of his conversation with Hitler, drawing attention to two subsidiary points on the way. The first was that the Poles and Hungarians would inevitably make claims for their minorities once the Germans had self-determination for themselves. The second was that, in Hitler's view, what Chamberlain called 'the smaller and weaker remnant of the Czechoslovak state' left after the Germans had gone would still remain 'a spearhead' in Germany's side because of the Russian alliance. On this latter point, however, he said, Hitler had had second thoughts and finally decided that with the Polish and Hungarian minorities gone too the state would be 'so insignificant that he would not bother his head about it'.[8]

Chamberlain thus rather successfully obscured the point that what he had agreed with Hitler would indeed probably reduce the Czechoslovak state to 'a weak remnant' of no significance. Further, in giving an otherwise fair account of the conversation's details, Chamberlain somehow skated over the fact that Hitler had made him accept a very different interpretation of the phrase 'self-determination' for the Sudetens from that with which he himself, talking of an 80 percent majority, had begun. In recounting that 80 percent was indeed the figure he had mentioned, he did not at this point actually make clear that Hitler had insisted on a straight 50 percent majority. Thus, when they considered, as he now told the French they must, the proposal that negotiations should be continued with Hitler on the basis of self-determination for the Sudetens, Hitler's interpretation of that phrase was presented without further definition as what they were discussing. It was a typical piece of Chamberlain sleight of hand, sharply belying the harmless impression which his wing collar and umbrella could sometimes convey to outsiders.

He now concluded his survey by stressing how dangerous the situation had been when he went to Berchtesgaden and telling the French of Goering's assurance to Henderson that as a result of the visit there was for the moment no need to be unduly anxious. Hitler,

161

said Chamberlain, had given his word and he himself 'had derived the impression whilst he was watching Herr Hitler and talking to him, that he would be better rather than worse than his word'. But he left the French with the urgent consideration that if they could not agree to self-determination Hitler's reply 'would be to give the order to march'.[9]

Daladier first astutely reminded the Prime Minister that it was only a few months since Goering had been assuring Henderson that Germany did not want to annex the Sudetens and here was Germany wanting to annex the Sudetens. But he was soon on the much less sure ground which awaited him on the main issue. They were now faced, he said vaguely, with 'facts and proposals which had never hitherto come under consideration'. He thought it was therefore better for the British to say first what they thought of the proposal.[10]

Chamberlain took the chance to reinforce his own view of it. He picked up Daladier's scepticism of Goering by saying that, at the time Goering made the remark, the Germans might well indeed have accepted something short of annexation. It was the fault of Beneš and his dilatory concessions which had made the only possible solution the one the Germans were now demanding. And he neatly returned the ball to Daladier's court by saying that it seemed to him that as the French were in a different position from the British because of their treaty obligation to the Czechs it was up to the French to say first whether they could accept the principle of that solution or not.[11]

Daladier, while deploying sound arguments why France should find the cession of the Sudetenland to Germany unacceptable, refused to commit himself to rejection of it. He stressed how painful it was for France to be considering something so painful for Czechoslovakia. 'It is always a most delicate matter to suggest to a friend and ally that he should submit to the amputation of one leg or, indeed, possibly of both legs.' He thought the loss of the Sudetenland would lead to the destruction of the Czechoslovak state once not only the Poles and the Hungarians but even the Slovaks too joined in the demand for minority secession. As for Hitler, Britain and France would not then have achieved a peaceful solution but be embarked on a dangerous policy encouraging Hitler to continue his march eastwards. The Poles, for all their present illusions, would soon find a Führer in the Polish corridor: '. . . To accept the proposal put forward could only result in increasing the general tension in the political life of Europe.'[12] But he still failed to draw the logical conclusion from all this and once again asked Chamberlain to say what he thought.

This game in which each side tried to place responsibility for what was about to happen on to the other continued for much of the rest of the morning of September 18. The deep French ambivalence between what they felt they ought to do and what they wanted to do became more and more apparent as Daladier spoke. At times his twisting and turning in the agony of France's dilemma became almost ridiculous. France, he said, had already defined her position. '. . . In all honour and morality, France had no right to regard her engagements as null and void . . .' It was true that certain suggestions had been made that France was not prepared to fulfil her obligations but such suggestions could be ignored. He did not think, 'and in this I am expressing the views of the French Government and the French people, that France could desert her ally. No Frenchman would be capable of committing such a crime . . .' But then, once more, rather than coming to any conclusion on the basis of such reasoning he said he would 'prefer to hear what conclusions had been reached by the British Government who had had more opportunity to examine the position'.[13]

He knew perfectly well from what Chamberlain had said so far what the British Government's conclusions were – but for the time being all that seemed important was to defer the moment when France had to go along with them.

Halifax now entered the game, beginning with a pious remark which appeared to dismiss what was really at the heart of the discussion. Nothing, he said, was further from their (the British) thoughts than that the French Government should fail to honour their obligations to the Czechoslovak Government. But very slowly, by a process of circumlocutory self-deception on both sides, they came round to the main purpose of the meeting. In this process Halifax's style was invaluable. Could there, 'in the judgement of the French Government', possibly be some means of reconciling their Treaty obligations with the fulfilment of the condition which the Prime Minister had made quite clear was essential for continuance of the negotiations with Hitler? If he might speak frankly, it was these very obligations which bound them to come to a decision on the proposal. It would in fact be impossible whatever action Britain, France or the Soviet Union took to give effective protection to the Czechoslovak state. We might fight a war against German aggression but he did not think that at the Peace Conference afterwards the statesmen would redraft Czechoslovakia in her present boundaries.[14] At which point Chamberlain shrewdly suggested they should adjourn for lunch to enable the French to consult among themselves and if necessary contact Paris.

They came back two hours later and it soon became clear that the French had somehow managed to square the Sudeten circle. The idea of a plebiscite was still unacceptable but 'it might be possible', said Daladier, 'to consider some sort of cession of a part of the territories occupied by the Sudeten areas.' The next question was to decide exactly how large a part. This time Chamberlain did reveal Hitler's implacable condition that not 80 but 50 percent German populations should be the determining figure. Daladier did not demur. Bonnet talked about the need to think in terms of transfer of population in certain cases rather than of territorial areas because of 'the need to take geographical and strategic areas into account in order to make it possible for Czechoslovakia, amputated as she would have been, to defend herself'. When Chamberlain realistically pointed out that there would be no point in his going back to see Hitler if he had to tell him that Beneš had agreed only to the cession of a limited area, 'whereas Herr Hitler had in mind something very much bigger', the responsibility for making population transfers and some as yet vague territory adjustments was shuffled off on to the idea of an 'international commission' to be set up. Beneš would, however, have to be warned now of the scale of transfer of territory contemplated.

The question then arose of some guarantee for what Chamberlain had already called 'the remnant of Czechoslovakia'. Chamberlain himself brought the subject up, but only it seemed to stress that such a guarantee would in fact be 'a very grave departure' for the British Government, 'a great liability and a serious source of embarrassment'. He said he might agree but thought conditions would have to be attached such as that Czechoslovakia should abandon its pact with the Soviet Union. Halifax's contribution was that the Czechs would have to agree to accept the British Government's advice on issues of peace or war.[15]

Daladier emphasised an aspect of the situation which British policy, beginning with the re-occupation of the Rhineland, had long studiously ignored. Some guarantee, he said, was vital to France because a certain German vulnerability in the east was part of France's own security. Chamberlain reluctantly listened to this and the meeting adjourned for two and a half hours for the British now to consider the matter of this guarantee. When they returned, Chamberlain announced that, in view of the great changes contemplated in the situation of Czechoslovakia, Britain was prepared to join in the guarantee.[16]

It was as if a sort of deal had been done. The rest of the meeting which after dinner went on until after midnight was concerned with the drafting of the joint warning to be sent to Beneš. The formula by which Daladier strove to save his dignity ran:

> It was certainly very distressing in view of France's very close relations with a friendly country, to whom she was bound by Treaty, for them to be obliged to examine a solution which would certainly give rise to strong feeling in Czechoslovakia and in France. But they had to consider the interests of European peace, and, as had been pointed out in the draft itself, they had to consider the interests of Czechoslovakia at this precise moment in the history of Europe.[17]

The Foreign Office official who saw Daladier and Bonnet off at Heston the next morning described them as looking 'wretched'.[18]

The feeling in France, though in some quarters indeed likely to be strong, would also be mixed. The domestic conflict there between left and right was reflected in attitudes to the international situation. Both the Franco-Soviet pact and the Czech-Soviet pact caused disquiet for a right troubled by the strength of an internal Communist Party. There could be no two ways about the strength of feeling now likely to be encountered in Czechoslovakia itself.

The pressure on the Czechs throughout the summer by both French and British to extract from them concessions to the Sudeten Germans within the structure of the state was nothing compared with what was now required to get them to cede the Sudetenland to

Germany altogether. Daladier himself before leaving the Downing Street meeting had stressed that 'the strongest pressure would have to be brought to bear on Dr Beneš'.[19]

Instructions for doing just this were sent to the British envoy in Prague, Basil Newton, within three hours of that meeting ending. He was told to concert at once with his French colleague, de Lacroix, and arrange a joint audience with Beneš to give him the message from the two governments. This was to the effect that for 'the maintenance of peace and Czechoslovakia's vital interests' those areas of Czechoslovakia with 'probably' over 50 percent German population would have to be handed over to the Reich. There was 'hope' that 'some international body including a Czech representative' would supervise the transfer and help deal with possible exchanges of population where necessary. Britain would be prepared to guarantee the boundaries of the new Czechoslovakia against unprovoked aggression (though this guarantee would not prejudice a further adjustment of frontiers in minority areas unless the result of unprovoked aggression). The message concluded with the statement that both the British and French Governments recognised 'how great is the sacrifice thus required of the Czechoslovak Government in the cause of peace', but because Chamberlain had to see Hitler again in less than two days 'we must ask for your reply at the earliest possible moment'.[20]

The French Council of Ministers had unanimously confirmed Daladier's decision by mid-day. Two hours later Newton and de Lacroix called on Beneš and delivered the message.

They found him 'greatly moved and agitated'. His first reaction was that as Czechoslovakia had not even been consulted he did not propose to reply. In any case he would have to refer the matter to his Government. He spoke bitterly though with self-control about the way he and his Government had been abandoned. He seemed to be wrestling with himself about what attitude to adopt. When Newton pointed out to him that he was about to receive an international guarantee of his new frontier in which Britain would participate, he pointed out in return that he had guarantees at the moment but they were proving of no value to him. Nevertheless Newton felt that though Beneš would not reply that day (Monday the 19th) he would in the end accept.[21] Wednesday, September 20 was the day on which Chamberlain was due to see Hitler on the Rhine at Godesberg.

As Beneš had indicated, the decision was not one for him alone. His immediately hostile response to the proposals was certainly representative of Czech opinion but there were some different degrees of emphasis in that opinion. Some politicians were likely to be, however sadly, more resigned than others to the inevitability of compromise. It was for Beneš above all a situation which had to be looked at practically as well as emotionally.

The Cabinet was unanimously for rejection. But the Generals told Beneš that the chances of long surviving a German attack without French help were slim. He consulted the Russians and received the usual assurance that they would certainly fulfil their obligations if the French did. In the light of the geographical difficulties, however, there was always doubt as to how valuable Russian help would be, quite apart from its conditional nature. Beneš's feelings about the Russians were in any case ambivalent enough to restrain him from asking them to override the condition, though Gottwald the leader of the Czech Communist Party suggested that he might.[22]

So, should Beneš pass the Cabinet's rejection on? He faced a whole series of dilemmas. His only real military hope was that the French would support him, along with the British and presumably the Russians. But the French and British were not supporting him or, rather, they seemed only to be supporting him if he would agree to the mutilation of his country. Was it not better to agree to that rather than for Czechoslovakia to accept the high risk of total annihilation in a war on her own? On the other hand, if Czechoslovakia did opt for that risk, might not the consciences of Britain and France be stirred and precipitate them into a world war on Czechoslovakia's behalf? Again, would such a world war, if brought about, really be better for Czechoslovakia than the suggested mutilation? The whole-hearted patriotic response that Czech public opinion was unquestionably ready to offer to such proposals was for him a luxury circumscribed by pragmatism. For the present he did the only thing he could do. While demonstrations in the streets called for national resistance, he played for time. For over twenty-four hours no answer came from Prague. The projected meeting between Chamberlain and Hitler at Godesberg had to be postponed to Thursday the 22nd.

As early as 11 a.m. on the Tuesday, Newton received information that the Czech Government were in fact likely to deliver a protest ahead of eventual compliance early that afternoon. But he was being unduly optimistic in passing this on to London. The French, on hearing that the Czech Cabinet were still undecided, sent de Lacroix instructions from Paris to tell Beneš that it 'would be folly and would mean war' if he refused. Newton associated himself with the *démarche* late that afternoon.[23] Two hours later a reply had still not arrived. It came at 7.45 p.m.

It was a rejection. It said that the Czechoslovak Government were convinced that the Franco-British proposal could not realise the object of peace, that the state would be mutilated in every respect, and that the balance of power would be destroyed. The offer of a guarantee was appreciated. The Czechoslovak Government was prepared to accept an arbitration award under the Czech-German Arbitration Treaty of 1936.[*] It addressed a final appeal to the British and French Governments to reconsider their point of view.[24]

Three hours later Newton telegraphed Halifax that he had it from a very good source that the reply should not in fact be regarded as final. He suggested that 'a kind of ultimatum' should be delivered to Beneš the next day. This would be to the effect that, unless the Czechs accepted the proposals 'without reserve', Britain would 'take no further interest in the fate of the country'. A similar suggestion went from de Lacroix to Paris.[25]

It was a suggestion which the British Ambassador in Paris had already been urging on the French. He had proposed that, unless Beneš's reply was 'an acceptance pure and simple, France and Great Britain would wash their hands of Czechoslovakia in the event of a German attack'.[26] Bonnet had not demurred. But at that moment, just before receipt of the Czech rejection, the British Foreign Office had been apprehensive about endorsing the idea since 'it would be used as evidence that we had pressed the French Government to evade their treaty obligations' which, as the American historian Telford Taylor emphasises, was what had been happening anyway.[27]

Now after a midnight conference in Downing Street between

[*]At the time of the re-occupation of the Rhineland, Beneš had in fact said that this Arbitration Treaty was nullified since it was linked to Locarno which the Germans had torn up. See above, p. 100.

Chamberlain, Horace Wilson, Halifax and the Foreign Office Under-Secretary Cadogan, instructions were sent to Newton at 1.20 a.m. – this was the morning of the day on which Chamberlain should have been going to Godesberg – to say that the Czech reply was inadequate and if persisted in would lead to an immediate German invasion. The Czechs were therefore begged to consider urgently and seriously 'before producing a situation *for which we could take no responsibility'.* If on reconsideration they felt bound to reject the British Government's advice they were 'of course . . . free to take any action that they think appropriate to meet the situation that may thereafter develop'. The original drafting of this last phrase had been 'the situation which the Czechs are creating'. But this had been amended tactfully in pencilled handwriting to 'the situation that may thereafter develop'. Newton was told to 'act immediately at whatever hour'.[28]

He and de Lacroix who had received similar instructions from Paris called on Beneš at 2 a.m. on September 21. They were with him for nearly two hours pressing home the significance of their instructions. If the Czechs persisted in their refusal to accept the proposals they would be left alone.

At 6 a.m. on September 21 Beneš met his Cabinet. They were indignant to hear of the 2 a.m. visit and there was some talk of moving the Government eastwards out of Prague and fighting. But the same set of dilemmas that had faced them all the day before had to be faced again. Asked whether the country should go to war without allies, the Generals said they could not recommend a war singlehanded against Germany. They thought they could last out about three weeks.[29] The meeting went on for two hours but the substance of the argument seems to have been decided early, for after half an hour Newton was telephoned by the Private Secretary of the Prime Minister Hodza to be told that the Government's reply was 'affirmative' and that an official reply would be sent as soon as possible.[30]

But once again there was a hitch – exasperating for Chamberlain, now preparing for his postponed visit to Godesberg on the following day. Most of the day went by without the anticipated official confirmation of the Czechs' acceptance. Not only the

*Author's italics.

169

Cabinet but the council representing all the political parties in the Coalition Government had to approve the decision to capitulate. The mood of depression at this council's meeting was summed up as 'defying description'. But the sense of revulsion was finally overcome and the decision accepted. Those politicians wishing to fight a war in isolation were in a clear minority. It was recognised that, quite apart from all the other disadvantages, Poland and Hungary would have to be fought as well.[31]

Throughout the day Britain and France had been stressing their impatience and anxiety over the continued delay while continuing to be reassured that a final acceptance would soon be available. The British Ambassador in Paris suggested that Bonnet should give the Czech Minister there 'a piece of his mind' and Bonnet promised to do so.[32] Soon afterwards the official draft of the Czech Government's change of mind and their acceptance of the British and French Governments' proposal to give the Sudetenland to Germany was finally handed to Newton in Prague. It ran:

> The Czechoslovak Government, forced by circumstances, yielding to unheard-of pressure and drawing the consequences from the communication of the French and British Governments of September 21, 1938 . . . accepts the Anglo-French proposals with feelings of pain . . . It notes with regret that these proposals were elaborated without previous consultation with the Czech Government . . .[33]

Perhaps conscience had led Newton earlier in the day to suggest to London that when this acceptance did finally come through it would be important to 'sweeten the pill' by showing appreciation of 'the far-sighted patriotism, moral courage and wisdom of the Czech Government and people'. He suggested too that the United States should associate themselves with such appreciation. 'If,' he added, 'the Czechoslovak public were made to realise that the great Anglo-Saxon democracies thought the decision a wise one in Czechoslovakia's own interests, it might make all the difference.'[34]

Nothing, least of all such patronage, could have 'sweetened the pill' for Czechoslovaks now out on the streets of Prague. Vast crowds collected spontaneously to demonstrate, their faces sombre, angry, bitter and aghast at news of the capitulation and of what was about to be done to their country by the removal of its mountain barrier against the Germans. 'Give us arms,' they cried. 'We paid for them.'[35]

It was a cry that could lead nowhere. Their frustrated patriotic fervour was all that was left now from a crisis which it seemed at last was over.

The next afternoon Chamberlain and Horace Wilson arrived at Godesberg on the Rhine and soon afterwards crossed the river to meet Hitler with the good news that the Czechs had accepted his solution to the problem of the Sudetenland.

But the crisis was not over at all. Only now did it move towards its climax.

CHAPTER EIGHTEEN

GODESBERG

WHILE THE CZECHS WERE STILL HESITATING ABOUT WHAT REPLY to send to the Anglo-French proposals first time round, the British Government had been at pains to reassure the Germans that the delay did not imply 'any element of uncertainty regarding Britain's political attitude or any evasion or wavering'.[1] But Hitler's attitude had actually been hardening. Encouraging both the Poles and the Hungarians to press Beneš on behalf of their own minorities, he told the Hungarians on the same day as the British message was received that he was determined to settle the Czech question even at the risk of war. The best thing, he said, would be to destroy Czechoslovakia; a country quite impossible to tolerate as an aircraft carrier in the heart of Europe. He was convinced that neither England nor France would intervene. He was going to present the German demands to Chamberlain at Godesberg with 'brutal frankness' and 'starkest realism'.[2]

Chamberlain, on the other hand, could leave for Godesberg with some grounds for self-satisfaction and even cautious optimism. He had after all now obtained the acceptance by his Cabinet, the French and the Czechs of the principle of the transfer of the Sudetenland – exactly what he had told Hitler at Berchtesgaden that he would try to obtain. There were even some concessions which he now hoped to be able to obtain from Hitler. He would try for a more favourable population transfer figure than the 51 percent he had agreed. It is, however, indicative of his approach to the whole problem that he regarded as a concession another point to which he hoped Hitler would agree, namely that Czech police and troops should be allowed to control any plebiscite in the areas not predominantly German while the Wehrmacht could have complete

172

control in the others. When at the meeting of the Inner Cabinet which preceded his departure Duff Cooper objected to this latter arrangement, Chamberlain said that he would at least begin by asking Hitler for an international force.

British public opinion, which was beginning to show some anxiety about the way the Czechs were being treated, would want at least an appearance of concessions. This requirement, together with details of some of the financial and social aspects of the intended transfer, were what he saw as the core of the coming discussion at Godesberg. Sir Horace Wilson, who accompanied him, later commented: 'I doubt whether he thought much about the political implications of failure.'[3]

Chamberlain reminded the journalists who saw him off on his flight from Heston of the much wider context of which the Czech Sudeten problem was for him only a part. The meeting was, he said, 'an essential preliminary to a better understanding between the British and the German peoples; and that, in turn, is the indispensable foundation of European peace. European peace is what I am aiming at, and I hope this journey may be the way to get it.'[4]

Chamberlain arrived with his party at his hotel on the east bank of the Rhine opposite Godesberg in time for lunch on Thursday, September 22. At 4 p.m. he set out across the river to see Hitler in his hotel on the other side. After a polite routine greeting in the lobby where Keitel, Himmler, Goebbels, Ribbentrop and others were standing, he and Hitler went upstairs alone with their interpreters and sat down in a room with a table covered in green baize. Hitler gestured to Chamberlain, as if to say: 'Your move.'[5]

Chamberlain told Hitler the good news that not only his own colleagues but the French and Czech Governments had agreed in principle to the cession of the Sudetenland. In moving on to the question of how this was practically to be achieved, he once again introduced 80 percent as the proposed figure of German majority to be transferred without discussion, suggesting 65 percent as the figure which would require a plebiscite. To offer rather less than what one was ultimately prepared to concede was after all the traditional way of doing a deal. He concluded with a matter which, while important for British public opinion, could also be presented to Hitler as something of a sweetener. Since Czechoslovakia was now to lose her carefully-built frontier fortifications, it was not unreasonable to offer her a guarantee of continued security. Britain was now prepared to guarantee her against unprovoked aggression. But this would be in place of her existing treaties. In other words, Czechoslovakia would no longer be an ally of the Soviet Union. She would become 'a neutral state'. Moreover, Chamberlain added, 'this guarantee would not necessarily mean that the present Czechoslovak frontiers would be guaranteed in perpetuity.'[6]

Hitler's interpreter Schmidt afterwards described Chamberlain at this point as leaning back with an expression of satisfaction, as much as to say, 'Haven't I worked splendidly during these five days?'[7]

He was in for what he afterwards described as 'a profound shock.' 'I'm sorry,' said Hitler, 'but that won't do any more.'[8]

Czechoslovakia, he said, was an artificial construction in which the Czechs wronged not just three and a half million Germans but also a million Hungarians, a hundred thousand Poles and several million Slovaks. His own concern of course was with the Germans but the demands now being made by others had his full sympathy. Chamberlain, he said, did not seem to realise how urgent the matter was. It now had to be settled definitely and completely by October 1 at the latest. There was only one possibility. A new frontier must be drawn at once, based on existing reliable maps of the language frontier, behind which the Czech army, police and all state authorities must at once withdraw, enabling German troops to occupy the area up to it. If the Czechs disputed the line of the language frontier he was perfectly prepared for a plebiscite to be held in the areas the German troops would be occupying though international commissions could be sent out in due course. He did not envisage the sort of majorities Chamberlain had been talking about but he 'would bow' (*sic*) to a majority.[9]

Chamberlain replied with puzzled disappointment. The Führer did not seem to understand that to get this far he, Chamberlain, had had to take his political life in his hands. He was being accused of betraying Czechoslovakia, yielding to dictators, etcetera, and had actually been booed when he left Britain that morning.

However, while describing as a 'difficulty' the arbitrary frontier line which Hitler was laying down and which he did not think British opinion would regard as fair, he tacitly accepted it as a difficulty which somehow had to be dealt with. Nor was anything more heard

174

from Chamberlain of 80 or 65 percent majorities. In fact he now went so far as to ask for reassurance that Hitler 'would be prepared to abide by a bare majority vote in the plebiscite'. He emphasised that Hitler had made his task 'no easier'.[10]

Hitler agreed (as he had done at Berchtesgaden where he equally well knew Keitel's deadline could not be brought forward before October 1) to tell Keitel to take no immediate military action. But he stressed that it was hard to hold his hand with the Czechs shooting German hostages while all the time he could rout the Czechs with a single armoured division. He said he had never thought the Prime Minister could achieve as much as he had done, which was why he had remained ready to move at a moment's notice.[11]

With this meagre laurel for his comfort Chamberlain agreed to adjourn the conversation. He withdrew with his mind full of foreboding.[12] There was to be a meeting the next morning.

The situation on the Czech-Sudeten border was now so dangerous with Sudeten Freikorps in total control of the Asch-Eger region and, as French intelligence reckoned, thirty-one German divisions in position waiting to move, that at 8.20 that evening, while Chamberlain was having dinner in his hotel at Godesberg, Halifax sent Newton instructions in Prague to tell the Czechs that the British and French could no longer take the responsibility of advising them not to mobilise. (This new move had been concerted with the French.) But he told Newton to delay for about an hour before actually delivering the message. Within that hour there was contact with Godesberg. The unsatisfactory nature of the negotiations there so far was made clear but Chamberlain recommended that all parties should for the moment refrain from further action. The suspension of the advice to the Czechs not to mobilise was thus in turn suspended (again in concert with the French).[13] Nothing could illustrate better the state of agitation in which both the Foreign Office and the Quai d'Orsay were living from hour to hour.

Chamberlain himself in his hotel at Godesberg was on the verge of despair.[14] It is greatly to his credit and testimony to the strength of conviction which had brought him so far that he did not at this stage decide to break off the meeting. Hitler's arbitrary frontier line with its 50 percent majority qualification corresponded in itself, as he told Halifax on the telephone that evening, 'very closely to the line we have been considering'.[15] But what he thought it was going to be very difficult for opinion in Britain to accept, and even opinion in the Cabinet, was Hitler's insistence on virtually immediate occupation by German troops. Indeed instead of going to meet Hitler again the next morning he sent him a letter in which he said he did not think Hitler had realised the impossibility of his putting forward a plan 'carrying out the principles already agreed upon' unless he could convince opinion in Britain, France and the world generally that it was being carried out in an orderly fashion and free from the threat of force. Even the Czechs, now tacitly almost relegated to a subsidiary role, would not regard it as in the spirit of the arrangement which the British and French had got them to accept.[16] In this way Chamberlain finally shifted the substance of the debate with Hitler away from anything to do with equity in the principle of transfer to the issue solely of the technique by which the transfer was to be implemented. It must be above all a technique acceptable to British, French and world opinion. This was what was now at stake. This was what the Munich Conference when it came – at the eleventh hour – was to be about.

Hitler's immediate reply was chilling. He cancelled the morning meeting and said he would reply formally in the afternoon. The British party sat down to a 'rather grim' lunch at which Chamberlain talked of Birmingham but in the course of which a telegram arrived from Halifax to say he was profoundly disturbed by the continued decision not to let the Czechs mobilise. He thought this should now be reversed. Horace Wilson telephoned London to say that Hitler's reply was still awaited and that the telegram had 'spoilt our luncheon'.[17]

When the reply eventually came across the Rhine it merely re-stated the stark demands of the day before. Even in Godesberg it was now recognised that withdrawal of the advice to the Czechs not to mobilise could hardly be delayed any longer. At 4 p.m. Halifax told Newton with Chamberlain's acquiescence to inform the Czechs that the advice against mobilisation was withdrawn. But he was to point out that such action might well 'precipitate action by others' and recommended them to avoid unnecessary publicity.[18]

In Godesberg Chamberlain kept his nerve. He allowed the

channel of negotiation with Hitler to remain open by replying that he wanted a precise memorandum of the German demands, together with a map so that he could present these formally to the Czechs. It would now be for them to decide, but he said he would forward it to them at once and ask for a reply at the earliest possible moment.[19] Thus tacitly was it implied that as far as Chamberlain at least was concerned the new terms had to be accepted.

Ribbentrop, in reply to Chamberlain's letter, said that the requested memorandum would be drawn up and explained later. Chamberlain had to wait until after dinner before further word came from across the Rhine.

In Prague, in spite of the British warning against publicity, news of the mobilisation leaked out before it was officially announced on the radio. It had an electrifying effect. Reservists rushed spontaneously to join their units. There was an overwhelming sense of relief and jubiliation on the streets.[20]

The official announcement came long after dark. By then Chamberlain had at last crossed the Rhine again to receive an explanation of the memorandum and map which spelt out the morning demands in detail. News of the Czech mobilisation arrived while the meeting was in progress. It did not improve an atmosphere already highly charged. After three hours, during which tempers rose and the customary courtesies of official diplomatic encounters sometimes almost failed, Chamberlain obtained only one marginally significant revision of the memorandum, namely a return to the 'unacceptable' date of October 1 as deadline for the military occupation of the Sudetenland rather than the date of September 26 (with completion by September 28) to which it had at first been advanced in the memorandum. Hitler, who at first, on hearing of the Czech mobilisation, had declared that that was the end of the matter and the Wehrmacht would now march, finally once again said he would stay his hand for the moment, while Chamberlain undertook to present the memorandum to the Czechs.[21]

And that was the end of the Godesberg meeting to which Chamberlain had come hoping that he might be on the very last lap of European appeasement. When, on return to his hotel at two o'clock in the morning, someone asked him, 'Is the position

177

hopeless, sir?' he replied: 'I would not like to say that. It is up to the Czechs now.'[22]

Back at Heston airport the next morning he returned to the theme he had expressed on leaving: 'I trust all concerned will continue their efforts to solve the Czechoslovakia problem peacefully because on that turns the peace of Europe in our time.'[23]

He was to continue his own efforts unceasingly for the next five days, at the end of which, by his own lights, he triumphed.

CHAPTER NINETEEN

MUNICH

IN PRAGUE PRESIDENT BENEŠ HAD A NEW PRIME MINISTER. HODZA had resigned, partly in response to public pressure, after the pre-Godesberg capitulation to the Anglo-French proposals. He had been replaced by General Syrovy, a one-eyed hero of that Czech Legion which had fought with the Russians against Austria in the First World War. An English translation of the Godesberg Memorandum went to his Government at six o'clock on the evening of the day Chamberlain got back to London, Saturday, September 24. The map and the German text arrived in Prague just before midnight having been driven down personally by the British Military Attaché from Berlin.[1] There was this time no recommendation one way or the other as there had been with the Anglo-French proposals. The Czechs were merely asked to transmit 'any reply' through Chamberlain and told that if they wanted to send someone to London he would be very happily received.[2]

When Chamberlain consulted his Cabinet that same afternoon and evening it was soon obvious that, though the Czechs could be expected to reject the Memorandum, their verbal reaction was not the most immediately important factor in the situation. In the interests of his all-preoccupying concern to preserve peace, what mattered most was to convince his Ministers that the Godesberg terms, for all their brutality against which he had properly protested during the night with Hitler, should not be the cause for breakdown of negotiations.

Chamberlain was still master of the Cabinet but had to work harder than before. He quickly stated his basic position, namely that 'having once agreed to cession, the sooner the transfer took place the better', but he faced openly the problem that the

179

Godesberg terms for the transfer did not look good and might well cause serious political difficulties. The Press was now striking an anxious note about the fate of Czechoslovakia. Eden had been criticising Chamberlain's policy in public. A Mass Observation Poll taken before he left for Godesberg had found 40 percent of those questioned opposed to his policy over Czechoslovakia and only 22 percent in favour, though a further 28 percent were undecided. Addressing the Cabinet he did everything he could to make them consider that the only possible course was to keep the line to Hitler open. He was convinced that Hitler was a man of his word and that when he had said, as he had done, that the Sudetenland was his last territorial demand in Europe he had meant it, that Hitler now trusted him, that beyond all this Czech question lay the all-important chance of a final Anglo-German understanding. He even went so far as to use as argument the thought he had had when flying back over London that morning. He had imagined a German bomber on the same course above the thousands of homes below him and 'had felt that we were in no position to justify waging a war to-day to prevent a war hereafter'.[3]

There was more opposition in the Cabinet than before. Duff Cooper with some minority support argued for a complete change of front towards Hitler, for recognition that he could not be trusted, and for positive support for the Czechs and British general mobilisation so that the Germans should understand quite clearly where Britain stood and still perhaps draw back from war. He was even to consider resignation at this stage but was to be talked out of this by Chamberlain.

A temporary shift in attitude on the part of Halifax was even more worrying for Chamberlain, though the shift was expressed in the Foreign Secretary's classically enigmatic style. He was not quite sure that his and the Prime Minister's minds 'were still altogether as one. Nevertheless he thought it right to expose his own hesitations with complete frankness.'

'Hesitations' was the right word. In an exchange of notes across the Cabinet table while the meeting proceeded and during which Chamberlain told Halifax his change of view had been 'a horrible blow' to him and Halifax had replied that he felt 'a brute', it emerged that unlike Duff Cooper he actually wanted the Czechs to agree but did not feel that they should be coerced into doing so.[4]

180

Chamberlain was in a strong moral position in the argument. All his Ministers until this moment had supported that policy of surrendering the Sudetenland which had led to the present crisis. Now they were really just shying away from the policy's consequences. Chamberlain, like Hitler in his very different way, had not wavered, though he was now confronted with the possibility that he might have to do so.

Skilfully, he turned the divisions in the Cabinet, in which in any case he had majority support, to his own advantage. It was impossible, he said, for a Cabinet that was not unanimous to prepare convincingly for war. So they must wait until the French who were arriving that evening had been consulted. Awaiting them, Chamberlain in his own mind must have felt a certain confidence that in that coming meeting each party would be able to get the other off the Czechoslovak hook. The gist of a number of telegrams from the British Ambassador in Paris (Sir Eric Phipps, who when in Berlin had been no lover of the Nazis) was that the majority of Frenchmen were against war and that even if they fought their heart would not be in it.[5]

On the Sunday evening of the 25th when Daladier and Bonnet again arrived in London, the Czech envoy Jan Masaryk gave Halifax the formal Czech response to the Godesberg terms. Having stated that the Czech Government had accepted the previous Anglo-French demands 'under extreme duress' and on the understanding that no further demands would be made on them they said they were now faced with 'a *de facto* ultimatum of the sort usually presented to a vanquished nation and not a proposition to a sovereign state which has shown the greatest possible readiness to make sacrifices for the appeasement of Europe . . . The proposals go far beyond what we agreed to in the so-called Anglo-French plan. They deprive us of every safeguard for our national existence. We are to yield up large proportions of our carefully prepared defences . . . Our national and economic independence would disappear . . . The demands in their present form are absolutely and unconditionally unacceptable. Against these new and cruel demands my Government feel bound to make their utmost resistance . . .'[6]

No one having the interests of the sovereign state of Czechoslovakia at heart could reasonably quarrel with any of these words.

181

But Chamberlain had long had at heart a cause which he judged far more important than Czechoslovakia and the two were, as he saw it, mutually exclusive.

The Czech Government's statement ended: 'We rely upon the two great democracies, whose wishes we have followed against our own judgement, to stand by us in our hour of trial.'

The French and British Ministers were due to meet in a few hours' time. Chamberlain, knowing that Masaryk would be quick to get maximum publicity for the statement, took what seemed to him the most necessary step of all in the circumstances. That evening he asked the German chargé d'affaires in London, strictly confidentially, to inform the German Foreign Office that the Czech 'final rejection' of the Godesberg Memorandum when it appeared was *not* to be taken as the last word. The same evening Henderson in Berlin telephoned a message from Chamberlain that the Führer should not trust reports of any negotiations between British, French and Czechs unless they came from him personally.[7] He was still just managing to keep the line open. But how much longer could he do this? Hitler's deadline on the Godesberg Memorandum was October 1. But the British were still acting on the presumption that the dates which Hitler had first given at Godesberg – the Czechs to start a withdrawal on September 26 to be completed by September 28 – made September 28 the day on which he would march unless persuaded not to.

The next three days until the calling of the Munich Conference was a period of continuously self-generating international tension in which only Chamberlain and Hitler and those who served them kept any sort of certain touch at all. Each of these knew what the other was after although the situation was easier for Hitler who was prepared to go for his objective whatever Chamberlain did. Hitler's only uncertainty was over whether, in obtaining what he was bound to obtain one way or another, he wanted to do so by peace or war. War brought with it the advantage that it would enable him at once to smash Czechoslovakia as he had already decided to do. On the other hand war with Czechoslovakia brought with it the danger that it might involve him – though he thought this unlikely – in a major war with Britain and France which he would have preferred not to happen at this stage. Whether or not he was aware of the Generals' plot against him he was certainly aware that some of his Generals, though not those he trusted like Keitel and Jodl, were uneasy about his decision to risk war so soon.

Chamberlain's uncertainty revolved round this uncertainty of Hitler's. If Hitler had in fact decided to get by war what he would get anyway if he waited, then obviously there was nothing Chamberlain could do to prevent him. This doubt certainly gave him some anxious moments. Political circumstances too placed Chamberlain at a greater disadvantage. Firm as was his control of his Cabinet he could not have Hitler's authoritarian command over those on whom he depended. Moreover he had to take into account a public opinion which he could not condition and which increasingly reflected disturbed emotions about Czechoslovakia to which he, in his single-mindedness, was not subject. On the other hand the public sense of apprehension at the approach of a new war bringing horrors no one could foresee worked to his advantage. For Hitler, who had no horror of war, the German public's fear of war, expressed openly by their welcome in the streets for Chamberlain, was a partial restraint.

Chamberlain's immediate task was to deal with the French. He must have felt instinctively that in the end their ambivalence would bring them round behind his view that a Czech rejection should not be 'the last word' and in favour of keeping the line open to Hitler. But he knew that it would be a tortuous and at times unpleasant business as indeed it proved to be. Both Daladier and one of the British Foreign Office advisers in attendance were to remember the meeting long afterwards with anguish and embarrassment.[8]

Daladier began tartly by saying that the French had not had time to examine the Godesberg Memorandum in detail because they had only received it that morning, which he regretted.[*] But he said the French Council of Ministers had that afternoon totally rejected the method now proposed by which Hitler demanded to occupy by force that territory which the Czechs 'as a heavy sacrifice' had agreed to cede.[9]

Chamberlain wasted no time. He denied that what the Germans were demanding to do was to take the territory by force. They were taking over areas which it had already been agreed they should have

---

[*]He seems to have been referring to the French translation and possibly also the map because the British Ambassador in Paris had delivered the document itself the night before (DBFP, 3rd Series, Vol. II, p. 583).

and German troops were only going in there to preserve law and order.

It was as if his own objections of two days before to the methods by which the transfer was to take place had never existed. Insofar as they continued to talk about the Godesberg terms Chamberlain seemed concerned here only to explain them now as not unreasonable. But he quickly switched from the Memorandum itself to the point on which the French were most sensitive: what did they actually propose should be done now?

Return to the Anglo-French proposals, said Daladier. And what if Hitler would not? 'Each of us would have to do his duty,' said Daladier, or as he re-phrased it after Chamberlain had once again reminded him that the Godesberg Memorandum was Hitler's last word: 'Each of us would do what was incumbent upon him.'

Chamberlain then moved into the heart of the matter. 'Were we to understand from that that France would declare war on Germany?' The matter was very clear, said Daladier, and then proceeded to make clear that it was not. He said what he had often said before, namely that France had always said she would fulfil her obligations, and he spoke of a million French reservists already called up.

No doubt, said Chamberlain, he had considered the next step after that: 'It would be of great assistance to His Majesty's Government to hear from M. Daladier whether the French General Staff had got some plan.'

When Daladier repeated what he had said in the past, namely that of course France could not send help directly to Czechoslovakia by land but could materially assist by drawing off a large part of the German army in the west, Chamberlain persisted, with the affected patience of a skilled cross-examiner, that he hoped M. Daladier would not think he was bringing pressure to bear upon M. Daladier unduly in these questions but 'one could not go into so great a conflict with one's ears and eyes closed . . . It was essential to know the conditions before taking any decision.' He would therefore like further information on certain points which had troubled British Ministers in the past. And he handed him over to the Chancellor of the Exchequer, Sir John Simon, a lawyer with long experience of skilled cross-examination.

In such a tone, bordering on offensiveness, did Britain's

184

consultation with her closest ally proceed in this moment of crisis possibly as serious as any in her history. When for instance Simon asked Daladier if the use of the French air force over Germany were contemplated and Daladier hedged by saying vaguely that he had certainly considered that and remarked that indeed in all wars recently, particularly in Spain, aerial attack had figured, Simon said he would 'repeat his question as it seemed to have been misunderstood'. He wished to ask in what way the French air force might be used. Of course he received no clear answer but then the point of the exercise was to expose the French lack of reliable determination. Inasmuch as the French revealed this they did not come well out of the encounter either.

But when the meeting was resumed the next morning something quite else was afoot. Chamberlain began the proceedings by saying that the speech Hitler was due to make that night would doubtless reveal his intentions. He stated, apparently quite happily now, that if Czechoslovakia were attacked France 'would fulfil her obligations'. In which case, he added in a phrase which, if taken seriously, would have given a curious new twist to British policy, Britain would come to France's assistance 'if France were in danger'. But his mind was on other things.

Talks were proceeding simultaneously between the Minister for Defence and his Chiefs of Staff and the French Chief of Staff General Gamelin who had come over that morning to expound rather more precise details of the theory of France's actions in the event of war than had been forthcoming the day before. Gamelin said that France would in fact declare war within four to five days of a German attack on Czechoslovakia (to give time for Paris to be evacuated) and that she would bomb industrial targets in the Ruhr and the Saar. On land she would advance immediately into Germany (though the French army was only about one third mobilised at present) until she met serious opposition when she would withdraw to the protection of the Maginot Line. Such reality as this talk contained – and it was minimised for practical purposes by the fact that British army and air chiefs present were not at liberty to disclose to Gamelin what help they could give the French if necessary – was at least the only military reality available should war come in two days' time. But it was already being jostled out of the limelight by

185

another reality more in keeping with Chamberlain's sense of how the crisis should be handled.

At a further Cabinet meeting late the night before he had proposed a new initiative which the Cabinet had approved. This was to send a personal letter that day to Hitler which would be taken to Germany at once by his trusted adviser Sir Horace Wilson. He now told Daladier who expressed his entire agreement, apparently with some relief. The acceptable face of the Entente was again restored.

In reasoned and friendly tones the letter proposed a conference between German and Czech representatives to discuss the way in which the transfer of the Sudeten German areas should take place by agreement. The key phrases in the letter were 'a settlement by negotiation remains possible' and 'the only differences between us lay in the method of carrying out an agreed principle'. Its penultimate paragraph ran. 'A conference such as I suggest would give the confidence that the cession of the territory would be carried into effect but that it would be done in an orderly manner with suitable safeguards.'[10]

There was no specific mention in the letter of other Powers attending such a conference, but since the idea came with Anglo-French approval the assumption could be that they would have a part in addition to the Germans and the Czechs.

The idea for some form of conference between Germany, Czechoslovakia and other powers had in fact been suggested by Chamberlain to Masaryk when the latter delivered the Czech rejection of the Godesberg terms the previous day. But all that the Czechs were now told for the moment was that the Wilson letter in no way prejudiced the position of the Czechoslovak Government, and that it simply substituted the process of negotiation for violent action.

In an age fifty years later when international crises automatically invite the attention of all large Powers, it may seem incongruous that the solution to a problem likely to cause another world war was still being sought on the relatively parochial level of individual national diplomacy. Certainly Chamberlain had revolutionised traditional diplomacy at a stroke by his personal message to Hitler of a fortnight before. He was persisting with the direct personal approach in the new letter being taken by Wilson. But there was

186

as yet no hint that the conference of which he spoke would be anything but a conventional one at which the interested parties could confer to resolve differences. Only the trend of events under his influence so far suggested that this could hardly be so. Within three days the notion was to be transformed into a meeting on a quite different scale. The Conference at Munich, Chamberlain's signal achievement, was to be one which did not seriously discuss but imposed a solution, and which, moreover, imposed it on one of the parties who was not even represented.

Curiously, independent suggestions that the European scene required something in the nature of a more overall view than that obtainable at the national diplomatic level had been circulated earlier in the year by the two great Powers which to-day dominate any consideration of world affairs: the United States and the Soviet Union. The latter, peripherally involved only through its rather remote alliances with France and Czechoslovakia, had proposed an international conference to deal with the problem of Germany soon after the Austrian *Anschluss* but the approach had been dismissed as too one-sided by both Halifax and Chamberlain. Halifax had actually criticised it as 'designed less to secure the settlement of outstanding problems than to organise concerted action against aggression'.[11] A more obviously high-minded initiative had been proposed two months earlier by President Roosevelt but that too had been summarily dismissed.

Looking back now from near the end of the twentieth century to the year of Munich it is difficult to realise that the United States, which had long been a Power of vast economic strength and is to-day one of the two great Powers in control of the peace of the world, could seem then quite marginal to the prospects of peace or war in Europe. But a positive wish in the United States to remain isolated from the snares of European politics had been of paramount concern there ever since Congress, refusing to ratify the Versailles Treaty and US membership of the League of Nations, had established isolationism as something of a patriotic doctrine. The doctrine had been legally enshrined in two Neutrality Acts in Roosevelt's own Presidency. Nevertheless Roosevelt himself was a man of broad liberal idealism with a belief in internationalism as well as being a patriotic American, and thought often with concern of the ominous uncertainties of the European scene. In January

187

1938 he had most secretly suggested to Chamberlain that the United States Government, in parallel with Chamberlain's own admired efforts to bring about appeasement, could take a moral, political and economic initiative to bring the nations of the world back on to the desired path of peace and decency in international relations from which they were evidently in danger of straying.

It was vague talk if densely formulated but Roosevelt was taking some personal political risk in putting forward such a basically non-isolationist proposition. He was politely snubbed by Chamberlain for his pains. The Prime Minister felt there was some danger of such an initiative actually getting in the way of what His Majesty's Government were trying to do and asked the President 'to consider whether it would not be wiser to consider holding his hand for a short while . . .' Indeed he said elsewhere that he viewed the initiative 'with the gravest concern', though he did not actually say so to Roosevelt. His Permanent Under-Secretary was unable to persuade him to put any suggestion of future encouragement or support into his reply.[12]

Perhaps it was as a result of this experience that, when at the time of the Czech May crisis the US Ambassador in Paris, William Bullitt, wrote an eloquent and emotional personal letter to Roosevelt asking him to propose a Four Power Conference at the Hague, he stirred little interest in Washington.[13] Between Berchtesgaden and Godesberg however the President had understandably felt an even more urgent concern for the way things were going in Europe and had again very secretly suggested to the British Ambassador that the Western Powers might call a world conference to which Hitler should be invited and which he, Roosevelt, would attend if it could be somewhere other than Europe, say the Azores.[14] But Chamberlain's mind was not on the Azores.

Roosevelt delivered two urgent public appeals to Europe for peace as the crisis got worse between September 26 and 28, the last addressed directly to Hitler. It is conceivable that they may have made some oblique impression somewhere in Hitler's mind. But though naturally welcomed by Chamberlain they were not of real importance to him. The first appeared on the morning of Wilson's trip to Germany. The second, on the 27th, pointed out specifically that negotiations were still open and that nothing stood in the way of widening their scope into 'a conference of all nations directly interested in the present controversy . . . such a meeting to be held immediately in some neutral spot in Europe . . .'[15]

But Roosevelt's activity was on the sidelines. (For domestic political reasons he even had to disown any US obligations in the message.) If the negotiations were still open, and they only just were, it was by now entirely thanks to Chamberlain. And if a conference was to be held, which it was, this was thanks to Chamberlain too. Hitler, and oddly Mussolini, would decide that it should be held not in a neutral spot but at Munich. Daladier would come too.

On the afternoon of September 26 Halifax had seemed to want to make clear that the message Wilson was taking to Hitler was the last word. This was the nearest thing to bluff in the whole process since Chamberlain had gone to Berchtesgaden. As if Daladier and Gamelin were as firm as they tried to sound, the Foreign Office issued a statement which declared that if, in spite of all Chamberlain's efforts, a German attack was made on Czechoslovakia 'the immediate result must be that France will be bound to come to her assistance, and Great Britain and Russia will certainly stand by France'.[16] It is true the statement did immediately add that it was 'still not too late' for settlement by negotiation, but it was the strongest British *démarche* on the European scene for years. A further instruction was sent to Wilson, who had by then reached Berlin, to make plain to Hitler that French intervention, followed by British, was 'an inevitable alternative to a peaceful solution'.[17]

But when Wilson managed to see Hitler that afternoon he had such a rough reception that he judged it advisable not to deliver this part of the message for the time being. Hitler was in a state of excitement before the speech he was to deliver that evening at the Berlin Sportpalast. When Wilson began by saying that the Godesberg terms had shocked British opinion, Hitler interrupted him at once to say that 'in that case there was no use talking any more'. When Wilson went on to point out that Chamberlain had actually managed to get his Cabinet, the French and the Czechs to agree to the incorporation of the Sudetenland in the Reich, Hitler interrupted again 'in staccato accents' to say that the problem must be solved forthwith without further delay. Gestures and exclamations of disgust and impatience accompanied such further

189

attention as he was prepared to give Wilson and at one point he even started to walk out of the room. What was happening, he said, was that Germany was being given something in theory but faced with 'boggling and delaying' when it came to giving it in practice. 'Germany was being treated like niggers, one would not dare to treat even the Turks like that.'

He now had even sharper demands than at Godesberg. 'On October 1 I shall have Czechoslovakia where I want her.' If, in the next two or three days, he did not know for certain that the territory would be well cleared of Czechs, he might go in earlier. He must have an affirmative reply by Wednesday the 28th.

'Midnight?' asked Henderson, the Ambassador, who was accompanying Wilson.

'No, 2 p.m.,' said Hitler.

But there were faint glimpses of hope. Given Wilson's understanding of the real object of his visit he was right by his own standards not to mention the *démarche* he had been given. Hitler asked if the suggestion that the Czechs should send a representative to him meant that Britain was abandoning her role as intermediary? He seemed relieved to hear Wilson say 'No', and that '*we still hoped to exercise a useful influence on the Czechs and we believed we could push through a quick agreement in accordance with the basic German requirements*'.[18]*

Hitler agreed to meet again the next day.

That evening his speech was broadcast to the world. It was a passionate uncompromising denunciation of the Czechoslovak state full of an urgent sense of impending action. There was a passing not unfriendly reference to Chamberlain and to an offer by the British Legion to help keep order in the plebiscite areas (which he said he had accepted) but it was punctuated by vicious personal attacks on Beneš.

'The decision now lies in his hands,' he concluded. 'Peace or War!'[19]

This was of course exactly what Chamberlain, Halifax and Wilson thought too. The pressure on the Czechs was on again. Moreover the British Government was anxious to show the Germans that it was on from their side. The day before, Halifax had

*Author's italics.

190

been at pains to have Hitler assured that when the Czechs said, as they apparently had done, that their decision to mobilise had been with 'the advice and approval' of their British Government this had definitely not been so; the British, he said, had merely discontinued taking responsibility for the Czechs not mobilising.[20] Now, after Hitler's speech and his attack on Beneš, it was decided that it was useless to go on suggesting that the Germans and Czechs should meet. Chamberlain immediately issued a statement. Hitler, he said, clearly had no faith that the Czech agreement to the Anglo-French proposals would be carried out. 'These promises,' he said, 'were made not to the German Government direct, but to the British and French Governments in the first instance. Speaking for the British Government we regard ourselves as morally responsible for seeing that the promises are carried out fairly and fully, and we are prepared to undertake that they shall be carried out with all reasonable promptitude.'[21] The term 'morality' had not figured much in the crisis hitherto.

That morning, Tuesday the 27th, Wilson went to see Hitler for the second time. Before doing so he had sent a message to Chamberlain saying that the Czechs 'should now be told starkly how matters stand'. They did not seem to realise that they were in danger of being completely overrun. Their best course seemed to be 'to withdraw troops from areas to be occupied leaving Germany to effect a bloodless occupation'.[22]

The objections to the Godesberg terms were now plainly being made not on the grounds that they were in themselves unacceptable but on the grounds that the Czechs would not accept them. There was only one conclusion to draw.

Wilson found Hitler quieter this time, though he still interjected brusque comments when Wilson was talking. In the light of the Prime Minister's public statement that morning Wilson asked Hitler if he had anything to give him which Chamberlain could use 'even at the eleventh hour'.[23] Wilson made the present British position clear enough, by conceding, 'if the Czechs accepted well and good . . .' Hitler said decisively that the only way to avoid war was by putting pressure on the Czechs and he begged Chamberlain to do all he possibly could to induce the Czechs to accept.

Wilson did this time manage to make the *démarche* that, if France went to help Czechoslovakia in hostilities against Germany, Britain

191

would have to join her, but he did so in a manner so prevaricating as to remove from it most of such firmness as it might have contained. He again said if the Czechs accepted 'well and good' but if not, and Germany attacked, France would have to fulfil her obligations with Britain in support. But here he took advantage of Daladier's formula. France had not said specifically that she would attack, only that she would fulfil her obligations. 'We do not know exactly in what form the French would decide to fulfil their obligations.'[24]

None of this was any longer really at the centre of the discussion. 'I will still try to make those Czechos sensible,' Wilson said aside to Hitler as he left.[25]

Early that evening Chamberlain sent a message to Beneš. 'I feel bound to tell you . . .,' it began in schoolmasterly tones.[26] It continued with the information that the Germans would attack 'almost immediately' unless the Czechs accepted the German terms by 2 p.m. tomorrow, the 28th. This would result in Bohemia being overrun. 'Nothing that any other Power can do will prevent this fate for your own country and people . . . His Majesty's Government cannot take responsibility of advising you what you should do but they consider that this information should be in your hands at once.'[27]

The implication was obvious. It was the situation after the Anglo-French proposals all over again except that this time, since Chamberlain himself had found Godesberg unreasonable, the pressure had to be applied in a rather less forthright manner.

Henderson, who was advising London to put 'the strongest pressure' on Prague,[28] had a word in the ear of the Czech chargé d'affaires in Berlin who had spoken to him of 'dying with honour'. Henderson said he thought nothing could be more honourable than for Beneš to tell the world he was yielding to overwhelming force rather than plunging the world into a war which would ruin his own country and perhaps Europe too. He thought Beneš would go down in history as a far greater man if he surrendered, now, territory which after all he had undertaken to surrender within a few months' time.[29]

The same evening (September 27) Hitler's formal reply arrived to the letter Chamberlain had sent through Wilson. It reiterated Hitler's determination to act. The Czechs were just trying to drag out negotiations to delay the final settlement. He had no faith in the assurances of the Czech Government, which was why immediate occupation of the territories was necessary as a guarantee that the settlement would take place smoothly and quickly. The letter though totally adamant on this point did have some subtler significant passages to encourage Chamberlain.

In the first place Hitler was prepared now to guarantee the remainder of the Czech state. But it was the last paragraph of all which gave most grounds for optimism. Having said that the Czechs were just trying to manoeuvre England and France into a war on Czechoslovakia's behalf he concluded:

> I must leave it to your judgement whether, in view of these facts, you consider that you should continue your effort, for which I should like to take this opportunity of once more sincerely thanking you, to spoil such manoeuvres and bring the government in Prague to reason at this very last hour.[30]

The letter arrived at the Foreign Office just after Chamberlain had finished the BBC broadcast in which he gave his first public account for some time of what had been going on (Parliament had been recalled for the next day). A broad outline of events had of course been available through the newspapers while, as Chamberlain now put it, he was 'flying backwards and forwards across Europe and the position was changing from hour to hour'. But what few ordinary citizens could have sensed for sure until that broadcast was the full trend, behind the scenes, of British policy towards Czechoslovakia. Chamberlain talked of all the letters he had received in recent days, mainly from women, thanking him for his efforts for peace.

> It has been heart-breaking to read of the growing anxiety they reveal and their intense relief when they thought, too soon, that the danger was past. If I felt my responsibility before, to read such letters has made it seem almost overwhelming. How horrible, fantastic, incredible it is that we should be digging trenches and trying on gas masks here because of a quarrel in a far-away country between people of whom *we*[*] know nothing. It seems still more impossible that a quarrel which has already been settled in principle should be the subject of war . . .

[*]Chamberlain's spoken emphasis.

The phrases even then were enough to make a listener, apprehensive of other things beside the approach of war, sit up. The British people knew quite a lot about the quarrel; it had been in all the newspapers for months. Later came the complementary sentence:

> However much we may sympathise with a small nation confronted by a big and powerful neighbour, we *cannot* in all circumstances undertake to involve the whole British Empire in war simply on her account.[31]

But no one had ever suggested such a thing in *all* circumstances. And was the size of the country really a relevant criterion? What about Belgium? Such debating points were quite irrelevant. Chamberlain's purpose was not to convince by logic but to make it easy, if the way were still open, for the British public to support him when he took it.

He had said in the broadcast that he was prepared to go to Germany a third time if he thought it would do any good. At the moment he did not see any more that he could usefully do.

At a Cabinet meeting shortly after the broadcast he confronted the fact that even if he wanted to use the line still just open to Hitler he was facing formidable difficulties at home. The Czechs were not yielding to the schoolmasterly pressure he was putting on them and if the Czech Minister in Berlin had passed on Henderson's view of Beneš's honour it had made small impression. Indeed later that night was to come the formal Czech rejection of Hitler's terms together with a proposal for an international conference. Now at this late Cabinet meeting there came, in addition to the anticipated opposition from Duff Cooper wanting a firmer line, renewed trouble from Halifax. The Foreign Secretary himself came round to saying that 'we could not in the end force the Czechs to do what we believe to be wrong' – even though of course he had been prepared to try and persuade them to do it. Wilson found Chamberlain that evening tired and uncertain and worried about what he was going to say to the House of Commons next day. At 10.30 p.m., after the Cabinet meeting, the American Ambassador, Joseph Kennedy, who saw him, found him depressed. But, having come so far and having in mind such a clear and determined view of what was the right thing to do, he was not going to give in.[32]

The options were closing. If, as he assumed, Hitler would move at 2 p.m. on the following afternoon something new had to happen quickly. The second appeal from Roosevelt direct to Hitler discussed with Kennedy could do no harm but was not, in his view, centrally relevant. There was however someone else more centrally placed who though representing a less powerful nation could be of service. Chamberlain had taken great care to repair relations with Mussolini after the Ethiopian disaster. Earlier in the day a message had been received from the British Ambassador in Rome, the Earl of Perth, which heralded a whole new series of decisive moves.

Chamberlain now saw the sort of opportunity for which he had been seeking. Perth suggested that the British Government should draw to Mussolini's attention the declaration which the Prime Minister had made that day about Britain's moral responsibility to see the Sudeten transfer through fully and promptly, and his own refusal to abandon efforts for peace. Now at 11 p.m., after the Cabinet meeting and his session with Kennedy, instructions were sent to Perth to act along those lines.[33]

Next morning, the 28th, just after ten o'clock, Perth saw Ciano, Mussolini's son-in-law and his Foreign Minister. Ciano asked him if the British Government were in fact officially asking Mussolini to persuade Hitler to accept Chamberlain's offer to help see the matter through. Perth said, 'Yes.'

'Then,' said Ciano, 'there is no time to be lost; it is a question of hours not days.'

He left at once to see Mussolini. Mussolini's vanity, further flattered by a personal appeal to him from Roosevelt of which news had just come through, reinforced a true reluctance to see the European peace disturbed. He telephoned his Ambassador in Berlin to ask Hitler to delay any action by twenty-four hours.[34]

Chamberlain sent another personal message to Hitler. He had drafted it at seven o'clock that morning without consulting either his Cabinet or Halifax. Only to Horace Wilson had he said he would have one more try. This was an unabashed personal undertaking to satisfy Hitler immediately. The message ran:

After reading your letter I feel certain that you can get all essentials without war and *without delay*. I am ready to come to Berlin at once to discuss arrangements for transfer with you and

representatives of Czech Government, together with representatives of France and Italy *if you desire.**

The message was repeated to Paris, Washington, Prague and
Rome.[35]

How would Hitler react?

He knew that he could get the Sudetenland without difficulty
either peacefully through Chamberlain's assistance or by invasion.
The latter however brought a risk, but only a risk, of general war.
Partly he was in a mood to take that risk, removing Czechoslovakia
at one fell swoop and adding a new dimension to the catalogue of his
spectacular successes. On the other hand the Commander-in-
Chief of his Army, von Brauchitsch, was begging his Chief of Staff
Keitel not to let him do more than take the Sudeten areas.[36]

Impatient as he was of this sort of advice from Brauchitsch Hitler
knew quite well that his armed forces and his defensive system in
the west would be much better equipped for war later. There was
also another consideration. Overwhelmingly enthusiastic as was his
popular support in Germany there was no evidence that the
German people shared his philosophical indifference to the issue of
peace or war in its own right. On the contrary, the enthusiasm with
which Chamberlain had been welcomed in the streets as a
harbinger of peace on the occasion of both his visits to Germany
had been a pointer to their mood. Gestapo reports[37] too said that
civilian morale was worried about a war. Hitler had just had a
further disagreeable experience in this context. With a view to
encouraging a martial spirit in the Berlin population he had, the
previous afternoon, ordered an armoured column to parade
through the streets as evidence of the might and splendour of the
Reich's capability in the present crisis. He himself had observed
from a window of the Chancellery how anxiously the parade was
watched by passers-by without any of the enthusiasm it had been
intended to stimulate.[38]

Throughout the past few days of unwavering public determina-
tion and firmness he had always taken care not specifically to reject
Chamberlain's continually expressed wish to keep the line open.
Now on this morning of decision, with both Mussolini and
Chamberlain asking him to agree to some sort of peace conference,

*Author's italics.

196

came news of Britain precautionary mobilisation of her fleet. He afterwards said that it was this which tipped the balance in his mind.[39] He responded favourably to Mussolini's appeal: he agreed to postpone general mobilisation for twenty-four hours. The news was telephoned to London at 1 p.m., less than two hours before Chamberlain was due to give his account of the past fortnight to the recalled House of Commons.[40] In the meantime Hitler had received Chamberlain's letter proposing what amounted to a five-power conference. After he had telephoned Mussolini it was agreed to arrange one. Which was how at 2.40 p.m. on the afternoon of September 28 the Italian Ambassador appeared before him for the third time that day to interrupt his lunch and tell him, 'Tomorrow eleven o'clock Munich'. Munich had been decided on as Mussolini found Berlin too far. This information made Hitler laugh.[41]

Invitations were sent out to Britain, France and Italy. Chamberlain had spoken of a meeting at which Czechoslovakia would be present. But no invitation to attend was sent to Czechoslovakia. In accepting, neither Chamberlain nor Daladier made any stipulation about a Czech presence. But Chamberlain sent a message to Beneš assuring him that he would 'have the interests of Czechoslovakia fully in mind'.[42] Halifax that evening asked the Czechs to have someone available to go to Munich at short notice on the following day.[43] Beneš telephoned Newton to beg that 'nothing may be done in Munich without Czechoslovakia being heard. It is a most terrible thing for her if negotiations take place without her being given an opportunity to state her case . . .'[44] When the Czechs the next day sent only qualified agreement to a provisional plan of a newly-proposed detailed plan for speedy transfer of the Sudeten territory which Chamberlain had worked out before making his last appeal to Hitler, they were told by Halifax that he hoped they would not 'render more difficult the Prime Minister's already delicate task by formulating objections . . .' Concrete results could only be expected from Munich '. . . if the Czech Government are prepared at this stage to give Mr Chamberlain a wide discretion and not to tie his hands'.[45] By the time that message was sent, Chamberlain had already been using his discretion in Munich for more than two hours.

The story of the scene in the House of Commons the day before has often been told. Alec Dunglass, Chamberlain's Private Secretary, handed him a note of Hitler's agreement to a conference just as

197

he was ending his analysis of recent events with an account of Mussolini's intervention of that day. Chamberlain, before leaving the House to make his preparation for Munich, said there could be no Member whose heart did not leap at the news. The good wishes of the leaders of both Labour and Liberal Oppositions bore him out. Each knew that if the Munich Conference preserved the peace it would be at the expense of the Sudetenland and the Czech fortifications. This, as Chamberlain had said in his broadcast, had already been agreed to in principle. But Clement Attlee's only mild qualification of the peace of which they were all 'desirous' was that it should not neglect principles. Archibald Sinclair for the Liberals did say he hoped the Czechoslovak state in its new frontiers would 'have a chance of economic survival and complete freedom'. Only the single Communist Member, Gallacher, spoke out to say he would not be a party to what was going on there and protested 'against the dismemberment of Czechoslovakia'.[46]

Halifax told the Russians next morning that he was sorry they could not be at the Conference but obviously Hitler would not have them. They said they hoped Czechoslovakia would be represented and Halifax said Chamberlain was bearing that in mind. The scene at Heston airport next morning is equally familiar from regular replay of the newsreels over many years. 'It's going to be all right this time,' Chamberlain had said to the crowds in Downing Street as he left. At the airport he spoke, rather in the tones of some elderly governess: 'When I was a little boy I used to repeat: if at first you don't succeed, try, try, try again,' and he quoted Hotspur from Shakespeare's *Henry IV* saying that he would pluck the flower safety from the nettle danger.

What is less familiar is the realisation that for all the dramatic background of tension, the anxious enthusiasm with which Chamberlain and Daladier were seen off on the morning of September 29 to Munich, and the suspense which prevailed in the world throughout the day, there was really nothing to be decided there which had not been decided or implicitly decided already.

As the first sentence of the Agreement itself was to declare: the cession to Germany of the Sudeten German territory had already been agreed in principle. The debate since then had been about Hitler's hurry to get it. Once the Conference had been called, the issue of peace or war no longer hung in the balance. Hitler was

198

unlikely to invade the Sudetenland by unilateral action now that he knew he could get it 'without delay' with British and French approval. The British and French by their presence at Munich were recognising that the only way to stop Hitler from going to war for the Sudetenland was to let him have it at once. As Hitler himself put it when the Conference started at about half past twelve that day, their task there was to absolve from the character of violence his action in taking the Sudetenland.[47] And this task was what the Munich Conference, which needed just over half a day for the purpose, satisfactorily accomplished.

It accomplished it in three sessions with breaks for lunch at 3 p.m. and dinner at 9 p.m. It was not like a formal conference at all. There was no conference table. In a large long room on the first floor the four participants sat down one end on arm-chairs and sofas round the fireplace, over which hung a portrait of Bismarck. No one acted as chairman. Hitler, in the morning session, looked now and again rather pointedly at his watch. There was no formal agenda. Everyone knew what they were there to do. But the actual proceedings were, as one British official described them, a 'hugger-mugger' business. The organisation, commented Wilson, was 'very imperfect'.[48]

The detailed arrangements for the German take-over of the Sudetenland were based on a draft memorandum put forward by Mussolini, though in fact, unknown to the British and French, it had been approved by Hitler in Berlin the day before and telephoned through to Mussolini to produce as if it were his own. The British and French approved it for discussion at once.

This plan as finally agreed after careful examination, detailed drafting and some discussion of specific boundaries and the property rights of departing Czech farmers, provided for evacuation by Czech forces and occupation by German forces of predominantly German areas to begin on October 1, the date on which Hitler had always said it should.

But there were, on the face of it, clear improvements on the Godesberg terms. Instead of the occupation happening all at once, it was to take place in five stages, the first four being the occupation of limited demarcation areas by October 7 while the rest of the predominantly German areas were to be occupied by October 10. These were now to be defined by an international commission which the agreement set up.

199

The British were surprised by what they called the 'moderation' of the German demands and the degree of latitude left to the international commission.[49] The international commission would be composed of representatives of Germany, Britain, France, Italy and Czechoslovakia. Further, there were areas designated for a plebiscite to be held under the auspices of the international commission by the end of November.

One real difficulty arose over the question of whether or not a Czech representative should be present at the Conference while these matters were worked out and agreed. Chamberlain argued quite persistently that one should be there, not on the grounds of equity but because if Britain had to guarantee that the Czechs would carry out the provisions of the agreement he needed to have Czech assurances that they would. When Daladier too argued for a while for a Czech presence Hitler said that if they were going to have the Czechs' consent to every detail they would be there for a fortnight. He then said that it was impossible because there was no Czech representative present with the authority to speak for the Czech Government.

This was untrue. There arrived in Munich that afternoon by plane from Prague both the Czech Minister to Berlin and the Czech Foreign Minister's *chef de cabinet*, Hubert Masarik, appointed by Beneš to act as observers on behalf of the Czech Government. They were brought from the airport in police cars with Gestapo escort to the hotel where the British were staying. There they were confined to their rooms with a police guard on the doors and prevented from leaving while the Conference progressed. Their first contact with a British official was not until seven o'clock in the evening when they were able to hear how the fate of their country was being decided.[50] Chamberlain had by then given up his attempt to have them represented and Daladier with a certain masochistic logic had explained that, as he had in the previous week accepted responsibility for ceding the Sudetenland without consulting the Czechs, in spite of the fact that France had a treaty with Czechoslovakia, he would not press the point if the inclusion of a Prague representative was going to cause difficulties; it was necessary to get on with things quickly.[51]

The British scored one effective point when they succeeded in getting the Hungarian and Polish claims for their minorities removed from the main agreement where they would have seemed to carry

200

equal status with the Sudeten claim. This question was now moved to an annex which merely declared that it was a matter for settlement between the respective governments; if they could not settle it within three months the heads of government would meet again. A further annex to the agreement stated that the British and French Governments were standing by the offer they had made in the original Anglo-French proposals to guarantee the new boundaries of Czechoslovakia. Germany and Italy would do so too when the Hungarian and Polish adjustments were settled.

The air of unreality at Munich was characterised by the often desultory manner in which the Conference proceeded, with the four principals sometimes sitting around awkwardly making conversation as their advisers drifted inconsequentially in and out. The deed was done just before midnight but not signed until just before two o'clock the next morning, after what Horace Wilson called 'long delays due to inefficient organisation and lack of control'.[52] Chamberlain and Daladier then summoned the Czechs, still waiting in their hotel, to tell them what they had done. In the rather unpleasant words of Horace Wilson who accompanied the Prime Minister, the Czechs were 'given a pretty broad hint' that – having regard to the seriousness of the alternative – the best course was for them to accept 'what was clearly a considerable improvement upon the German memorandum'. One of the Czech observers, Masarik, described Chamberlain as yawning a lot while this went on. Wilson concluded his written summary of the events of that day with the observation that Russia had not been mentioned once during the entire Conference.[53]

Next morning Chamberlain went by arrangement to see Hitler in his private apartment at 16 Prinz Regenten Platz. The conversation began with mutual congratulations on what they had achieved. Chamberlain then addressed a plea to Hitler that should the Czechs 'be mad enough to refuse the terms and attempt resistance' he trusted that he would not bomb Prague or kill women and children in air attacks.[54]

It was the least he could do for them in the circumstances.

Hitler said he would always try to spare the civilian population from air attacks and stressed that he had in the past been anxious for an international ban on aerial bombing altogether. The conversation continued on the subject of aerial bombardments for some time before Chamberlain finally brought it round to the point of his visit. He wanted their agreement of the day before to give hope for better Anglo-German relations and a greater European stability altogether. He asked if Hitler would sign a statement which he had prepared.

'When?' asked Hitler.

'Immediately,' said Chamberlain.[55]

They then went over to a table and signed the sheet of paper Chamberlain had prepared and of which he thoughtfully had two copies, one for himself and the other for the Führer.

The Munich Agreement, declared the paper, was 'symbolic of the desire of our two peoples never to go to war again'. The signatories declared that they would continue their efforts to remove possible sources of difference and thus contribute to assure the peace of Europe.

Dunglass, Chamberlain's Private Secretary, said years later that he thought Hitler signed in rather a perfunctory manner and Spitzy, Ribbentrop's adjutant, heard Hitler say to a remonstrating Ribbentrop shortly afterwards that the paper was of no significance.[56]

For Chamberlain it was of tremendous significance. It took the crisis of the past few months with its resolution at Munich on to that higher level to which the whole of his foreign policy aspired. This moment could see the beginning of that permanent appeasement of Europe for which British policy itself had striven for so many years – the final phase at last of fair adjustment in the post-Versailles era.

This was why Chamberlain felt able to wave the sheet of paper so ecstatically at the airport when he got home. The reception he received from the crowds there and in London itself was more just an expression of overwhelming relief that the threat of war had been removed, coupled with gratitude and admiration for the man whose stamina and persistence had removed it. The sensation of success went to his head and he made what even Horace Wilson thought afterwards was the mistake of proclaiming from his window in Downing Street that he had brought back peace with honour. The Press the next day was almost unanimous in tribute.[57]

Daladier, the French Prime Minister, left Munich in some trepidation. Whichever way one looked at it, the French had suffered a major diplomatic defeat. When the aircraft arrived over Le Bourget and the pilot saw the crowds below, he circled round the airport and asked Daladier for instructions. Daladier decided to go down to face his destiny. He expected boos and execrations. Instead he was received with waved hats and cheering. Going through the door of the plane Daladier stopped in astonishment. He turned to Leger, head of the French Foreign Office and said '*Ces gens sont fous.*'

From Daladier that night there came no talk of peace with honour as he waved to the cheering crowds from his window. He smiled, but the smile broke as he waved.[58]

In Berlin there was an appropriate atmosphere of triumph. Henlein was on the platform to welcome Hitler under a banner 'The Sudetenland thanks the Führer'. Paradoxically it was the beginning of the end for him; he was to become a relatively unimportant figure. It was after all his territory too that was now being taken over by the Reich.

Hitler himself seems to have felt, strangely in the light of what he had achieved, rather thwarted by the fact that he had not in the end broken Czechoslovakia by war.[59] This state of mind perhaps reflected a genuine emotional as well as tactical ambivalence of the past fortnight's crisis as to whether peace or war was the most desirable way of resolving it. So much success was now his as a result of Munich that he could feel disappointment that the success had not been total in the style he knew would eventually be his. On the other hand to the German people his triumph seemed all the greater because it had been achieved without the war they had been dreading. An awareness of their relief partly accounted too for his sense of frustration.

For one group in Germany, Munich dealt a devastating blow to hopes and plans. For those Generals, diplomats and political survivors of Weimar who had plotted a *coup d'état* in the event of Britain and France standing firm, confidence was destroyed. It was to be many years before, in very different circumstances, they thought they saw an opportunity again.

For Czechoslovakia too the blow was in every sense devastating. Though Beneš met with his Generals at Hradčany the next morning there could be no chance of resisting now. They had, after all, decided only the week before that even with the possibility of France and Britain being drawn in afterwards (which plainly no longer existed) the risk was too great to take. The Government issued a statement. It accepted the decisions of the four Powers at Munich. It added: 'The Czechoslovak Government at the same time registers its protest before the world against this decision which was taken unilaterally and without its participation.' 'We were deserted. We stand alone,' said the new Prime Minister Syrovy in a broadcast that evening.[60]

In the vast underground network of fortifications in the Sudetenland of which Field Marshal von Blomberg himself had once said 'they would present extreme difficulties to our attack', the order to evacuate and abandon them was now given.[61]

'To all units of the Czechoslovak army,' echoed an impassive martial voice through the bunkers and deep concrete corridors, 'you are listening to an announcement of the Commander-in-Chief's office. In order to safeguard the peace the Czechoslovak Government on September 30 accepted the Munich Agreement. On the morning of October 1 the German army will begin the occupation of the border areas. The Czechoslovak defence will not be activated . . . The Czechoslovak defence will not be activated . . .'[62]

The soldiers who now had to retreat were in some cases having to abandon not only their country's defences but their homes. Many wept as they went, even hoping for a day or so that it might still be possible to fight.[63] But the Czechoslovak army had been efficient and well-disciplined. The Czechoslovak defence system was not activated.

Among the Czech people the feeling was one of total betrayal. One of the leading Czech poets of the time, Frantisek Halas, wrote a poem which was recited across the nation:

> The bell of treason is tolling
> Whose hand made it swing?
> Sweet France,
> Proud Albion,
> And we loved them.[64]

CHAPTER TWENTY

EPILOGUE

THE SUBSEQUENT HISTORY OF THE AGREEMENT IS STRAIGHT-forward enough, though melancholy to record.

In the debate on Munich which took place in the House of Commons on October 3, 1938, it was still possible for Chamberlain and his relieved supporters to maintain that they had won something at Munich that had not been available at Godesberg. Even Duff Cooper in his speech on the resignation into which his conscience had finally driven him saw 'great and important differences' between the two positions and admitted that it had been 'a great triumph for the Prime Minister that he was able to acquire them'.[1]

Chamberlain made the most of these differences. He could now afford to be unambiguous in public and made no attempt to argue that the four Powers had been talking about anything at Munich other than finding 'an orderly instead of a violent method of carrying out an agreed decision' to hand over the Sudetenland to Germany.[2] It was on the difference between the 'unacceptable' terms of Godesberg and those which he had now accepted at Munich that he asked to be judged.

Some of his argument was thin from the start, particularly looked at from the point of view of Czechoslovakia.

Munich, he stressed, was an agreement between four Powers to carry out a plan; Godesberg had been a bald ultimatum with a six-day time limit.

Godesberg had demanded an immediate occupation and evacuation of arbitrarily designated predominantly German territories to start in six days' time; Munich arranged for such occupation to take place in stages over ten days with an 'interna-

205

tional commission' designating the final boundaries. (A Labour Member pointed out later in the debate that the real time difference was thus not in fact ten days but seventy-two hours.)[3]

The international commission was now to determine the more closely mixed population areas in which plebiscites were to be held, instead of such areas being determined by Germany as at Godesberg. At Godesberg these plebiscite areas were to be occupied at once by German troops; Munich laid down occupation by 'an international force'.

Munich, like Godesberg, required Czech evacuation of the territories without damaging installations, but there was no clause in the Munich Agreement, as there had been in the Godesberg terms, to the effect that cattle and foodstuffs might not be removed.

A right of personal option into or out of the transferred territories could be exercised within six months of the agreement; there had been no such option under the Godesberg terms.

Finally there was to be under the Munich Agreement a guarantee by Britain and France of Czechoslovakia's new frontiers.

However, as a Conservative Member was to ask, if, as was suggested, the British people had not been prepared to fight for the old frontiers of Czechoslovakia, would they be prepared to fight for the new ones?[4]

The debate lasted four days and Chamberlain won comfortably on a motion which approved 'the policy of His Majesty's Government by which war was averted in the recent crisis' and supported 'their efforts to secure a lasting peace'. Eden in his speech had made clear that for him the question which had first troubled him in the train from Berlin to Moscow in 1935 was finally resolved: foreign affairs could not indefinitely be conducted 'on the basis of "stand and deliver". Successive surrenders bring only successive humiliation, and they, in their turn, more humiliating demands.'[5] He abstained in the division. It was to his credit that by however fragmented a process he had, at last, come to accept that 'appeasement' was bankrupt.

Chamberlain, after four days in which he had been 'charged with cowardice, with weakness, with presumption, and with stupidity' by Opposition Members who had happily cheered him off to Munich, fell back on the argument which was the basis for his wide popular appeal. 'I have been accused,' he said of his treatment by the

Opposition, 'of bringing the country to the edge of war, and I have been denied the merit of having snatched it back to safety.'[6]

Munich had saved the peace. But then Godesberg would have done that too if he had agreed to it without consulting the Czechs as he had agreed Munich. In the context of policy, his case rested on the superiority or otherwise of the Munich agreement as contrasted with the Godesberg terms. The strength of that case rested almost entirely on the credibility of 'the international commission'. It did not do so for long. On the day before the vote in the House of Commons was already taken the hollow character of 'the international commission' was already being revealed.

The commission was composed of British (Henderson), French, Italian and Czech Ambassadors to Berlin together with the German Foreign Office State Secretary von Weizsäcker. But when they met in Berlin for the first time on October 1 it was the German General Staff, in the form of von Brauchitsch and Keitel, who were the true German representatives behind von Weizsäcker.

The Commission's immediate task was to determine the fifth zone of occupation of preponderantly German character to be completed by October 10. The Czechs proposed that the 1930 census should be taken as the basis for determining which areas were predominantly German. Von Brauchitsch and Keitel were busy at the time working out the General Staff's plan for the final destruction of Czechoslovakia. They wanted the maximum gain at once. They insisted on use of the 1910 census of the Austro-Hungarian Empire in which the language most in daily use in the area rather than mother-tongue had been the test of the area's nationality. Vastly more territory thus became considered predominantly German than would otherwise have been the case, approximately the same amount, in fact, as Hitler had demanded in the Godesberg Memorandum.

The British, French and Italian Ambassadors concurred in the decision to use the 1910 census. The decision was presented to the Czechs as a *fait accompli*, an ultimatum with the October 10 time limit. 'Notwithstanding all our objections and protests no changes were made in it,' declared the Czechoslovak Government in a broadcast on October 7.[7] The Italian Ambassador on the commission had been rather more sympathetic to the Czech claim than the British and French. But it was clear that the Czech 'membership' of the international commission was an empty formality.

Henderson later gave three reasons for siding with the Germans on this all-important decision for the final frontier. First, he said, he hoped it would obviate the need for plebiscites. This in fact it successfully did because the Germans thus acquired most of the more doubtful areas and saw no more need for plebiscites. Secondly, said Henderson, 'to pin the Germans down to a line of their own choosing' would make it more difficult for them to change it; 'and, thirdly . . . the German contention was actually, in my opinion, the better founded of the two theses.'[8]

The new frontier, in the laconic words of the Royal Institute of Foreign Affairs, 'closely resembled the frontier demanded by Hitler in the Godesberg Memorandum'.[9]*

As for the clause in the Munich Agreement by which people had a six-month option to enter or leave the transferred territories, this never had any application at all. Thousands of Czechs, anti-Nazi Germans and German Jews wisely fled from their homes before the incoming German troops. A London Lord Mayor's fund was raised to help them and a British party flew to Prague on October 10, the day when the Germans moved to the approximate Godesberg position, to consult about the fund's distribution. They found that the Germans were insisting on all registered residents of the occupied areas being returned forthwith and the Czech Government was complying. Refugees were being sent back forcibly. General Syrovy, whom the British party asked to grant temporary respite in this procedure, refused. 'In this affair,' he told them bitterly, 'we have been willing to fight on the side of the angels, now we shall hunt with the wolves.'[10]

John Wheeler-Bennett, one of the party to whom this remark was addressed, himself later summed up the whole dismal consequence of Munich as follows:

> Within a week of signature, therefore, the Munich Agreement, with the concurrence of all the signatory powers, was stripped of even those few limitations which had been laid on Nazi demands. No vestige of success remained to Mr Chamberlain and

*See maps, pp. xiii and xiv.

208

M. Daladier – save that this victory for German arms had been a bloodless one.[11]

It would be charitable to leave it there. But history does not dispense charity. For Czechs, possibly the only hopeful clause in the Munich Agreement consisted of the British and French offer to guarantee the state's new frontiers against unprovoked aggression. On October 5 the Government said in the House of Commons that they felt 'under a moral obligation to Czechoslovakia to treat the guarantee as now in force'.[12]

When in March 1939 Hitler, with the help of von Brauchitsch and Keitel, was ready to implement the vow he had made ten months before to smash the Czechoslovak state, he did so using the instrument of a Fascist secessionist movement in Slovakia which asked for his help and which, with his sanction, on March 14 proclaimed an independent Slovak state. Asked in the House of Commons about the Munich guarantee of the frontiers Chamberlain first replied that as no unprovoked aggression had taken place the guarantee did not apply. Hours later, with German motorised infantry pouring through the streets of Prague, Chamberlain again turned his attention to the Munich guarantee. It had, he said, always been regarded as being only of a transitory nature and with Slovak independence the moral obligation had ceased to exist.[13]

'No vestige of success' for Chamberlain? Fifty years after the event and more than forty years after those words were written, the judgement should not pass unquestioned. It is now possible, though still painful, to put on one side feelings about what happened to Czechoslovakia and ask whether, in not being prepared to go to war for the territorial integrity of Czechoslovakia, Chamberlain did the right thing.

Chamberlain himself would hardly have put the question in that way. He acted as he did because, under pressure, he thought it was the right thing to do to let the Germans have the Sudetenland, both as an action in itself and in the interests of the British Empire. It was right, he thought, because the Czechoslovak state had not been particularly well constructed at Versailles, and if, by letting the Germans have that territory, there was hope at last of fully appeasing the German spirit which Versailles had made so aggressive, then it was in the interests of the British Empire to do so.

Sentiment for Czechoslovakia never troubled him; sentiment for the British Empire, which required international peace and prosperity, did. The worst thing that can be said about him, judging him by his own lights, is that he was too ready to suppose that Hitler would act within his own (Chamberlain's) conventions because he so much wanted him to do so. When, in September of the following year, he reluctantly had to accept that this had been an illusion and declare war, he had no sentiment for Poland either. He went into a war for the British Empire and while Poland was being destroyed the only British attacks were on German naval ports to counter the menace the German navy presented to shipping on British supply lines.

Chamberlain's emphasis in 1938 was not on the question: would it be better to fight now rather than later, but on the question how to avoid war even at considerable cost – as Munich showed. We, however, knowing for certain that Hitler was realistically deter-mined to carry through the policy envisaged in *Mein Kampf*, and that there was thus to be a war, ask a question of our own: would it have been better to fight Hitler in September 1938 than in September 1939?

The argument often subsequently put forward in justification for Munich, to the effect that it gained time, was not immediately widely used and only really began to take shape retrospectively after Hitler's entry into Prague and the eventual outbreak of war itself. Even after Prague Chamberlain himself said in the House of Commons that he did not want to be diverted from his pursuit of peace.[14] In spite of pressure from the Conservative group round Churchill, little was done in a hurry after Munich to put Britain on a more warlike footing. What was done was mainly in terms of defence against air raids rather than rearmament. Chamberlain even made a scornful remark in Cabinet late in October 1938 about people wanting expenditure on new armament programmes 'as though one result of the Munich Agreement had been that it would be necessary to *add* to our rearmament programme'.[15]*

Even retrospectively the 'gaining-time' argument for Munich does not hold up very well. There was certainly one very important respect in which Britain was better equipped for the sort of war that

*Chamberlain's emphasis.

had developed by 1940 in that more squadrons of Hurricane and Spitfire eight-gun fighters were then available for her defence. But, if one asks how else Britain was better equipped then than two years earlier in comparison with the Germans, there are virtually no military results to help with an answer. The Germans, who had been positively preparing for war and who by then had had the experience of moving their armies into Czechoslovakia and fighting a modern *blitzkrieg* in Poland, had taken immeasurably better advantage of the time. Curiously the argument about gaining time had been looked at the other way round by Halifax after the *Anschluss*. He said then: 'It may well be true that Germany's superiority in arms may be greater a year or two hence than it is now, but this is not a good argument for risking disaster now.'[16]

Accepting that there was virtually no question of Britain going to war intentionally at the time of Munich, as opposed to being dragged into it, it is impossible not to ask the question: would it not have been better in September 1938 if Hitler had been given no option but to attack or pull back, and, if he had attacked, France had then honoured her obligations and Britain supported her?

There are many telling points to be made in favour of the argument but since the discussion is hypothetical many telling counter-arguments too. The Czech army of thirty-six divisions was modern and efficient, almost certainly more effective than the gallant Polish army which became Britain's ally instead a year later. The massive fortifications on the Czech frontiers, which were handed over to the Germans by the Munich Agreement, should have been a formidable hindrance to German invasion and were certainly respected by the German General Staff.

On the other hand the experience of 1940 was to show that the even more massive fortifications of the French Maginot Line, on which the Czech fortifications were modelled, could be irrelevant before a German army moving with innovative tactical brilliance. All the strongest Czech defences could have been outflanked and made irrelevant by a lightning masterstroke across the waist of Czechoslovakia from north and south.

The Germans, apart from not having had the advantage of an extra year's armament and military experience, would have been weaker in the west where the West Wall was not in 1938 far advanced. And while Russian action might well have remained enigmatic the Germans could not have been certain that they would not attack as they were able to be after the Nazi-Soviet pact of 1939.

It can however also be argued that even had the Czechs been able to hold out far longer than the Poles it would have done them no more good. British military strategy had been based for years on the theory that the next war would be won by bombing. The British army was not conceived for a major continental role. Practical allied help would have been no more likely to reach Czechoslovakia than it did Poland. Czechoslovakia would have been obliterated as Poland was.

But does that mean that it was not right to go to war over Poland? This too can be argued if moral considerations about the character of the German New Order are left out of account, which Chamberlain was always inclined to do however much he might deplore it.

There are further questions about Czechoslovakia. Would the Dominions, who had strongly approved Chamberlain's appeasement, have supported Britain in war in 1938 as they did in 1939? They were mostly opposed to the idea of risking war at the time of Munich. And was not the United States even more closely wedded to neutrality in 1938 than 1939?

There is one more difficult hypothetical conundrum, and perhaps the most unanswerable of all. If Britain and France had stood more firmly behind the Czechs, might not the plotting German Generals have been able to act and remove Hitler altogether thus preventing any war at all? They showed no particular talent for a *coup d'état* in 1944 but conditions were far less favourable then.

The hypothesis game can be played almost endlessly. But after fifty years there is still one simple certainty: whether Munich was right or wrong something dreadful happened there.

Shortly afterwards Jan Masaryk, son of the founder of Czechoslovakia, made a statement in London:

I have repeated lately that my little country has paid almost the supreme price in trying to preserve European democracy. And I say to you that if it is for peace that my country has been butchered up in this unprecedented manner I am glad of it. If it isn't, may God have mercy on our souls.[17]

In the light of what was to happen it is still difficult, even fifty years afterwards, not to find those words disturbing.

APPENDIX I

THE COVENANT OF THE LEAGUE OF NATIONS

THE COVENANT OF THE LEAGUE OF NATIONS FORMED PART 1 OF THE TREATY of Versailles. It consisted of 26 Articles.

Under Articles 12, 13 and 15 Member Nations were obliged to submit disputes either to arbitration or to the League Council, and in no case to resort first to war. They agreed to carry out in full good faith any award made and not to resort to war against a Member of the League who complied with it.

Article 16 ran as follows:

'Should any Member of the League resort to war in disregard of its covenants under Articles 12, 13 or 15 it shall *ipso facto* be considered to have committed an act of war against all other Members of the League which hereby undertake immediately to subject it to the severance of all trade or financial relations, the prohibition of all intercourse between their nationals and the nationals of the covenant breaking State, and the prevention of all financial, commercial, or personal intercourse between the nationals of the covenant breaking State and the nationals of any other State whether Members of the League or not.

It shall be the duty of the Council in such case to recommend to the several Governments concerned what effective military, naval or air force the Members of the League shall severally contribute to the armed forces to be used to protect the covenants of the League . . .'

Under Article 17 States which were not Members of the League were, when in dispute, either with a League Member or another non-Member, invited to accept the obligations of Membership. If they refused and resorted to war against a Member of the League the provisions of Article 16 would be applicable against it. If both States refused, the Council 'may take such measures and make such recommendations as will prevent hostilities and will result in the settlement of the dispute'.

APPENDIX II

THE MUNICH AGREEMENT

GERMANY, THE UNITED KINGDOM, FRANCE AND ITALY, TAKING INTO consideration the agreement, which has been already reached in principle for the cession to Germany of the Sudeten German territory, have agreed on the following terms and conditions governing the said cession and the measures consequent thereon, and by this agreement they each hold themselves responsible for the steps necessary to secure its fulfilment:–

1. The evacuation will begin on the 1st October.

2. The United Kingdom, France and Italy agree that the evacuation of the territory shall be completed by the 10th October, without any existing installations having been destroyed and that the Czechoslovak Government will be held responsible for carrying out the evacuation without damage to the said installations.

3. The conditions governing the evacuation will be laid down in detail by an international commission composed of representatives of Germany, the United Kingdom, France, Italy and Czechoslovakia.

4. The occupation by stages of the predominantly German territory by German troops will begin on the 1st October. The four territories marked on the attached map will be occupied by German troops in the following order: the territory marked No. I on the 1st and 2nd of October, the territory marked No. II on the 2nd and 3rd of October, the territory marked No. III on the 3rd, 4th and 5th of October, the territory marked No. IV on the 6th and 7th of October. The remaining territory of preponderantly German character will be ascertained by the aforesaid international commission forthwith and be occupied by German troops by the 10th of October.

5. The international commission referred to in paragraph 3 will determine the territories in which a plebiscite is to be held. These territories will be occupied by international bodies until the plebiscite has been completed. The same commission will fix the conditions in which the plebiscite is to be held, taking as a basis the conditions of the Saar plebiscite. The commission will also fix a date, not later than the end of November, on which the plebiscite will be held.

6. The final determination of the frontiers will be carried out by the international commission. This commission will also be entitled to recommend

to the four Powers, Germany, the United Kingdom, France and Italy, in certain exceptional cases minor modifications in the strictly ethnographical determination of the zones which are to be transferred without plebiscite.

7. There will be a right of option into and out of the transferred territories, the option to be exercised within six months from the date of this agreement. A German-Czechoslovak commission shall determine the details of the option, consider ways of facilitating the transfer of population and settle questions of principle arising out of the said transfer.

8. The Czechoslovak Government will within a period of four weeks from the date of this agreement release from their military and police forces any Sudeten Germans who may wish to be released, and the Czechoslovak Government will within the same period release Sudeten German prisoners who are serving terms of imprisonment for political offences.

ADOLF HITLER
NEVILLE CHAMBERLAIN
ÉDOUARD DALADIER
BENITO MUSSOLINI

Munich,
   September 29, 1938

Annex to the Agreement

His Majesty's Government in the United Kingdom and the French Government have entered into the above agreement on the basis that they stand by the offer, contained in paragraph 6 of the Anglo-French proposals of the 19th September, relating to an international guarantee of the new boundaries of the Czechoslovak State against unprovoked aggression.

When the question of the Polish and Hungarian minorities in Czechoslovakia has been settled, Germany and Italy for their part will give a guarantee to Czechoslovakia.

ADOLF HITLER
NEVILLE CHAMBERLAIN
ÉDOUARD DALADIER
BENITO MUSSOLINI

Munich,
   September 29, 1938

Declaration

The Heads of the Governments of the four Powers declare that the problems of the Polish and Hungarian minorities in Czechoslovakia, if not settled within three months by agreement between the respective Governments, shall form the subject of another meeting of the Heads of the Governments of the four Powers here present.

ADOLF HITLER
NEVILLE CHAMBERLAIN
ÉDOUARD DALADIER
BENITO MUSSOLINI

Munich,
   September 29, 1938

Supplementary Declaration

All questions which may arise out of the transfer of the territory shall be considered as coming within the terms of reference to the international commission.

ADOLF HITLER
NEVILLE CHAMBERLAIN
ÉDOUARD DALADIER
BENITO MUSSOLINI

Munich,
   September 29, 1938

Composition of the International Commission

The four Heads of Government here present agree that the international commission provided for in the agreement signed by them to-day shall consist of the Secretary of State in the German Foreign Office, the British, French and Italian Ambassadors accredited in Berlin, and a representative to be nominated by the Government of Czechoslovakia.

ADOLF HITLER
NEVILLE CHAMBERLAIN
ÉDOUARD DALADIER
BENITO MUSSOLINI

Munich,
   September 29, 1938

APPENDIX III

POPULATION OF CZECHOSLOVAKIA BY RACE, 1930 CENSUS

Czechs	7,447,000
Germans	3,231,000
Slovaks	2,309,000
Hungarians	691,000
Ruthenians	549,000
Poles	87,000

NOTES

This book's special indebtedness to certain secondary sources will be apparent throughout these references, in particular the Documents on British and German Foreign Policy published by HMSO, Telford Taylor's encyclopaedic *Munich: The Price of Peace*, Keith Middlemas's *Diplomacy of Illusion*, the late Elizabeth Wiskemann's *Czechs and Germans*, Ronald Smelser's *The Sudeten Problem 1933–1938*, Gordon Craig's *Germany 1866–1945* and *The Times*.

Chapter 1

1 David Irving, *The War Path*, p. 149.
2 A. J. P. Taylor, *The Origins of the Second World War*, p. 189.

Chapter 2

1 *The Times*, 23 Nov 1987.
2 The easiest access to the full text of the Treaty of Versailles is through the supplement to the issue of *The Times* dated 28 June 1919.
3 Gordon A. Craig, *Germany 1866–1945*, pp. 425–28.
4 *The Times*, 30 June 1919.
5 *Hansard* 5th series, Vol. 117, Col. 1213.
6 *The Times*, 30 June 1919.

Chapter 3

1 Craig, op. cit., p. 450.
2 Ibid.
3 Ibid., p. 35.
4 Adolf Hitler, *Mein Kampf*, p. 193.
5 Ibid., pp.282–86, 306–09.
6 Ibid., pp. 284, 283.
7 Ibid., p. 289.
8 Ibid., p. 194.

9 Ibid., p. 309.
10 Shiela Grant Duff, *The Parting of the Ways*, p. 198.

Chapter 4

1 Quoted Craig, op. cit., p. 519.
2 Golo Mann, *The History of Germany since 1789*, p. 578.
3 Quoted William L. Shirer, *The Rise and Fall of the Third Reich*, p. 151.
4 Quoted Alan Bullock, *Hitler: A Study in Tyranny*, p. 162.
5 Quoted Bullock op. cit., p. 182.
6 Quoted Shirer, op. cit., p. 252.

Chapter 5

1 *The Times*, 17 Sept 1933.
2 Ibid.
3 Ibid., 3 Feb 1933.
4 Ibid., 8 Mar 1933.
5 Ibid., 14 May 1932.
6 Ibid., 19 Sept 1932.
7 Ibid.
8 Ibid., 4 Mar 1933.
9 Ibid., 31 Jan 1933.
10 Ibid., 16 March 1933.
11 Ibid., 15 May 1933.
12 Ibid., 11 May 1933.
13 Ibid., 27 May 1933.
14 Ibid., 16 May 1933.
15 Ibid., 17 May 1933.
16 Ibid., 16 Oct 1933.
17 Ibid., 14 Nov 1933.
18 Labour Party Conference, 1919.
19 *The Times*, 15 Oct 1933.
20 Ibid., 6 July 1934.

Chapter 6

1 The information in this chapter relies heavily on Elizabeth Wiskemann's excellent academic work, *Czechs and Germans*, Oxford 1938, completed in that year for the Royal Institute of International Affairs. It is particularly valuable inasmuch as it could be written free from the emotive impact of the Czech crisis and the Munich Agreement which followed publication.
The early chapters of Ronald Smelser, *The Sudeten Problem 1933–1938*, London 1975, have also been helpful.

2 Austrian Parliamentary Debate, 17 Sept 1917, cited in Wiskemann, op. cit.,
   p. 77.
3 Ibid., p. 83.
4 Ibid., p. 90.
5 Ibid., pp. 122–3.
6 Ibid., pp. 201–2.

Chapter 7

 1 *The Times*, 23 Nov 1933.
 2 Ibid., 13 Jan 1934.
 3 British White Paper, quoted *The Times*, 1 Feb 1934.
 4 *The Times*, 7 Feb 1934.
 5 Ibid., 28 Nov 1933.
 6 Ibid., 16 Dec 1933.
 7 *Reichsgesetzblatt*, 26 Mar, cited in *The Times*, 10 Apr 1934.
 8 *The Times*, 23 Jan 1934.
 9 Ibid., 12 Mar 1934.
10 Ibid., 24 Mar 1934.
11 Ibid., 26 Mar 1934.
12 Ibid., 24 Mar 1934.
13 Ibid., 19 Apr 1934 and 24 Mar 1934.
14 Quoted J. Wheeler-Bennett, *The Disarmament Deadlock*, p. 222.
15 *The Times*, 1 June 1934.

Chapter 8

 1 *The Times*, 9 July 1934.
 2 Ibid., 7 July 1934.
 3 Ibid.
 4 *Hansard* 5th Series, Vol. 292, Cols. 693, 697.
 5 Ibid., Cols. 2440, 2444.
 6 *Hansard* 5th Series, Vol. 295, Cols. 875, 877.
 7 *The Times*, 13 Nov 1934.
 8 Ibid., 13 Nov 1934.
 9 Ibid., 12 Jan 1935.
10 Ibid., 16 Jan 1935.
11 Ibid.
12 Richard Lamb, *The Ghosts of Peace*, p. 4.
13 *The Times*, 9 Jan 1935.
14 Ibid., 4 Feb 1935.
15 Ibid., 16 Feb 1935.
16 Ibid., 21 Feb 1935.
17 Ibid., 16 Jan 1935.
18 *Hansard* 5th Series, Vol. 299, Col. 104.
19 *Hansard*, ibid., Col. 45.

20 *The Times*, 5 Mar 1935.
21 Ibid., 18 Mar 1935.
22 Ibid., 19 Mar 1935.
23 Documents on British Foreign Policy, 2nd Series, Vol. XII, pp. 663–4.
24 Ibid., pp. 666–7.
25 Ibid., pp. 667, 672–3.
26 Ibid., pp. 677, 679–80, 686.
27 *The Times*, 21–23 Mar 1935.
28 DBFP, 2nd Series, Vol. XIII, p. 697.
29 Ibid., pp. 693–96.
30 Ibid., p. 695.
31 *The Times*, 25 Nov 1935.
32 Ibid.
33 Ibid., 22 Nov 1935.

Chapter 9

1 Documents on British Foreign Policy, 2nd Series, Vol. XI, pp. 704, 784.
2 Documents on German Foreign Policy, Series C, Vol. 3, pp. 1040–1.
3 DBFP, 2nd Series, Vol. XII, p. 716.
4 Ibid., p. 721.
5 DGFP, Series C, Vol. 3, p. 1059.
6 DBFP, 2nd Series, Vol. XII, pp. 728, 730, 740.
7 Ibid., pp. 703–39.
8 Ibid., p. 745.
9 Ibid., p. 744.
10 *The Times*, 27 Mar 1935.
11 Ibid., 29 Mar 1935.
12 DGFP, Series C, Vol. III, pp. 1091–1103.
13 *The Times*, 29 Mar 1935.
14 Ibid., 4 Apr 1935.
15 DBFP, 2nd Series, Vol. XII, p. 752.
16 Ibid., pp. 755–6.
17 Ibid.
18 Ibid., pp. 766–9.
19 Ibid., p. 785.
20 Ibid., pp. 785–6.
21 Ibid., pp. 799–800.
22 Ibid., pp. 813–17.
23 Ibid., p. 847.
24 *The Times*, 10 Apr 1935.
25 DBFP, 2nd Series, Vol. XII, p. 827.
26 Ibid., pp. 827–8.
27 Ibid., pp. 829–30.
28 Ibid., p. 829.

Chapter 10

1 Documents on British Foreign Policy, 2nd Series, Vol. XII, pp. 862–914.
2 Ibid., p. 868.
3 Lamb, *op. cit.*, p. 11.
4 DBFP, 2nd Series, Vol. XII, p. 865.
5 *The Times*, 30 Apr 1935.
6 Ibid., 22 May 1935.
7 Ibid., 23 May 1935.
8 Ibid., 28 May 1935.
9 Ibid., 29 May 1935.
10 Ibid., 8 June 1935.
11 Ibid., 19 June 1935.
12 Ibid., 24 June 1935.
13 Ibid.
14 DBFP, 2nd Series, Vol. XIII, pp. 447–8.
15 Ibid., p. 446.
16 *The Times*, 1 July 1935.
17 Ibid.
18 Ibid., 12 July 1935.
19 Ibid., 23 July 1935.
20 Ibid., 4 Oct 1935.
21 Ibid., 2 Oct 1935.
22 Ibid., 4 Oct 1935.
23 DBFP, 2nd Series, Vol. XV, pp. 264–8.
24 Ibid., p. 268.
25 Ibid.
26 DBFP, 2nd Series, Vol. XIV, pp. 712–3.
27 DBFP, 2nd Series, Vol. XV, p. 487.
28 Ibid., pp. 488–93 and pp. 514–16.
29 Ibid., pp. 564–5.
30 Ibid., pp. 569–70.
31 Ibid., p. 611.
32 Ibid., p. 615.
33 Ibid., pp. 624–6.
34 Ibid., pp. 641–3.
35 Ibid., p. 652.
36 Ibid., p. 660.
37 DBFP, 2nd Series, Vol. XVI, pp. 22–3.
38 Quoted Telford Taylor, *Munich*, p. 135.
39 *The Times*, 9 Mar 1936.
40 DBFP, 2nd Series, Vol. XV, p. 86.
41 Ibid., p. 152.
42 Ibid., p. 158.
43 Ibid., p. 151.
44 Ibid., p. 125.

45 Ibid., p. 51; *Hansard* 5th series, Vol. 309, Col. 1812.
46 A useful resumé of British Press reaction appeared in *The Times* 9 Mar 1936.
47 Quoted Telford Taylor, op. cit., p. 245.
48 DBFP, 2nd Series, Vol. XV, pp. 60, 64.
49 Ibid., pp. 64–5.
50 *Hansard* 5th Series, Vol. 310, Cols. 1443–4.
51 Ibid., Col. 1541.
52 *The Times* 21 Mar 1936.
53 *Hansard* 5th Series, Vol. 310, Col. 1446.

Chapter 11

1 William Shirer, op. cit., p. 361.
2 Alan Bullock, op. cit., p. 345.
3 Documents on British Foreign Policy, 2nd Series, Vol. XVI, p. 268.
4 Ibid., p. 228.
5 Ibid., p. 298.
6 Ibid., p. 302.
7 Keith Feiling, *The Life of Neville Chamberlain*, p. 296.
8 Andreas Hillgruber, *Germany and the Two World Wars*, p. 56.
9 DBFP, 2nd Series, Vol. XVI, pp. 287–8.
10 Ibid., Vol. XV, pp. 582–3.
11 Ibid., p. 589.
12 Ibid., Vol. XVI, p. 112.
13 Ibid., p. 144.
14 Ibid., Vol. XII, pp. 866–7.
15 Bullock, op. cit., p. 360.
16 Ibid., p. 362.
17 Ibid., p. 363.
18 Hillgruber, op.cit., p. 57.
19 Shirer, op.cit., pp. 376–80 and Taylor, op. cit., pp. 288–302.
20 Shirer, op. cit., p. 375.

Chapter 12

1 Montgomery Hyde, *Neville Chamberlain*, p. 1.
2 Keith Feiling, op. cit.
3 Ibid., p.252.
4 Documents on British Foreign Policy, 2nd Series, Vol. XIX, p. 205.
5 Ibid., p. 94.
6 Ibid., p. 101.
7 Ibid., p. 209.
8 Ibid., pp. 336–7.
9 Ibid., p. 338.
10 Ibid., p. 367.
11 Ibid., p. 380.

12 Ibid., p. 383.
13 Ibid., p. 447.
14 Ibid.
15 Ibid., pp. 471–2.
16 Ibid., pp. 518–20.
17 DBFP, 2nd Series, Vol. XIX, p. 405.
18 Ibid., p. 494.
19 *The Times*, 10 Nov 1937.
20 Telford Taylor, op. cit., p. 262.
21 DBFP, 2nd Series, Vol. XIX, pp. 540–51 and 571–5; Avon, *Facing the Dictators*, pp. 513–16; Telford Taylor, op. cit., pp. 309–12.
22 DBFP, ibid., pp. 580–1.
23 Ibid., pp. 597–600, 621.

Chapter 13

1 Documents on British Foreign Policy, 2nd Series, Vol. XIX, p. 669.
2 Telford Taylor, op. cit., p. 338.
3 Ibid., p. 343.
4 Ibid., p. 367.
5 Brook Productions Interview with Sir Geoffrey Cox for television documentary, *Munich: The Peace of Paper*, 1987.
6 David Irving, op. cit., p. 88.
7 DBFP, 2nd Series, Vol. XIX, pp. 738, 889.
8 Ibid., p. 746, p. 886.
9 Ibid., p. 872.
10 Ibid., p. 908.
11 Ibid., p. 904.
12 Ibid., p. 929.
13 Ibid., pp. 924–5.
14 Ibid., p. 926.
15 Ibid., p. 967.
16 Ibid., p. 976.
17 Keith Middlemas, *Diplomacy of Illusion*, p. 181. For an account of the luncheon, see also Winston Churchill, *The Gathering Storm*, pp. 243–4.
18 Middlemas, op. cit., p. 191–2.
19 Ibid., p. 188.
20 Ibid., p. 204.

Chapter 14

Much of the argument for this chapter is based on Ronald Smelser's authoritative *The Sudeten Problem 1933–1938: Volkstumpolitik and the Formulation of Nazi Foreign Policy* (London, Dawson, 1975).

1 Documents on German Foreign Policy, Series D, Vol. 2, p. 15.

2 Ibid., pp. 49–62.
3 Documents on International Affairs, 1938, Vol. 2, p. 125.
4 DGFP, Series D, Vol. 2, p. 198.
5 DIA, 1938, Vol. 2, pp. 130–7.
6 Ibid., p. 139.
7 Smelser, op. cit., p. 224.
8 Ibid.
9 DGFP Series D, Vol. 2, p. 273.
10 Smelser, op. cit., p. 222: Celovsky, *Münchener Abkommen*, p. 157.
11 DGFP, Series D, Vol. 2, p. 300.
12 *Munich: The Peace of Paper* (TV).
13 Telford Taylor: op. cit., pp. 390–2 and pp. 654–5. Documents on British Foreign Policy, 3rd Series, Vol. I, p. 356.
14 *Munich: The Peace of Paper* (TV).
15 DGFP, Series D, Vol. 2, p. 358.
16 DIA op. cit. pp. 145–6 (Chamberlain's Speech of May 30).
17 *Munich: The Peace of Paper* (TV), Sir Frank Roberts (British Foreign Office).
18 Ibid., Baron Juniac (French Foreign Office).
19 DIA, 1938, Vol. 2, p. 164.
20 Ibid., p. 166.
21 Ibid., pp. 175–6.
22 Ibid., pp. 166–8.
23 Sir Geoffrey Cox, former Foreign Correspondent of the *Daily Express*, *Munich: The Peace of Paper* Part II (TV).
24 DIA, 1938, Vol. 2, p. 169–71.
25 Ibid., p. 177.
26 Ibid., p. 178.
27 Ibid., pp. 218–24.

Chapter 15

1 David Irving op. cit., pp. 122–3.
2 Ibid., p. 124.
3 Peter Hoffman, *The History of the German Resistance*, pp. 69–80.
4 Ibid., pp. 81–96.
5 Ibid., pp. 66–8.
6 Documents on British Foreign Policy, 3rd Series, Vol. I, p. 332.
7 DBFP, 3rd Series, Vol. II, pp. 277–278.
8 Ibid., p. 280.
9 Ibid., p. 686.
10 DBFP, 3rd Series, Vol. I, p. 366.
11 Ibid., p. 357.
12 Ibid., p. 217.
13 Ibid., p. 419.
14 Ibid., p. 499.
15 Ibid., p. 623.

16 Ibid., p. 470–71.
17 Ibid., p. 467.
18 Documents on International Affairs, 1938, Vol. 2, p. 148.
19 DBFP, 3rd Series, Vol. I, pp. 564–5.
20 *Munich: The Peace of Paper* (TV) (Evidence of Reinhard Spitzy, Ribbentrop's adjutant).
21 Ibid.
22 Ibid.
23 DBFP, 3rd Series, Vol. I, pp. 545–6.
24 *Munich: The Peace of Paper* (TV).
25 DBFP, 3rd Series, Vol. II, p. 74.
26 Ibid., p. 54–5.
27 Ibid., p. 63.
28 Ibid., pp. 135, 137.
29 Ibid., pp. 167, 229.
30 Ibid., p. 220.
31 Ibid., p. 219.
32 *Munich: The Peace of Paper* (TV) Stalin's interpreter, Berezhkov.
33 DBFP, 3rd Series, Vol. I, p. 161.
34 Ibid., Vol. II, pp. 41–6, 104, 126, 161.
35 Ibid., pp. 125–6.
36 *History of the Times, 1912–1948*, pp. 929–34.
37 DIA, 1938, Vol. 2, pp. 189–90.
38 Ibid., pp. 192–3.
39 *Hansard* 5th Series, Vol. 339, Col. 12.
40 *Munich: The Peace of Paper* (TV) Nemec.
41 Documents on German Foreign Policy, Series D, Vol. 2, p. 827.
42 Ibid., p. 812.
43 DBFP, 3rd Series, Vol. II, p. 314.

Chapter 16

1 Keith Middlemas, op. cit., pp. 299–300.
2 Ibid., pp. 314–17.
3 Keith Feiling, op. cit., p. 357.
4 Middlemas, op. cit., p. 333.
5 Documents on British Foreign Policy, 3rd Series, Vol. II, p. 314.
6 Documents on German Foreign Policy, Series D, Vol. 2, p. 754.
7 Ibid., p. 763.
8 Feiling, op. cit., p. 364.
9 Ibid., pp. 363–4.
10 DGFP, Series D, Vol. 2, p. 785.
11 Middlemas, op. cit., p. 339.
12 Ibid., pp. 347–8.
13 Feiling, op. cit., pp. 366–7.
14 Middlemass, op. cit., p. 188.

15 Feiling, op. cit., p. 367.
16 DBFP, 3rd Series, Vol. II, pp. 338–51; DGFP, Series D, Vol. 2, pp. 786–98; Documents on International Affairs, 1938, Vol. 2, p. 221.
17 Telford Taylor, op. cit., p. 737.

Chapter 17

1   Documents on German Foreign Policy, Series D, Vol. 2, pp. 828–9.
2   Inskip Diary, Middlemas, op.cit., p. 348.
3   Documents on British Foreign Policy, 3rd Series, Vol. II, p. 367.
4   Middlemas, op.cit., pp. 348–9.
5   DBFP, 3rd Series, Vol. II, p. 370.
6   Ibid., p. 400.
7   Ibid., p. 373.
8   Ibid., p. 376.
9   Ibid., pp. 376–9.
10 Ibid., pp. 379–80.
11 Ibid., p. 380.
12 Ibid., pp. 380–2.
13 Ibid., pp. 383–4.
14 Ibid., pp. 384–5.
15 Ibid., pp. 387–4.
16 Ibid., pp. 394–7.
17 Ibid., pp. 397–9.
18 Telford Taylor, op. cit., p. 784.
19 DBFP, 3rd Series, Vol. II, p. 398.
20 Ibid., pp. 404–5.
21 Ibid., pp. 416–17.
22 Telford Taylor, op. cit., p. 786.
23 DBFP, 3rd Series, Vol. II, pp. 419–20.
24 Ibid., pp. 424–5, 434–6.
25 Ibid., p. 425.
26 Ibid., p. 422.
27 Telford Taylor, op. cit., p. 787.
28 DBFP, 3rd Series, Vol. II, pp. 437–8.
29 Telford Taylor, op. cit., pp. 790–1.
30 DBFP, 3rd Series, Vol. II, pp. 438–9. Telford Taylor, op. cit., p. 790 (footnote).
31 Hubert Ripka, *Munich: Before and After*, quoted by Telford Taylor, op. cit., pp. 791–2.
32 DBFP, 3rd Series, Vol. II, pp. 440, 443–4
33 Documents on International Affairs 1938, Vol. 2, p. 217.
34 DBFP, 3rd Series, Vol. II, p. 439.
35 *Munich: The Peace of Paper* (TV) Edward Goldstücker, Sir Geoffrey Cox.

Chapter 18

1 Documents on German Foreign Policy, Series D, Vol. 2, p. 848.
2 Ibid., pp. 863–5.
3 Middlemas, op. cit., pp. 360–4. The extent to which I have made use of Keith Middlemas's lucid analysis of the Cabinet Papers in this period will already be apparent.
4 *The Times*, 23 Sept 1938.
5 Telford Taylor, op. cit., p. 806, quoted from Ivone Kirkpatrick (Chamberlain's Foreign Office interpreter), *The Inner Circle*.
6 Documents on British Foreign Policy, 3rd Series, Vol. II, pp. 464–5.
7 Paul Schmidt, *Hitler's Interpreter*, p. 96.
8 Telford Taylor, op. cit., p. 806, quoted from Kirkpatrick, op. cit.
9 DBFP, op. cit., pp. 465–6. For an account of the Godesberg conversation of 22 September 1938, see also German Documents, Series D, Vol. 2, pp. 870–9.
10 Ibid., p. 467; ibid., (German) p. 875.
11 Ibid., p. 473.
12 *Hansard* 5th Series, Vol. 339, Col. 20.
13 DBFP, op. cit., pp. 459–63.
14 Middlemas, op. cit., p. 366, quoting memorandum by Sir Horace Wilson.
15 DBFP, op. cit., p. 477.
16 Ibid., p. 482.
17 Telford Taylor, op. cit., p. 812.
18 DBFP, op. cit., p. 483.
19 Telford Taylor, op. cit., p. 810.
20 *Munich: The Peace of Paper* (TV), Edward Taborsky (Secretary to Czech Prime Minister Hodza) Edward Goldstücker.
21 Telford Taylor, op. cit., pp. 814–17.
22 *The Times*, 24 Sept 1938, quoted by Telford Taylor.
23 Documents on International Affairs, 1938, Vol. 2, p. 224, quoted by Telford Taylor.

Chapter 19

1 Documents on British Foreign Policy, 3rd series, Vol. II, p. 512.
2 Ibid., p. 511.
3 The important Cabinet meetings immediately after Godesberg are dealt with at length from primary sources in Telford Taylor, *Munich*, pp. 820–7, and Keith Middlemas, *Diplomacy of Illusion*, pp. 374–80. The brief survey in this chapter is indebted to them both.
4 Telford Taylor, op. cit., pp. 824–5.
5 DBFP, 3rd Series, Vol. II, pp. 520, 513.
6 Documents on International Affairs, 1938, Vol. 2, pp. 236–8.
7 Documents on German Foreign Policy, Series D, Vol. 2, pp. 933, 936–7.
8 Leonard Mosley, *On Borrowed Time*, pp. 52, 481.

9 DBFP, 3rd Series, Vol. II, pp. 520–41.
10 Telford Taylor, op. cit., pp. 859–62; Middlemas, op. cit., pp. 386–7.
11 Telford Taylor, op. cit., p. 634.
12 DBFP, 2nd Series, Vol. XIX, pp. 726–32, 737–9, 743.
13 Telford Taylor, op. cit., pp. 4–5.
14 Reynolds, *The Creation of the Anglo-American Alliance*, p. 35.
15 DIA, 1938, Vol. 2, pp. 266–7.
16 DBFP, 3rd Series, Vol. II, p. 550.
17 Ibid.
18 Ibid., pp. 552–3, 554–7.
19 DIA, 1938, Vol. 2, p. 260.
20 DBFP, 3rd Series, Vol. II, p. 517.
21 Ibid., p. 559.
22 Ibid., p. 653.
23 Ibid., p. 564.
24 Ibid., pp. 564–7.
25 DGFP, Series D, Vol. 2, p. 965.
26 DBFP, 3rd Series, Vol. II, p. 570.
27 Ibid.
28 Ibid., p. 574.
29 Ibid., pp. 578–9.
30 Ibid., pp. 576–9.
31 DIA, 1938, Vol. 2, p. 271.
32 Middlemas, op. cit., p. 396.
33 DBFP, 3rd Series, Vol. II, p. 561.
34 Ibid.
35 Ibid., p. 587.
36 David Irving, op. cit., p. 148.
37 Ibid.
38 Telford Taylor, op. cit., p. 877.
39 Irving, op. cit., p. 148.
40 DBFP, 3rd Series, Vol. II, p. 590.
41 Irving, op. cit., p. 149.
42 DBFP, 3rd Series, Vol. II, p. 599.
43 Ibid., p. 601.
44 Ibid., p. 604.
45 Ibid., pp. 614–15.
46 *Hansard* 5th Series, Vol. 339, Cols. 5–28.
47 DGFP Series D, Vol. 2, p. 1004.
48 Quoted by Telford Taylor, op. cit. p. 29.
49 Ibid., pp. 30–1; DBFP, 3rd Series, Vol. II, p. 631.
50 Telford Taylor, op. cit., p. 38; *Munich: The Peace of Paper* (TV).
51 DGFP, Series D, Vol. 2, p. 1008.
52 DBFP, 3rd Series, Vol. II, p. 633.
53 Ibid., p. 634.
54 Ibid., p. 636.

55 Ibid., p. 640.
56 *Munich: The Peace of Paper* (TV).
57 Middlemas, op. cit., pp. 404, 407.
58 *Munich: The Peace of Paper* (TV).
59 Ibid., Reinhard Spitzy; Wheeler-Bennett, *Munich: Prologue to Tragedy*, p. 331.
60 DIA, 1938, Vol. 2, p. 327.
61 Wheeler-Bennett, *Munich*, p. 13.
62 *Munich: The Peace of Paper* (TV) Czechoslovak archive film.
63 Ibid., Karel Doudera.
64 Ibid., Edward Goldstücker.

Chapter 20

1 *Hansard* 5th Series, Vol. 339, Col. 36.
2 Ibid., Col. 42.
3 Ibid., Col. 503, Philip Noel-Baker.
4 Ibid., Col. 247, Brigadier-General Spears.
5 Ibid., Col. 87.
6 Ibid., Col. 344.
7 Documents on International Affairs, 1938, Vol. 2, pp. 336–7.
8 Wheeler-Bennett, *Munich*, p. 193, quoting Henderson, *Failure of a Mission*, p. 175.
9 DIA, 1938, Vol. 2, p. 322.
10 Wheeler-Bennett, op. cit., p. 198.
11 Ibid., p. 194.
12 *Hansard* 5th Series, Vol. 339, Col. 303.
13 Wheeler-Bennett, op. cit., p. 353; *Hansard* 5th Series, Vol. 345, Col. 437.
14 *Hansard* 5th Series, Vol. 345, Col. 435–40.
15 Middlemas, op. cit., p. 421.
16 Ibid., pp. 186–7.
17 *Munich: The Peace of Paper* (TV) Newsreel film.

SELECT BIBLIOGRAPHY

Alan Bullock: *Hitler: A Study in Tyranny*, (London 1952) (Penguin Paperback, 1962)

Avon, *see* Eden

Winston S. Churchill: *The Gathering Storm* (London, Paperback, 1985)

Alfred Duff Cooper: *Old Men Forget*, (London 1954)

Gordon A. Craig: *Germany 1866–1945*, (Oxford University Press, Paperback, 1986)

Documents on British Foreign Policy (HMSO)

Sheila Grant Duff: *The Parting of Ways, A Personal Account of the Thirties*, (London: Unwin Paperbacks, 1984)

Anthony Eden: *Facing the Dictators* (London 1962)

Keith Feiling: *The Life of Neville Chamberlain*, (London 1970)

German Documents on Foreign Policy (HMSO)

Martin Gilbert and Richard Gott: *The Appeasers*, Houghton Mifflin (Boston 1963)

Andreas Hillgruber: *Germany and the Two World Wars*, Trans. by W. C. Kirby, (Harvard, London 1981)

Adolf Hitler: *Mein Kampf*, (Hurst and Blackett, London 1939)

Peter Hoffman: *The History of the German Resistance, 1933–1945* (Cambridge, Mass. 1979)

H. Montgomery Hyde, *Neville Chamberlain*, (London 1976)

David Irving: *The War Path: Hitler's Germany, 1933–1939*, (London, Paperback 1978)

Richard Lamb: *The Ghosts of Peace*, (Russell, Salisbury 1987)

William McElwee: *Britain's Locust Years* (London 1962)

Golo Mann: *The History of Germany since 1789*, (London, Paperback 1987)

Keith Middlemas: *Diplomacy of Illusion* (London 1972)

Leonard Mosley: *On Borrowed Time* (London 1969)

David Reynolds: *The Creation of the Anglo-American Alliance* (London 1981)

Hubert Ripka: *Munich: Before and After* (London 1939)

Keith Robbins: *Munich 1938* (London 1968)

Royal Institute of International Affairs: *Documents 1938, Vols 1 & 2* (Oxford 1942)

Paul Schmidt: *Hitler's Interpreter* (London 1951)
William Shirer: *The Rise and Fall of the Third Reich* (London, Paperback 1964)
Ronald Smelser: *The Sudeten Problem 1933–1938* (London 1975)
A. J. P. Taylor: *The Origins of the Second World War* (London 1962)
Telford Taylor: *Munich: The Price of Peace* (London 1979)
History of The Times, 1912–1948 (London 1952)
John Wheeler-Bennett: *The Disarmament Deadlock* (London 1934)
John Wheeler-Bennett: *Munich: Prologue to Tragedy*, (London 1948)
Elizabeth Wiskemann: *Czechs and Germans* (Oxford 1938)

INDEX

Abyssinia, see Ethiopia
Air Force, German; forbidden by Versailles: 7; Baldwin acknowledges creation of: 53; theoretically non-existent: 57
Air Ministry, German: increasing expenditure: 45–6
Air Sport Federation, German: 45, 52
Albania: 20
Albert Hall: 78
Alsace-Lorraine: 7, 27(fn)
Anglo-German Naval Agreement (1935): foreshadowed: 65–6, 77; negotiated and signed: 78–9; Eden's justification of: 79–80; Chamberlain on: 80; aftermath: 83
Austria, Empire: 6, 14, 24, 35, 207; disintegration: 36; republic of: 37, 56, 65; *Anschluss* foreshadowed: 111–14; implemented: 116–23; referred to: 109, 126–8, 140–1, 187, 211
Asch-Eger region: 175
Attlee, Clement: 58, 198
Auschwitz: 21
Azores, The: 188

Baldwin, Stanley, Lord President of the Council 1931–35, Prime Minister 1935–37: on armament options: 45; remembers German claim aright: 53; on German air force: 53; becomes Prime Minister: 77; on 'difficult' French: 78; close to *The Times*: 79; regrets distrust of Germans: 80; wins General Election (1935): 81; Cabinet awaits Eden: 84–5; retires: 105; and possible meeting with Hitler: 113

Baltic States: 51
Barthou, French Foreign Minister: criticises Britain: 49; strives for 'Eastern Locarno': 50–2; murdered: 55
Bayerische Motorenwerke: good profit from aircraft engines: 45
BBC: 193
Beaverbrook, Lord: 33, 89
Beck, Col. Josef, Polish Foreign Minister: 70
Beck, General Ludwig: moves towards coup d'état: 138–9
Belgium: reparations deliveries to: 6; and occupation of Ruhr: 9; and Locarno, 18; of more interest to Britain than Austria: 65; smaller than Czechoslovakia: 194
Beneš, Edward: and foundation of Czechoslovak State: 14, 34; and Swiss model: 37–8; meets Eden: 70; reacts to Rhineland: 100; warns about German designs: 109; interviewed by *Spectator*: 110; optimistic at Christmas: 124; signs Czech-Soviet Pact: 128; negotiations with Henlein: 129, 133; orders partial mobilisation (May crisis): 131; and Karlsbad points: 135; courteous to Runciman: 136; under British and French pressure: 141–4; confident: 145; alliance with Soviet Union: 146; accepts Karlsbad points: 148; and Berchtesgaden talks: 164; pressure from Britain and France: 166; his dilemmas: 167; rejects Anglo-French proposals, to receive ultimatum: 168 and fn; consults Generals and Cabinet: 166–9; accepts proposals 'with pain': 170; and new

234